D0805754

PROPHECY
AND THE
PHILOSOPHY
OF
MIND

PROPHECY
AND THE
PHILOSOPHY
OF
MIND
TRADITIONS OF
BLAKE AND SHELLEY

TERENCE ALLAN HOAGWOOD

THE UNIVERSITY OF ALABAMA PRESS

Publication of this book has been assisted, in part, by financial assistance from the Andrew W. Mellon Foundation and the American Council of Learned Societies.

Library of Congress Cataloging in Publication Data

Hoagwood, Terence Allan, 1952–
  Prophecy and the philosophy of mind.

  Bibliography: p.
  Includes index.
  1. English poetry—19th century—History and
criticism. 2. Blake, William, 1757–1827. Jerusalem.
3. Shelley, Percy Bysshe, 1792–1822. Prometheus unbound.
4. Prophecies in literature. 5. Philosophy in
literature. 6. Romanticism—England. I. Title.
PR590.H52 1985   821'.7'09384   83-6896
ISBN 0-8173-0177-1

To Kimberly Hoagwood

Contents

List of Illustrations ... viii

Preface ... ix

Note on Citations ... xiii

Prologue: "The Eternal, the Infinite, and the One" ... 1

One: Prophecy and the Philosophy of Mind ... 11

Two: "Humanity Divine": Blake's *Jerusalem* ... 59

Three: "The Prophecy Which Begins and Ends in Thee": Shelley's *Prometheus Unbound* ... 131

Epilogue: "The Sublime System" ... 187

Notes ... 192

Bibliography ... 226

Index ... 237

List of Illustrations

1. House of Death (color print), 100
2. Ezekiel (line engraving), 100
3. *Illustrations of the Book of Job*, no. 13, 101
4. Isaiah Foretelling the Destruction of Jerusalem (drawing on wood block), 102
5. Plate 12 of *For the Sexes: The Gates of Paradise*, 103
6. Elohim Creating Adam (color print), 104
7. Satan Exulting Over Eve (color print), 104
8. The Great Red Dragon and the Woman Clothed in the Sun (watercolor), 105
9. Plate 1 of *Jerusalem*, copy A, 106
10. Plate 1 of *Jerusalem*, copy E, 107
11. Plate 12 of *America*, 108
12. Death's Door (white-line engraving), 109
13. Plate 15 of *For the Sexes: The Gates of Paradise*, 110
14. Illustration for *The Grave*, no. 11 (designed by Blake and engraved by Louis Schiavonetti), 111
15. Plate 24 of *The Book of Urizen*, copy B, 112
16. Plate 13 of *Milton*, copy A, 113
17. Plate 2 of *Jerusalem*, copy A, 114
18. Plate 2 of *Jerusalem*, copy E, 115
19. Frontispiece of *For the Sexes: The Gates of Paradise*, 116
20. *Paradise Lost*, The Creation of Eve (watercolor), 117
21. Plate 3 of *Jerusalem*, copy A, 118
22. Plate 4 of *Jerusalem*, copy A, 119
23. Plate 6 of *Jerusalem*, copy A, 120
24. Plate 14 of *Jerusalem*, copy A, 121
25. Plate 33 of *Jerusalem*, copy A, 122
26. Plate 37 of *Jerusalem*, copy A, 123
27. Pencil drawing for Plate 37 of *Jerusalem*, 124
28. Plate 50 of *Jerusalem*, copy A, 125
29. Plate 58 of *Jerusalem*, copy A, 126
30. Plate 63 of *Jerusalem*, copy A, 127
31. Plate 75 of *Jerusalem*, copy A, 128
32. Plate 76 of *Jerusalem*, copy A, 129
33. Plate 99 of *Jerusalem*, copy A, 130

Preface

Research for this book began innocently, with two short articles, each devoted to the relation of a particular Blake text to one philosophical predecessor. As will happen, the issues enlarged, or my understanding of them increased; soon it was not two writers but two traditions whose relationships interested me. One of these traditions is Christian—the tradition of biblical prophecy and its exegesis, especially in England. The other tradition is apparently secular—Enlightenment epistemology. Both traditions have an important place in the political thought, literature, and action of the eighteenth and nineteenth centuries, and I came to understand that these lines of thought converge in interesting ways, and, further, that their convergence is one major project of English Romanticism.

This book is not, however, merely a study of intellectual backgrounds. One would no longer present Blake or Shelley as an enraptured visionary poet who surprisingly owns a sober conceptual heritage. Instead, it is the case that an epistemology and a metaphysic are embodied in these poets' masterpieces; their poetic forms and their philosophical project are essential to one another. In *Jerusalem* and in *Prometheus Unbound*, the poets do not merely betray the influence of philosophical texts; they transform the traditions that they inherit, largely by unifying those traditions in the multidimensional forms of poetic and (for Blake) pictorial art. Prior relations subsisted between Christian biblical commentaries and secular philosophies of mind, but the poets' splendid unification of these traditions is revolutionary.

The interest of this study increased for me, as I came to understand that what cognitive psychologists are now discovering about the activities of the mind in the production of knowledge is anticipated and confirmed in the work of earlier philosophers and inspired visionaries. For a professional's guidance through the contemporary literature of cognitive psychology, I am indebted to Kimberly Hoagwood: beyond references and interpretations, she provided several thorough readings of the manuscript of this book, at more stages than a normal patience could bear.

It is a pleasure to record a major indebtedness to Joseph Anthony

Wittreich, Jr., who first guided me through the scriptural commentaries and their literary relevance to the Romantic poems. Wittreich also supervised the doctoral dissertation (at the University of Maryland) on which this book is largely based. My debts to Wittreich's published work are recorded in my notes, but his careful guidance at that early stage of preparation, I gratefully acknowledge here. I wish also to express my appreciation for help provided by other members of that dissertation committee—of the Department of Philosophy, Professor James Lesher, and, of the Department of English, Professors John Howard, Calhoun Winton, and Gayle Smith. Also at the University of Maryland, the late John Kinnaird was both informative and encouraging as my philosophical interest in Romanticism increased, and I add therefore this tardy acknowledgement of his help.

This book was written while I held faculty posts at the following colleges and universities, in sequence: Vassar College, The University of Maryland, The American University, and The Pennsylvania State University. Research and writing were further carried on at the British Museum (Department of Prints and Drawings); The Tate Gallery, London; the Library of Congress; the Newberry Library; and the Folger Shakespeare Library. The faculties, staff, and resources of *all* these institutions have been helpful, providing material, guidance, encouragement, inspiration, and support of various kinds. A grant from the College of Liberal Arts at The Pennsylvania State University helped to procure photographs for the illustrations in this book, and so did a further grant from the Office of Academic Affairs at the Altoona Campus of The Pennsylvania State University; for that grant and for helping to defray the cost of essential travel, I wish to thank particularly Dr. Kjell Meling, Director for Academic Affairs, The Pennsylvania State University, Altoona.

At the University of Maryland, Rod Jellema thoughtfully arranged my administrative responsibilities so that I could both meet them and also write a draft of this book; Michael Marcuse was considerate in that way, with regard to my teaching schedules, and so I thank them both.

At the University of Alabama Press, this book has met with unusual courtesy, expertise, and patience, for which I am grateful to Malcolm M. MacDonald, Director, and all the Press staff. For careful copy editing, I thank Hilde L. Robinson.

For permission to reproduce the illustrations in this book, I thank the following persons and institutions: The Tate Gallery, London (and particularly Martin Butlin); the Trustees of the British Museum; the British Library; the National Gallery of Art, Washington, D.C. (Rosenwald Collection); the Collection of Paul Mellon; Mrs. Charles J. Rosenbloom (and, for photography, Larry Ostrom of the Art Gallery of Ontario, Toronto); The Pierpont Morgan Library; The Huntington Library, San Marino, California; and the Library of Congress, Washington, D.C. (Lessing J. Rosenwald Collection).

Finally, I wish to thank Barbara Hoagwood, my mother, for being helpful and supportive when that was most needed, and Kimberly Hoagwood, my wife, to whom this book is dedicated—she has been attentive until this project has become "one passion in twin-hearts."

T. A. H.

Note on Citations

Quotations from Blake's works are from *The Poetry and Prose of William Blake*, ed. David V. Erdman, rev. ed. (Garden City, N.Y.: Doubleday, 1970). References to this book are supplied parenthetically in the text. Citations for poems refer to plate (or page) and line number; citations for prose works refer to the page number in the Erdman edition, abbreviated as *E*. The following abbreviations for Blake's works have been used in parenthetical citations:

A.R.O.	*All Religions are One*
F.Z.	*The Four Zoas*
J.	*Jerusalem*
M.	*Milton*
M.H.H.	*The Marriage of Heaven and Hell*
V.L.J.	*A Vision of The Last Judgment*

When in the documentation I supply letter abbreviations for individual copies of Blake's works, I follow G. E. Bentley, Jr., *Blake Books* (Oxford: Clarendon Press, 1977).

Quotations from Shelley's *Prometheus Unbound* are from the text of Lawrence John Zillman, *Shelley's "Prometheus Unbound": The Text and the Drafts. Toward a Modern Definitive Edition* (New Haven: Yale University Press, 1968), abbreviated as *P.U.* Quotations from Shelley's letters are from *The Letters of Percy Bysshe Shelley*, ed. Frederick L. Jones, 2 vols. (Oxford: Clarendon Press, 1964), which I have abbreviated as *Letters*. Quotations from Shelley's other works are from *The Complete Works of Percy Bysshe Shelley*, ed. Roger Ingpen and Walter E. Peck, 10 vols. (London: Ernest Benn; New York: Charles Scribner's Sons, 1926–30). Poetry citations refer to act (or canto) and line number. I have used the abbreviation, *Prose*, for volumes 5–7 of the Ingpen and Peck edition, and have supplied volume and page numbers in parentheses.

Quotations from George Berkeley are from *A Treatise Concerning the Principles of Human Knowledge* (1710), in *The Works of George Berkeley Bishop of Cloyne*, ed. A. A. Luce and T. E. Jessop (London: Thomas

Nelson and Sons, 1949), 2:1–113. Parenthetical citations refer to paragraph numbers.

Quotations from John Locke are from *An Essay Concerning Human Understanding* (1690), ed. Alexander Campbell Fraser, 2 vols. (1894; rpt. New York: Dover Publications, 1959). Parenthetical citations refer to book, chapter and paragraph numbers.

PROPHECY
AND THE
PHILOSOPHY
OF
MIND

PROLOGUE

"The Eternal, the Infinite, and the One"

The greatest Romantic poems challenge their readers with syntheses of cultural history. Thus M. H. Abrams writes that "these poets were part of a comprehensive intellectual tendency which manifested itself in philosophy as well as in poetry," and which caused political change.[1] This fact of literary history is expressed more majestically by Shelley himself: poetry is "the root and blossom of all other systems of thought" (*Prose*, 7:135). To elaborate the structure of a poet's metaphysics, as Earl R. Wasserman has done for Shelley, is to unfold the poems.[2] He who knows only poems knows little of them.

William Blake also understood that intellectual creeds shape imaginative works, a fact that Sir Leslie Stephen has articulated in a philosophical context.[3] Northrop Frye begins with the poet's case against Locke and proceeds to his vision of the City of God.[4] The theater of Blake's intellectual war includes these traditions, philosophical and religious. Accordingly, to disparage "outside readings" while trying to interpret *Jerusalem* is literary blind man's buff;[5] Blake's art simply cannot be understood without reference to philosophical and religious tradition. To understand the radical transformations to which Blake subjects those traditions requires knowledge of the relevant systems of thought. These systems, synthesized, constitute what Blake said every poem must be: "a perfect Unity" ("On Homers Poetry," *E.*, p. 267).

The following chapters study *Jerusalem* and *Prometheus Unbound*, attempting to show that each of these poems is just such a unity. An explication of these texts must identify, unfold, and relate different systems of thought. The poets have deliberately entangled contradictory traditions, which battle within the poems; we find ourselves, as the poets intended, engaged in intellectual struggle. The outcome of

1

this struggle is a complete revolution in one's reading of poetry, as Frye has argued;[6] it is a revolution of thought.

Four questions still require attention from readers of *Jerusalem* and *Prometheus Unbound:* the question of their context, of their real subject, of their symbolic technique, and of their literary form. These questions are difficult because the poems present contradictory evidence, but their answers are suggested by this very fact. First, we must recognize that, contrary to the pronouncements of Matthew Arnold and T. S. Eliot, the masterpieces of Romanticism are difficult precisely because their authors knew so much. They knew, for example, what modern criticism is still learning: the literature of prophecy and the philosophy of mind. They knew that a prophecy submits tradition to the transfiguring light of imagination; and they knew that contraries generate progression. In consequence, the greatest prophecies of the Romantic period, *Jerusalem* and *Prometheus Unbound,* assume these contrary contexts: prophecy and the philosophy of mind.

Contradictory evidence also perplexes interpretation of other works by Blake and Shelley. Some evidence suggests that these are political writers: Blake entitled a poem *The French Revolution,* for example, and Shelley began *The Revolt of Islam* with a discussion of the French Revolution. David V. Erdman and Kenneth Neill Cameron, among others, argue that this political interest pervaded the poets' careers;[7] other poems certainly suggest this interpretation. One of Blake's prophecies concludes with "A Song of Liberty" that in turn climaxes with the prophetic declaration that "Empire is no more!" (*M.H.H.*). Another prophecy explicitly celebrates the American Revolution. In *A Philosophical View of Reform* Shelley celebrates both the weakening of "the strength of . . . Empire" and also "the just and successful Revolt of America" (*Prose,* 7: 5, 13). These statements do not display merely historical interest: Blake names his hero Albion and locates his revolution within that figure; Shelley writes that "meanwhile England, the particular object for the sake of which these general considerations have been stated on the present occasion, has arrived, like the nations which surround it, at a crisis in its destiny" (*Prose,* 7:19). We are evidently reading revolutionaries.

The nature of the revolution that Blake and Shelley treat is complicated. Blake demands "Mental" and not "Corporeal War" (*M.,* preface). His revolutionary agent, Orc, who "stamps the stony law to dust" ("A Song of Liberty"), also stands with Jesus, who is the "Human

Imagination" (*F.Z., E.*, p. 358; *M.*, 3:3). Shelley's "Ode to Liberty" invokes not armies or parties but "bright minds" and "human thoughts . . . alone." He celebrates Florence's resistance to "Empire" because it produced "superiority . . . in literature and the arts" (*Prose*, 7:5). When he discusses the French Revolution, Shelley writes of "metaphysics" (*The Revolt of Islam*, preface). *A Philosophical View of Reform* describes the new epoch by pointing to Bacon, Spinoza, Hobbes, Bayle, Montaigne, Locke, Berkeley, Hume, and Hartley. Shelley condemns the new aristocracy because "they poison the literature of the age" (*Prose*, 7:29), and repeatedly makes this intellectual focus apparent, reminding us that "poets and philosophers are the unacknowledged legislators of the world" (*Prose*, 7:20). If we conclude that Blake and Shelley write of revolution, we must also admit that they refer this revolution to the mind.[8]

In fact, both Blake and Shelley write explicitly about the philosophy of mind. Blake's first illuminated works are tractates on epistemology; he cites Bacon, Newton, and Locke all his life; and he affirms that "Mental Things are alone Real" (*V.L.J., E.*, p. 555). Shelley speculated on metaphysics, concluding that "beyond the limits of perception and of thought nothing can exist" (*Prose*, 7:59). Further, both writers involved their poetic art with these philosophical issues, Blake declaring that he will not cease from mental fight and that "painting, as well as poetry and music, exists and exults in immortal thoughts" (*A Descriptive Catalogue, E.*, p. 532). Shelley is equally explicit about the mental reference of his art: just as his metaphysical speculations are committed to compelling "the mind to a rigid consideration of itself" (*Prose*, 7:342 n.), so his greatest poem's imagery is "drawn from the operations of the human mind" (*P.U.*, preface).

Openly religious language further complicates their poetry. Blake's greatest poem, *Jerusalem*, takes its title from the Bible, and in that poem and elsewhere he refers his revolution, his philosophy, and his art to Jesus. Blake painted and wrote a commentary on the Last Judgment, defining his grand theme; his watercolor "The Great Red Dragon and the Woman Clothed in the Sun" points us nominally to the same source, the Book of Revelation, and symbolically to Blake's interpretation of it. Even if Mary Shelley had not told us that the Bible was Shelley's constant study, we would know that *A Philosophical View of Reform* names Jesus Christ "that great Reformer" (*Prose*, 7:5); that Shelley claimed that "the Being who has influenced in the most memorable manner the opinions and the fortunes of the human species, is Jesus Christ" (*Prose*, 6:227); that Shelley wrote "On the Moral Teaching of Christ"; and that a late and major poem, *Hellas: A Lyrical Drama*, begins with a Herald of Eternity and includes Christ among its characters. We must not forget that these prophets against empire lodged their art in a biblical tradition.

Jean H. Hagstrum has identified two relevant strains of a prophecy's meaning, "the story of the universe and the story of the age." Although I have preferred to identify three, to include the story of the perceiving mind, I agree with Hagstrum that "in no classical [or Romantic] work of prophecy can the two [or three] strains be disentangled."[9] Simultaneously to perceive different levels is necessary for understanding Blake's composite art of poems and designs; it is also necessary for understanding the multiple meanings that enrich both *Jerusalem* and *Prometheus Unbound*. The reader's task is a difficult one: "Thought can with difficulty visit the intricate and winding chambers which it inhabits" (*Prose*, 7:64). The interpreter's goal must be, like the poets', a synthesis rather than a dissection of multiple strains. To examine the syntheses achieved in *Jerusalem* and *Prometheus Unbound* is to attempt to answer the four questions with which I began; to answer them is to define Romantic visionary art.

These poems exhibit a literary form that still requires adequate definition. Their figurative technique and visionary symbolism await precise formulation. Their subject (mind and its metaphor, history) belongs to the visionary aesthetic tradition; that subject is also consistent with philosophical tradition. Because the *form* of prophecy and the *philosophy* of mind require explanation, I shall have to outline those traditions in some detail.

First, however, it will be useful to describe the poets' characteristic multiplicity of meaning. Their symbols have many levels of reference. Some are drawn from mythologies: like Shelley, Blake modifies every myth that he uses, and both poets show prodigious knowledge of mythic traditions. In addition, their prophecies have a contemporary frame of reference that usually involves political facts. These two levels of reference collapse when Blake combines biblical and British place names, as Frye has explained;[10] they also combine when Christ appears in *Hellas*, a poem whose preface cites contemporary political events (Wasserman has explained this strategy).[11] Beyond these levels, prophecy is sublime allegory: it does not predict specific temporal events, but refers to an eternal present in the mental life of mankind. Such interiority does not contradict prophecy's historical reference, but combines with it to achieve a multiplicity that Revelation's interpreters have traditionally expounded. Those commentators regularly explain that book's symbols of tyranny, for instance, whose historical counterparts embody an eternal idea. If we consider also the literal level of a visionary narrative, as Dante does (in *The Convivio*) and as Henry More does (in his biblical commentaries), then our interpretation will be fourfold.

More specifically, *Jerusalem* and *Prometheus Unbound* exploit three points of contact between prophecy and the philosophy of mind. Briefly, prophecy is traditionally understood to commit itself to an idealistic philosophy of being. British empirical philosophy also led its practitioners to idealism, notably in Berkeley's *Principles of Human Knowledge*, but also in other major texts of the period. A related methodological point of contact is the visionary concentration of mental activity: prophets, their exegetes, and empirical philosophers study chiefly perception—and more specifically, vision. Newton's *Opticks*, Berkeley's *A New Theory of Vision*, and virtually all other major empiricist texts focus on the mind's activity when it sees; so do most explicators of the vision of Saint John. Finally, the central symbolic pattern of biblical prophecy is the overthrow of spiritual tyranny. Empirical idealism is also based on a pattern of intellectual liberation, clearly expressed in Descartes' *Discourse on Method* and repeated by Descartes' major successors. The prophet and philosopher both narrate a revolution of mind in order to effect a renovation of vision.

Such an ambition is more than a theme: it is a vocation. The techniques and purposes that I have described characterize the masterpieces of Blake and Shelley, and they also characterize their careers. In order to define the pattern that is most beautifully but obscurely elaborated in *Jerusalem* and *Prometheus Unbound*, I shall first explicate a few shorter and simpler works by Blake and Shelley. Equipped with the model that these shorter works provide, and with the traditions outlined in my next chapter, we shall be prepared to approach *Jerusalem* and *Prometheus Unbound*.

Blake's *Visions of the Daughters of Albion* identifies its own form, by its title. The theme of the poem is tyranny and its overthrow; and to achieve the visionary multiplicity of meaning, Blake has neatly divided his poem into three sections, which he separates by a refrain. The first section, which continues to plate 2, line 20, treats the subject of political tyranny by reference to the enslavement of America. Bromion declares:

> Thy soft American plains are mine, and mine thy north & south:
> Stampt with my signet are the swarthy children of the sun:
> They are obedient, they resist not, they obey the scourge:
> Their daughters worship terrors and obey the violent: . . .
>
> (1:20– 23)

This section also treats the issue of commercial slavery: Theotormon hears "the voice of slaves beneath the sun, and children bought with money" (2:8).

The second section of the poem incorporates the symbolism of slavery again, but in terms of empirical philosophy: Oothoon complains that "they told me that I had five senses to inclose me up. / And they inclos'd my infinite brain into a narrow circle" (2:31– 32). Theotormon makes this demand: "Tell me what is a thought? & of what substance is it made?" (3:23). Bromion refers to the dominion of "the infinite microscope" (4:16). The philosophy of the five senses, clearly, has replaced politics as the literal subject of the poem, but the paradigm of tyranny is preserved within this new frame of reference.

The third section of the poem addresses the "Creator of men! mistaken Demon of heaven" (5:3). Tyranny has shifted to the religious level of reference: Oothoon attacks the sacrament of marriage; she complains that Innocence converts to "religious dreams and holy vespers" (6:14), and that "Oothoon is the crafty slave of selfish holiness" (6:20). She curses, now, not political tyrants or the tyranny of the five senses, but the God of institutionalized Christianity: "Father of Jealousy. be thou accursed from the earth!" (7:12).

Thus Blake presents three visions of one symbolic act; he separates in space three actions whose time is one, thus providing three different perspectives on his unified theme. This technique is a visionary convention: Joseph Mede, Henry More, and Sir Isaac Newton call it *synchronism* in their commentaries on Revelation. The technique achieves symbolic multiplicity; it enables the poet to address at once all the levels of reference that I have listed above, and thereby to expand a reader's perception.[12]

The Marriage of Heaven and Hell also complains about the "senses five" (plate 7); it also concerns itself with cleansing the doors of perception (plate 14), and employs those same levels of reference. The *Marriage* begins with a poem, "The Argument," whose contemporary political reference has been conjectured by Erdman.[13] Joseph Anthony Wittreich, Jr., has elaborately unfolded the form of the *Marriage*, the form of prophecy;[14] Blake himself has indicated his genre by citing two prophetic chapters from Isaiah (on plate 3) and by using "the Prophets Isaiah and Ezekiel" as speaking characters (on plate 12). Furthermore, Blake discusses epistemological problems in the *Marriage*, using vocabulary that lodges his work in the mainstream of British philosophy. He has Ezekiel discuss "principles of human perception" (plate 12), thereby achieving in miniature a conflation of prophecy and epistemology. This conflation was already latent traditionally, as I shall subsequently show, but it was never so directly expressed.

Blake very nearly quotes a visionary theologian, Emanuel Swedenborg, and a secular philosopher, Paul Henri Thiry, Baron d'Holbach, inverting them both (plate 4). Blake's formulation of the "error" that "Man has two real existing principles Viz: a Body & a Soul" alludes to Swedenborg, whom he has named as the object of his attack and who had written "that the Spirit of a Man is his Mind" and that "the Mind of every one is his Internal Man, which is actually a Man, and dwelleth within the External Man, that maketh it's Body."[15] But for Holbach, as for Blake, this dualism is an error: "The more man reflects, the more he will be convinced that the soul, very far from being distinguished from the body, is only the body itself, considered relatively to some of its functions."[16] Blake's statement is a calculated inversion of Holbach's: "Man has no Body distinct from his Soul for that calld Body is a portion of Soul discernd by the five Senses." Swedenborg was wrong in positing a distinction, and so far Blake agrees with Holbach; but Holbach was wrong in assigning ontological priority to the body, or material portion of man. Blake has invoked and inverted his contrary contexts, sacred and profane; he has achieved a miniature marriage of heaven and hell, transfiguring both parties in their marriage. He has also overthrown the tyranny of materialism, which he continues to do, by means of this technique and others, throughout his career.

Later, Blake invokes another principle from Holbach, but at the same time he also embodies both his radical Christianity and his philosophical idealism. This brief passage, on plate 11, contains poetic theory too, and includes speculation on the activities of mind and the objects of knowledge: conflation of contexts enables Blake to achieve all these levels at once. Holbach had written that "the elements of nature were . . . the first divinities of man" and that "the elements were deified."[17] Blake writes that "the ancient Poets animated all sensible objects with Gods." This sentence recalls Holbach's, but it also recalls a theory of myth that was devised by the Cambridge Platonist, Henry More. Blake adds epistemological theory when he describes the attempt "to realize or abstract the mental deities from their objects." Both Holbach and Blake complain that by means of this deification "a system was formed, which some took advantage of & enslav'd the vulgar," but while this enslavement, for Holbach, was merely political, for Blake it also involved art ("poetic tales") and religion: "Thus began Priesthood." Holbach writes that "subsequent speculators no longer recollected the source from whence their predecessors had drawn their Gods," i.e., material objects.[18] Again Blake invokes Holbach in order to invert him: "Thus men forgot that All deities reside in the human breast." Poetic theory, religious history, philosophy, and political theory can and must be conflated, Blake implies, because they are all referable to a comprehensive mental unity, toward which visionary art aspires.

Blake states this doctrine of poetic unification in his brief essay "On Homers Poetry"; he implies it again when he expresses his intent in the *Marriage:* "The notion that man has a body distinct from his soul, is to be expunged; this I shall do, by printing in the infernal method, by corrosives, which in Hell are salutary and medicinal, melting apparent surfaces away, and displaying the infinite which was hid" (plate 14). Here Blake commits his art to the task of expunging philosophical materialism; the "apparent surfaces" are, at once, the copper of his plate, the supposed matter of the body, and the literal level of a symbolic image. His art will display "the infinite which was hid," and this is an aesthetic intention that places Blake in the line of biblical prophets whose hallmark is "the desire of raising other men into a perception of the infinite" (plate 13).

More lucid than the *Marriage,* Shelley's *Defence of Poetry* also expounds the visionary aesthetics that these poets share. Ezekiel had told Blake "that the Poetic Genius (as you now call it) was the first principle" of human perception (plate 12); Shelley agrees, affirming that "poetry is connate with the origin of man" (*Prose,* 7:109). Like Blake, Shelley argues that even primitive language is "vitally metaphorical"

(p. 111), drawing its vehicles from the sensible world and converting them to intelligible tenors: "In the infancy of society every author is necessarily a poet, because language is itself poetry; and to be a poet is to apprehend the true and the beautiful, in a word, the good which exists in the relation subsisting, first between existence and perception, and secondly between perception and expression" (pp. 111–12). Just as Holbach and Blake had done, Shelley identifies the common origin of allegory, religion, and law: "All original religions are allegorical. . . . Poets . . . were called, in the earlier epochs of the world, legislators or prophets; a poet essentially comprises and unites both these characters" (p. 112). Blake makes exactly those points on plate 11 of the *Marriage*; both writers differ from Holbach by exalting rather than execrating the poetic process that they describe.

Shelley defines the prophet by assigning him the same commitment that Blake had assigned him: a poet is a prophet, not because he predicts the future, but because he "participates in the eternal, the infinite, and the one" (p. 112). He is concerned not with "apparent surfaces" but with "the infinite which was hid"; "poetry lifts the veil from the hidden beauty of the world" (p. 117), which Shelley tells us "is infinite" (p. 131).

The symbolic terms of a poem are often drawn from contemporary events; "but the poet considers the vices of his contemporaries as the temporary dress in which his creations must be arrayed, and which cover without concealing the eternal proportions of their beauty" (p. 117). To the poet's vision, history is symbolic: "The true poetry of Rome lived in its institutions," whose beauty the imagination created "out of itself according to its own idea" (p. 125). Events, like the imagery of poems, have an intellectual and not a material cause; for this reason, "a poem is the image of life expressed in its eternal truth" (p. 115). If visionaries demand political change, it is because they demand intellectual revolution: they "want the poetry of life" (p. 134).

Thus Shelley identifies symbolic art with idealism and with revolution: their bases are absolutely identical. The unification that is poetic art is so comprehensive that poetry is called divine. Traditional religion is itself symbolic, a form to be penetrated, interpreted, to reveal "eternal truth" or "the infinite which was hid": "The distorted notions of invisible things which Dante and his rival Milton have idealised, are merely the mask and the mantle in which these great poets walk through eternity enveloped and disguised" (p. 129).

We cannot expect Shelley or Blake to write prophecies whose terms finally convert to historical meanings; plain prose could handle such matters more directly. Furthermore, the poets recognize that "there is no want of knowledge respecting what is wisest and best in morals, government, and political economy" (p. 134), and so those are not the goal of visionary art, which Shelley devotes to a grander purpose: "We want the creative faculty to imagine that which we know" (p. 134). As Blake had done, Shelley unifies the contexts—aesthetic, religious, philosophical, and political. His art treats them all at once because his art is an event of their common fountain: the human mind and its actions. He will use the historical facts of empire, but as a poet uses his other symbols: "They are the episodes of that cyclic poem written by Time upon the memories of men" (p. 125). It is the poet's task—and his readers'—to interpret them, to perceive the eternal truth, the *idea*, that individual symbols signify.

All these principles and strategies lodge Blake and Shelley in the prophetic tradition, but both writers effect a change in the prophetic paradigm. Blake firmly encloses his cosmic history "in the Human Brain" (*F.Z., E.*, p. 302), and Shelley writes that the transcendent power of inspiration "arises from within" (*Prose*, 7:135). This internalization arises, as I shall show, from a conflation of the visionary tradition with a philosophy of mind that reduces reality to ideas and ideas to the individual mind. The complex unification that Blake and Shelley describe, and that they achieve in *Jerusalem* and *Prometheus Unbound*, depends upon the simultaneous usage of contrary traditions, aesthetic and philosophical. Before approaching these poems, therefore, I shall first outline in greater detail those traditions and the relations that subsisted between them before they embraced in the flames of Romantic imagination, and a new art rose like Elijah.

ONE

Prophecy and the
Philosophy of Mind

B lake and Shelley selected the prophetic form for their master-
pieces precisely because that form is best adaptable for
embodying what Shelley called the "intellectual philosophy" (*Prose,*
6:196). That philosophy provides the content with which prophecy's
form becomes identified.[1] In *Jerusalem* and *Prometheus Unbound,* Blake
and Shelley entangle the contrary perspectives whose conflict is the
visionary drama. According to a traditional interpretation, when Saint
John says "Come and see," he refers at once to the tenor of his
prophecy—a revolution in vision—and its vehicle, vision itself.[2] The
structures and techniques of prophecy all serve to make its form match
its content. On one level, then, a prophecy *means* the intellectual effort
that it *exacts.*[3] Blake and Shelley, I shall argue, both recognized this
fusion of philosophy with form. To reconstruct the development of this
perception, it is necessary to begin with the intellectual doctrines—
the philosophy of mind—and then move to the fusion of this philosophy
with visionary form.

Blake and Shelley couched their intellectual premises in the terms of
Enlightenment philosophy, what Shelley called the intellectual philoso-
phy.[4] British philosophy in the seventeenth and eighteenth centuries
forms a coherent tradition because each major philosopher reacts
openly to his predecessor, wherever he does not repeat him. To study
Descartes (against whom the British philosophers reacted) and then
Locke, Newton, Berkeley, and Hume in order is to assemble intellec-
tual rather than merely chronological relations; it is to produce the body
of ideas that Blake and Shelley perceived. These philosophers were
concerned with religious problems: Descartes proved the existence of
God, although this part of his argument may be, intellectually, only an

artful dodge;[5] Locke proved the reasonableness of Christianity, although his arguments in the book by that name are based on a contradiction;[6] Sir Isaac Newton wrote commentaries on biblical prophecy; and Berkeley's *A Treatise Concerning the Principles of Human Knowledge* contains crucial theological passages.[7] Nevertheless, these philosophers form a tradition that eventually includes such profane thinkers as Hume and Holbach. Furthermore, their tools, most of their subjects, and their results almost never directly concern scripture.[8]

René Descartes initiated the activity that I shall trace in the British philosophers of the eighteenth century. Locke constantly reacts to him, and—beyond this special influence—Descartes' methods represent an almost cultural tendency; in fact, Descartes' methods were influential in forming that cultural tendency. Specifically, Descartes shifts philosophy into a special direction: the consideration of ways of knowing becomes a primary issue. The decline of scriptural authority may contribute to this individualizing tendency; it may be, too, as Karl Mannheim suggests, that the collapse of social stability also directs attention onto ways of knowing.[9] In the case of Descartes, that philosopher's interest in the skepticism of the Greeks and of Montaigne may be a stronger factor. But it is Descartes' effects rather than his antecedents that directly concern us here, and his intended effect was, he writes, to construct a new method of knowledge; this effort he began only when he had leisure to examine his ideas.[10] This preliminary statement suggests two of the four central principles of Descartes' philosophy. First, the individual philosopher is his own object of study. Descartes writes that he has never intended more than to try to reform his own ideas (p. 10). The philosopher's aims therefore shrink with his subject and so become circumscribed by the individual mind.

The second major principle of Descartes' philosophy is also implied in that preliminary statement: he studies the individual only, and, further, he studies the individual's ideas only. He studies first knowledge, not that which is known. This study is epistemology, and there is no clearer illustration of the science than the following statement: "The mental process of knowing a thing is distinct from, and can occur without, the mental process of knowing that we know it" (p. 15).[11] This intellectual involution is a result of the direct consciousness of multiplicity of ways of knowing; this consciousness, in turn, is a result of the decline in authority of traditional intellectual models. Other principles follow from this one.

The fact that Descartes is exclusively concerned with *reforming* his ideas, and the causes that enable him to do so, are consistent with the consciously revolutionary tendency of his method. At the outset of his discourse he writes that "as far as the opinions which I had been receiving since my birth were concerned, I could not do better than to reject them completely for once in my lifetime," replacing or resuming them only after destroying "the old foundations" and building anew (p. 9). Thus the preparation that Descartes assigns to himself has a revolutionary tendency: "This preparation would consist partly in freeing my mind from the false opinions which I had previously acquired" (p. 14).

Descartes' revolutionary focus is consistent with a fourth principle: he studies "mental process" because "nothing is unchanging." Accordingly, his definition of man is at once egocentric, ideational, and active: "I concluded that I was a substance whose whole essence or nature was only to think, and which, to exist, has no need of space nor of any material thing" (pp. 16, 21). His definition depends on a verb form because reality—mental reality—is a process.

Descartes' well-known first principle in fact depends on those four principles. He begins by resolving to "reject as absolutely false anything of which I could have the least doubt" (p. 20), and he discovers that only the activity of thinking remains undoubtable. Therefore "this truth, *I think, therefore I am*" becomes "the first principle of the philosophy" that he has been seeking (p. 21). Having thus reduced the first principle to mental reference, Descartes articulates a corollary that becomes important for his major successors. Concerning the nature of the reality of "sensible and corporeal entities," he writes that "although I might suppose that I was dreaming and that all I saw or imagined was false, I could not at any rate deny that the ideas were truly in my consciousness" (p. 23). Seeking certainty, he finds that he can rely only on ideal terms: the first principle of being is knowing, and being is therefore a mental act.

These principles affect the doctrine of innate ideas, which Locke attacks at such great length. Alexander Campbell Fraser has shown that Descartes' argument refers to the mind's faculties rather than to its contents.[12] This fact appears also in the concise statement of the doctrine by Descartes' philosophical correspondent, Henry More—and, as I shall be showing later, More relates this philosophy of knowing to his interpretation of biblical books, especially the Apocalypse. As Blake was to do, More defends the doctrine of innate ideas: More does not "mean that there is a certain number of ideas flaring and shining to the animadversive faculty like so many torches or starres in the firmament to our outward sight"; rather, the term *innate ideas* refers to "an active sagacity in the soul" that responds to small hints by producing clear conceptions.[13]

Blake's defense of innate ideas is similar: "Innate Ideas. are in Every Man Born with him," he writes, in his annotations to *The Works of Sir Joshua Reynolds;* and he makes his rationale clearer when, in the same work, he states explicitly: "I always thought that the Human Mind was the most Prolific of All Things & Inexhaustible" (*E.,* pp. 637, 646). Blake refers thus to what Henry More calls "the active sagacity in the soul." For both writers, then, the doctrine of innate ideas is consistent with the ideational and active elements in the philosophy of the period: the term designates a "mental process."[14] For the philosophers of mind, the doctrine is a tool with which they analyze the perception and generation of ideas. Mental activity having become the first principle of being, the importance of this process and its interpretive tools is evident.

An opposite formula also arose, after Descartes and More. Rather than study the mind's production of ideas, Sir Isaac Newton's enormously influential *Opticks* studies its reception of them. So too does the best-known work of Newton's friend and contemporary, John Locke. Each of these philosophers constructs a passive model of mind, in which an exterior agency—nature, usually—imposes ideas on the mind, which is, in turn, pictured as lifeless—a tablet of wax, a dark room, or shreds of flesh-tissue. The value of imagination and the intellectual nature of human reality are both profoundly affected by this shift in direction. Although Locke was not nearly so gratuitous and rootless a phenomenon as some scholars have pretended,[15] his thought can be treated as both representative and influential. Locke's work is puzzling: the man of the world who decided to clarify matters by setting out plain truths in his famous "historical, plain method" (introduction, par. 2) has, in fact, baffled his commentators by his ambiguity. A. A. Luce accurately observes that "Locke's use of the terms *idea, quality,* and *power* is vague and inconsistent."[16] This fact is especially troublesome because that list includes the most important terms for Locke's philosophy.

This paradox leads to another, this one visible in Locke's influence. Positively, Locke uses some readily available philosophical tools and approaches to advance intellectual philosophy and to define its purpose and direction more firmly than his predecessors had done. Negatively, he furnishes almost as much. He persists in repeating, as though he had shown them to be certainly true, doctrines that his own work persuasively disproves. Tuveson rightly observes that the importance of Locke's philosophy for aesthetics is derived from "the transference of the 'locus of reality' to the perceiving mind";[17] but, though Tuveson does not seem to recognize it, Locke never intended any such transference at all. That transference represents an activity that had been going forward before Locke wrote, as I hope is now evident, and the fact that he advanced the movement is at once one of the paradoxes of his work and one of his negative influences. The circumscription of reality by the perceiving mind is, I shall argue, an unforeseen and unintended consequence of Locke's first principle, and one that he steadfastly refused to accept; nevertheless, it is his legacy.

That first principle, put simply, is this: ideas are the only objects of knowledge. Locke's introductory definition of the term *idea* states that principle: an idea is "whatever it is which the mind can be employed about in thinking" (introduction, par. 8). The ambiguity of the interior or exterior locus of reality persists: "Whatsoever the mind perceives *in itself*, or is the immediate object of perception, thought, or understanding, that I call *idea*" (2.8.8). That first conjunction does not really connect two statements of the same thing, though it pretends to do so; the ambiguity is unsettling because all knowledge is circumscribed, in his philosophy, by whatever he does mean.

Hence Locke's famous contribution: all knowledge consists of ideas derived from two sources, sensation and reflection. The definitions of these two sources of ideas are especially important because they connect Locke's epistemology with the ontology on which it is based. His definitions therefore deserve to be quoted at length:

First, our Senses, conversant about particular sensible objects, do convey into the mind several distinct perceptions of things, according to those various ways wherein those objects do affect them. And thus we come by those *ideas* we have of *yellow, white, heat, cold, soft, hard, bitter, sweet*, and all those which we call sensible qualities; which when I say the senses convey into the mind, I mean, they from external objects convey into the mind what produces there those perceptions. This great source of most of the ideas we have, depending wholly upon our

senses, and derived by them to the understanding, I call SENSATION
(2.1.3).

This great source of most of the ideas that we have is riddled with
perplexities. First, Locke has almost surreptitiously posited some
external objects of which he is certain, but which are different from
ideas, which are all he knows; then he has posited a third thing,
different from the objects and the ideas, "what produces there those
perceptions." The distinction between sensation and perception is not
clear, and the sentence contains no explanation—or means of explain-
ing—what those things are which are not ideas, or how, if they are not,
we know them.

Locke's second source of ideas remains to be explained, and yet it
provides no clearer answers:

> Secondly, the other fountain from which experience furnisheth the
> understanding with ideas is,—the perception of the operations of our
> own mind within us, as it is employed about the ideas it has got;—
> which operations, when the soul comes to reflect on and consider, do
> furnish the understanding with another set of ideas, which could not be
> had from things without. (2.1.4)

The introspective and ideal nature of this second source of ideas
characterizes epistemology; it recalls Descartes' habits and suggests an
idealism with which Locke nevertheless does not come to terms.

Locke is now enabled to enumerate what we know: "We have the
ideas but of three sorts of substances: 1. *God* 2. *Finite Intelligences* 3.
Bodies" (2.27.2). Locke attaches a limitation to this knowledge be-
cause we cannot, he writes, identify "real essences; because we know
them not." Our faculties supply no more than "ideas which we observe
in" substances, ideas which are "more remote from the true internal
constitution from which those qualities flow, than . . . a countryman's
idea is from the inward contrivance of that famous clock at Strasburg,
whereof he only sees the outward figure and motions" (3.6.9). This
passage is evidently consistent with the limitation of knowledge by
ideas, but inconsistencies within the passage were to trouble the history
of philosophy for a long time to come. First, how the ideas which, by
earlier definition, "the mind perceives *in itself*," can now be "*in them*
[substances]" is at least as confusing as how unthinking substances

(which Locke calls *bodies*) can have ideas in them. Locke's own explanation of the inconsistency— "I would be understood to mean those qualities in the objects which produce them [ideas] in us" (2.8.8)— only begs the question by positing something other than an idea, and calling it an idea.

Another problem that troubled Locke's successors involves his analogy. Although the countryman's idea of the clock at Strasburg is limited to its "outward figure and motions," we can confidently discuss its concealed workings because they are perceptible to other people, such as clockmakers. But according to Locke's definition, no one knows more about those real essences of substances than what those remote ideas afford. To say that one is ignorant of a thing and then, in the same sentence, to claim knowledge about that thing, is to contradict oneself. This contradiction was evident to Locke's greatest critics, who did not like to be instructed about "this real constitution, or (as it is apt to be called) essence" (3.9.12) by someone who admits that he knows nothing whatever about it, that essence "being utterly unknown to us" (3.9.12).

That is precisely the problem with the materialism on which Locke claims his epistemology is based: that materialism is in fact refuted by his epistemology. The epistemology has never, as far as I know, been more clearly expressed than by Locke himself: "Since the mind, in all its thoughts and reasonings, hath no other immediate object but its own ideas, which it alone does or can contemplate, it is evident that our knowledge is only conversant about them" (4.1.1). This principle undercuts any attempt to claim knowledge about "real essences" other than ideas. When Locke explains the origin of ideas, he feels forced to posit something other than ideas. His knowledge, however, is only conversant about ideas, so that his nonideational terms are unintelligible to anyone who accepts his ideational premises, and the great philosophers who succeeded Locke did accept many of them. The problem that Locke left to his followers, then, was an abyss between objects and the mind, an abyss that his philosophy is unable to bridge. When he demonstrates materialism, Locke shows "the existence of particular external objects, by that perception and consciousness we have of the actual entrance of ideas from them" (4.2.14). But if we are only conscious of ideas, and those "objects" and that "entrance" are distinct from ideas, then we have, according to Locke's own reasoning, no such consciousness at all.

Locke's epistemology has similar consequences when he discusses that other sort of substance, God. He humanizes the idea of God in the same passage in which he claims to transcendentalize it. He writes that "even the most advanced notion we have of GOD is but attributing the same simple ideas which we have got from reflection on what we find in ourselves, and which we conceive to have more perfection in them than would be in their absence; attributing, I say, those simple ideas to Him in an unlimited degree" (3.6.11). Here, just as he had done with external objects, Locke first limits the mind, and then posits a gap that the limited mind cannot cross. This making of God in man's image is what we do "when we would frame as well as we can an idea of the First Being; who yet, it is certain, is infinitely more remote, in the real excellency of his nature, from the highest and perfectest of all created beings, than the greatest man, nay, purest seraph, is from the most contemptible part of matter; and consequently must infinitely exceed what our narrow understandings can conceive of Him" (3.6.11). If those things are "certain," they are by no means certainly shown by Locke's anthropomorphic argument. That argument has, as post-Lockian intellectual history demonstrates, rather a humanistic tendency than a transcendental one. Though his own apparent conclusions do not show it, to define God as a projection of the human mind is to render Him a psychological process. God becomes an attribution.[18]

Another psychological process, language, is also related to Locke's epistemology. He defines both the origin and the process of language: "The comfort and advantage of society not being to be had without communication of thoughts, it was necessary that man should find out some external sensible signs, whereof those invisible ideas, which his thoughts are made up of, might be made known to others" (3.2.1). Language is thus a system of visible signs of the invisible. Two elements of this definition warrant amplification.

First, the ontological dialectic of inner and outer, visible and invisible, is implied: Locke finds material origins for immaterial terms, including *spirit, angel,* and "all" names of immaterial things, "in all languages" (3.1.5). Second, if "words, in their primary or immediate signification, stand for nothing but the ideas in the mind of him that uses them" (3.2.2), then it is impossible to talk of anything other than ideas. This principle limits the sorts of things whose existence can be predicated: we confuse meaning and pervert the use of words "whenever we make them stand for anything but those ideas we have in our own minds" (3.2.5). An idealist could not ask for a more congenial theory of language.

On this issue, another contradiction arises. Figurative semantics, which are implied by Locke's definition of language, come under Locke's attack. He writes that figurative language is merely ornamental, and that "where truth and knowledge are concerned," figurative language is "a great fault" (3.10.34). This argument was a source of trouble to writers after Locke. It contains contradictions: Locke elsewhere shows that "real knowledge" and speaking of "things as they are" apart from ideas, which are the grounds of his attack on figurative language, are both impossible. Beyond this, a great poet, whose first professional principle is symbolic figuration, might well resent this final double-cross from a writer whose theory of language should have enabled him to know better. Furthermore, Locke's argument is too much like Plato the poet banishing poets from the Republic. Locke's metaphors are among the most famous in the English language: ideas are "imprinted" or "stamped" on the mind; the mind is "white paper, void of all characters, without any ideas." These metaphors are so popular that they are commonly thought, even now, to be self-evident truths, and not recognized as dubious and metaphorical parts of Locke's legacy.

The metaphor of Locke's on which I prefer to concentrate is that of vision. Locke did not invent the application of the language of bodily sight to intellectual perception; it had long been a commonplace of visionary theory, as I shall show when I come to examine that tradition. Locke does not acknowledge his debt to those visionary theorists whose metaphor he adopts, but his pervasive use of it testifies to unconscious or unadmitted interpenetration of doctrine. Locke writes that "the perception of the mind being most aptly explained by words relating to the sight, we shall best understand what is meant by *clear* and *obscure* in our ideas, by reflecting on what we call clear and obscure in the objects of sight" (2.29.2). That is, of course, an analogy, and not an explanation at all. Locke elsewhere extends the metaphor until he is writing as figuratively as any poet or visionary: external and internal sensation are "windows by which light is let into this *dark room*. For, methinks, the understanding is not much unlike a closet wholly shut from light, with only some little openings left, to let in external visible resemblances, or ideas of things without" (2.11.17). Sometimes Locke intensifies the tone of the metaphor until it becomes charged with emotion: he writes of intuitive knowledge, for instance, that it "is irresistible, and, like bright sunshine, forces itself immediately to be perceived, as soon as ever the mind turns its view that way; and leaves no room for hesitation, doubt, or examination, but the mind is presently filled with the clear light of it" (4.2.1). This joyous little passage does what metaphor ordinarily does: it intensifies thought with feeling. It is a perfect example of figurative language employed with evident relish, and is employed by a writer who banished such language from serious discourse as a "perfect cheat" (3.10.34).

The use of this metaphor is no less interesting than its history. The form of writing that traditionally pursued intellectual truth under the metaphor of vision and light is Christian theology, and especially visionary theology. This context is invoked, therefore, by Locke's central metaphor. I stress the point because it has been missed so often before. Tuveson, for example, points out the function of the metaphor of light and vision in Locke's *Essay*, but treats it as an outright invention of Locke's, uniquely pertinent to his new philosophy.[19] Such a view impairs understanding not only of the history of the metaphor, but of Locke himself: the history of a metaphor is the history of an idea. Applied to the study of imaginative literature, Tuveson's point of view leads to erroneous attributions of influence. In fact, relations of Locke's philosophy to prior systems of thought, including the philosophies of visionary aestheticians, are apparent in his central metaphor, vision. Neither is it always safe to take Locke's as the last word on such subjects. He not only knew about the work of the Cambridge Platonist and visionary theorist, Henry More, for example, but also cites it specifically (3.10.14). Locke disparages More's philosophy as opposed to his own, with regard to the theory of meaning, and yet there are evident, though unacknowledged, similarities between the two writers' theories, as I shall subsequently show. Both writers stress mental tenors of sensible imagery, for instance, and the metaphor of accession of light.

This same interpenetration of doctrine, based in large part on that same metaphor, is equally noticeable in the prodigiously influential work of Locke's friend and contemporary, Sir Isaac Newton. Newton's writings on vision—bodily and mental—express contrary perspectives, sacred and profane. His *Opticks* studies bodily sight, speculating on purely intellectual perception, and achieving unrivaled influence; his learned *Observations upon the Prophecies* brings tremendous knowledge and energy to the study of spiritual vision; and the salient point of contact of these books is Locke's central metaphor—vision. Just as Locke does, Newton assumes rather than proves exterior agency, be it matter or God, but, also like Locke, he writes on the question of perspective itself.

Although Newton's *Opticks* studies physical rather than metaphysical science, that work is based on philosophical assumptions, many of them Locke's. Conscious that his own concerns pass beyond physical mechanics and enter spiritual questions, Newton also addresses those spiritual questions in the *Opticks*, though tentatively: he deliberately extends the philosophical relevance of his book, pointing out that "if natural Philosophy in all its Parts, by pursuing this method, shall at length be perfected, the Bounds of Moral Philosophy will also be enlarged."[20] These philosophical bases and implications of Newton's work interested the Romantic poets, in a way in which merely physical mechanics could not. Of these bases, one set—the spiritualist set of assumptions—has attracted interpretation of Newton as a Neoplatonist.[21] In the General Scholium to the *Principia*, Newton writes that "we might add something concerning a certain most subtle Spirit which pervades and lies hid in all gross bodies,"[22] but he then stops short of explaining this theory—which he may have acquired from his colleague at Cambridge, Henry More—because he lacks space and "sufficiency of experiments."

In the *Opticks*, Newton seems to contradict the spiritual hypothesis by his absolute materialism, affirming that "even the Rays of Light seem to be hard Bodies" (p. 389). When he complicates his philosophy with his religion, here and again in his commentaries on the Bible, the result is generally materialism: the world and its maker are conceived as exterior agencies and as different in kind from human powers. "All material Things seem to have been composed of the hard and solid Particles . . . variously associated in the first Creation by the Counsel of an intelligent Agent. . . . Once form'd, it [the world] may continue by those Laws for many Ages" (p. 402). This conjunction of materialism and an external deity has two consequences in both Newton and Locke: first, purely ideal experience is invalidated; second, human mental activity—and especially imagination—loses value. Visionary philosophy and art plainly depend on those two values, and so subsequent visionaries must either reinterpret Newton's thought to employ it, as Shelley does, or else oppose it, as Blake does. To be able, later, to assemble the poets' reactions, it will be necessary here to chart their precursor's system.

The method by which Locke and then Newton invalidate purely mental reality involves the doctrine of secondary qualities. Locke writes that "primary qualities," which produce "solidity, extension, figure, motion or rest, and number" (2.8.9), differ from "secondary qualities," which produce "colours, sounds, tastes, &c." The difference invalidates purely visionary experience— *all* purely mental experience: our secondary ideas, according to Locke, do not even resemble the qualities, in bodies, which produce them. "The ideas of primary qualities of bodies are resemblances of them, and their patterns do really exist in the bodies themselves, but the ideas produced in us by these secondary qualities have no resemblance of them at all. There is nothing like our ideas, existing in the bodies themselves" (2.8.15). Locke includes the ideas of sight in the class of ideas that do not resemble exterior realities. He also, and for similar reasons, attacks the validity of visionary philosophy: *its* ideas also lack resemblance to exterior realities. Thus, Locke attacks *"enthusiasm:* which, laying by reason, would set up revelation without it. Whereby in effect it takes away both reason and revelation, and substitutes in the room of them the ungrounded fancies of a man's own brain, and assumes them for a foundation both of opinion and conduct" (4.19.3). Here Locke attacks more than a group of Dissenters; he attacks the philosophy that relies upon—that values—imagination. He thus denies ontological validity to the visions of the bodily eye, asserting that these visions (ideas of sight) do not resemble exterior realities; for a similar reason Locke invalidates purely mental vision: the "ungrounded fancies of a man's own brain" do not represent reality, which is conceived as exterior to the mind.

Newton similarly limits the value of both kinds of vision in the *Opticks*; he reduces visual experience to a condition of the perceiving mind. Such a condition does not represent the qualities in the objects which produce the ideas of sight. In light,

the Rays to speak properly are not coloured. In them there is nothing else than a certain Power and Disposition to stir up a Sensation of this or that Colour. . . . Colours in the Object are nothing but a Disposition to reflect this or that sort of Rays more copiously than the rest; in the Rays they are nothing but their Dispositions to propogate this or that Motion

into the Sensorium, and in the Sensorium they are Sensations of those
Motions under the Forms of Colours. (p. 125)

Vision thus affords no direct access to reality, which must instead be
deduced uncertainly from the system of illusions that vision supplies.
Similarly, the faculty of mental vision, imagination, is of little value,
Newton preferring to study "All the Colours in the Universe which are
made by Light, and depend not on the Power of Imagination" (p. 158).
God's activity created the universe; mankind's only discolors it: "If the
Eye be tinged with any colour (as in the Disease of the *Jaundice*) so as to
tinge the Pictures in the bottom of the Eye with that Colour, then all
Objects appear tinged with the same Colour" (p. 16). Blake alludes to
this statement of Newton's when he writes, "As the Eye—Such the
Object" (*E.*, p. 634). He converts the principle to a doctrine of mental
power, knowing that for Newton it was a statement of a crippling
limitation.

The Accordingly, Newton deviates from a central principle of both Des-
cartes and Henry More: the mind is *not* an active agent in the
production of its ideas, but rather a mechanical recipient: "Wherever
the Rays which come from all the Points of any Object meet again in so
many Points after they have been made to converge by Reflection or
Refraction, there they will make a Picture of the Object upon any white
Body on which they fall" (p. 14). This model of vision requires no
mental activity at all: in fact, the process is performed equally well
with inert lens and paper (pp. 14, 165), and its causes can be deduced
from a dead eye (p. 15). Relying on the doctrine of an external and
material world, on secondary qualities, and on a passive model of mind,
it is no coincidence that Newton adapts Locke's metaphors—including
the white paper and the dark closet, which are used over and over again
in the *Opticks*.

The subsequent history of these principles is itself a history of
eighteenth-century philosophy. Many thinkers exhibit both the posi-
tive and negative influence of Locke and Newton, but the most
important of their immediate successors was George Berkeley. In *A
Treatise Concerning the Principles of Human Knowledge,* he concentrates on
his subject—mind—even more completely than Locke had done. Like
many of the thinkers of the period, Berkeley constructs an epistemol-
ogy that conducts him to an implied ontology, and for him the two fuse.
His introductory comments on his own intellectual method, therefore,

have special importance. In those comments he makes plain a principle that will differentiate his work from Locke's: he will not assert a thing of which he has no idea or notion. If someone tells him of a thing and at the same time tells him that the thing is altogether imperceptible by any means, and that consequently no one has any idea of it, Berkeley withholds credence. This principle, obvious as it sounds, is in fact Berkeley's precise point of departure from Locke and Newton, and it is the first principle of his widely misunderstood philosophy.[23]

The introduction of the principle involves the doctrine of abstract ideas: Berkeley wishes to extricate himself "out of that fine and subtle net of *abstract ideas,* which has so miserably perplexed and entangled the minds of men" (introduction, par. 22). He cites the pasage from the *Essay Concerning Human Understanding* in which Locke explains the doctrine of abstraction by defining the abstract or general idea of a triangle. This "must be neither oblique nor rectangle, neither equilateral, equicrural, nor scalenon, but *all and none* of these at once" (4.7.9; cit. Berkeley, introduction, par. 13). Berkeley's discussion of this passage is an excellent illustration of his method: "If any man has the faculty of framing in his mind such an idea of a triangle as is here described, it is in vain to pretend to dispute him out of it, nor would I go about it. All I desire is, that the reader would fully and certainly inform himself whether he has such an idea or no" (introduction, par. 13). Berkeley identifies that of which the mind *is* capable: "Whether others have this wonderful faculty of abstracting their ideas, they can best tell; for myself I find indeed I have a faculty of imagining, or representing to myself, the ideas of those particular things I have perceived, and of variously compounding them and dividing them" (introduction, par. 10). What Berkeley denies is that the mind can frame an idea of qualities in separation "which it is impossible should exist so separated" (introduction, par. 10). This refusal to claim to conceive the inconceivable actually has controversial consequences. First, the denial restores the known world to perception. The principle involved is sometimes called, in other contexts, Romantic particularity; it is a basic principle of Berkeley's philosophy.[24]

Berkeley elaborates this concept with reference to Locke. He cites the *Essay Concerning Human Understanding,* where Locke argues that "words become general by being made the signs of general ideas" (3.3.6; cit. Berkeley, introduction, par. 11). Berkeley perceives the contradiction: "But it seems that a word becomes general by being made the sign, not of an abstract general idea, but of several particular ideas, any one of which it indifferently suggests to the mind" (introduction, par. 11). This, then, is the way in which Berkeley achieves his doctrine of particularity: for thinking, it is necessary to have particular ideas, whatever the scope of the thought. The principle is both useful and liberating: "He that knows he has no other than particular ideas, will not puzzle himself in vain to find out and conceive the abstract idea annexed to any name" (introduction, par. 24).

Another result of Berkeley's concentration on mind is a connection between his methodological statements and his conclusions, and between his epistemology and his ontology:

> The objects I consider, I clearly and adequately know. I cannot be deceived in thinking I have an idea which I have not. It is not possible for me to imagine, that any of my ideas are alike or unlike, that are not truly so. To discern the agreements or disagreements there are between my ideas, to see what ideas are included in any compound idea, and what not, there is nothing more requisite, than an attentive perception of what passes in my own understanding. (introduction, par. 22)

This point is skillfully made and placed. Its validity in context is self-evident; later it helps define Berkeley's entire view of the world. Considering his reader, Berkeley writes that "I do not see how he can be led into an error by considering his own naked, undisguised ideas" (introduction, par. 25). This is a statement of method, but also of purpose, and, as the following sections of the *Principles of Human Knowledge* make plain, it is a statement of Berkeley's philosophy, in which processes of knowing and being, previously linked by Descartes, fuse even more completely.

That fusion, Berkeley's most important contribution to philosophy, is accomplished in three paragraphs that begin the *Principles of Human Knowledge*. This condensed and artful part of his book is ably explicated by A. A. Luce, and need only be outlined here.[25] Section 1 begins with an epistemological statement that recalls Locke: "It is evident to any one who takes a survey of the objects of human knowledge, that they are either ideas actually imprinted on the senses, or else such as are perceived by attending to the passions and operations of the mind, or lastly ideas formed by help of memory and imagination, either compounding, dividing, or barely representing those originally perceived in the aforesaid ways" (par. 1). Section 2 adds another term to this now conventional formula of knowledge: "Besides all that endless variety of ideas or objects of knowledge, there is likewise something which knows or perceives them, and exercises divers operations, as willing, imagining, remembering about them. This perceiving, active being is what I call *mind, spirit, soul,* or *my self*" (par. 2). That seems scarcely to require saying; but it has important implications. The paragraph concludes with a deduction that seems equally obvious and, considered epistemologically, consistent with received and popular theory: "The existence of an idea consists in being perceived" (par. 2).

Then the controversy begins. If the argument of section 1 is accepted, then that of section 2 follows necessarily, and that of section 3 follows necessarily in turn. At once Berkeley solves the problem of Locke's contradictions and sets forward a new principle of being that is also a principle of knowing: "For as to what is said of the absolute existence of unthinking things without any relation to their being perceived, that seems perfectly unintelligible. Their *esse* is *percipi,* nor is it possible they should have any existence, out of the minds or thinking things which perceive them" (par. 3).

In my analysis of Locke's and Newton's philosophies, I have tried to indicate the problems that Berkeley is solving here. The unintelligibility to which he refers is precisely the confusion embodied in Locke's limiting his knowledge to ideas and then claiming knowledge of things other than ideas: Berkeley simply removes the contradiction. Newton's philosophy posits a reality totally alien to human awareness; Berkeley's philosophy restores that reality to the human mind. He does not say that what is perceived does not exist; he says precisely that it does exist, and by doing so he solves other problems of contradiction. Whereas Locke argues in some places that ideas are "in us," and elsewhere that they are "in them," in some unthinking material substance, Berkeley points out that "for an idea to exist in an unperceiving thing is a manifest contradiction" (par. 7); whereas Locke argues first that knowledge is only of ideas and then claims knowledge of the agreement or disagreement of ideas with something other than ideas, Berkeley points out that "an idea can be like nothing but an idea" (par. 8). In short, agreeing with Locke that only ideas are known, Berkeley limits ontological terms accordingly.

As in the argument on abstract ideas, here again Berkeley argues that his reader's introspection will prove his case. "When we do our utmost

to conceive the existence of external bodies, we are all the while only
contemplating our own ideas. But the mind taking no notice of itself, is
deluded to think it can and doth conceive bodies existing unthought of
or without the mind; though at the same time they are apprehended by
or exist in it self" (par. 23). Berkeley's *or* is placed so strategically that
his own insight and the misunderstanding to which it has been subject
for more than two hundred and fifty years are both explained by the
meaning of that one conjunction. The misunderstanding has occurred
among both matterists and subjective idealists, but Berkeley was of
neither school. Not all his followers have so misunderstood him, and the
quality of his positive influence requires at least a brief indication of
features of his philosophy that matterists and subjective idealists often
miss.[26]

A careful reading of the *Principles of Human Knowledge* shows that
Berkeley was no solipsist; he did not believe that all reality existed
only within his mind. He explicitly states his belief to the contrary:
"The table I write on, I say, exists, that is, I see and feel it"; further, "if
I were out of my study I should say it existed, meaning thereby that if I
was in my study I might perceive it, or that some other spirit actually
does perceive it" (par. 3). Berkeley even analyzes the process by which
he distinguishes between objects that are the product of his mind and
those that are not (pars. 28–29): if Berkeley were to kick a rock, he
"should say it existed" because, not in spite, of his philosophy. This is a
theory of being that is based on a theory of knowing; it is a mental,
though not a subjective, model of reality that he deduces from his
model of mind. Whereas Locke asserts the existence of three sorts of
substances, while showing that he has knowledge of only one, Berkeley
writes that "there is not any other substance than *spirit*, or that which
perceives" (par. 7). Here, as in section 2, Berkeley identifies *spirit* with
mind, and he solves the problems created by the confused statements
about "real essences" that trouble the work of his great predecessor: he
argues, as Blake was to argue, that "Mental Things are alone Real"
(*V.L.J., E.*, p. 555).

The nature of this "mind" is therefore of great importance; and
Berkeley's elaboration of its definition is an influential part of his
philosophy. He has called *mind* an "active being," in section 2, and its
activity is a central element in its definition: "A spirit is one simple,
undivided, active being: as it perceives ideas, it is called the *under-*

standing, and as it produces or otherwise operates about them, it is
called the *will*" (par. 27).

Reality is wholly circumscribed by mind; the mind is by definition
active; the result is a view of reality as process. This process view links
Berkeley's thought with that of many successors, including Kant. It is
Kant, in fact, who is generally credited with articulating this idea and
its importance; my point is that this emphasis on the mind as an active
agent was suggested prior to Kant, and in Britain—by Berkeley. This
assumption—that mind is active in the formation of its knowledge—is
widespread and current still: Jean Piaget discusses this tendency of
modern epistemology, and a recent book on cognitive psychology, a
discipline that is itself an emerging phenomenon, argues the point as
controversial. Ulric Neisser points out that "in its continuity, its cyclic
nature, its dependence on continuously modified schemata—perceiv-
ing is a kind of doing."[27] Though neither Piaget nor Neisser acknowl-
edges the fact, this amounts to a restatement of Berkeley's point. In this
new context, the argument is still controversial: Neisser has to argue,
with all the energy of current controversy, that "the perceiver is ac-
tive,"[28] because a passive model of mind, a vestige of Locke's philoso-
phy, also generally unacknowledged, persists in modern psychology.
Between Berkeley's time and our own, the problem of the active
processes of mind and, consequently, of reality has involved the ener-
gies of other kinds of thinkers, too—many of them poets as well as
philosophers. Chief among these poets are Blake and Shelley.

Some correlative principles of Berkeley's philosophy are also impor-
tant to his successors. One of them is the deduction that "the cause of
ideas is an incorporeal, active substance or spirit" (par. 26). Thus, there
are only spiritual causes, and so "philosophers amuse themselves in
vain, when they inquire for any natural efficient cause, distinct from a
mind or *spirit*" (par. 107). This point, too, Blake later repeats: "Every
Natural Effect has a Spiritual Cause, and Not / A Natural" (*M.*,
26:44–45). Thus Newton's search for natural causes comes under
attack by Berkeley (pars. 97–98, 110–17) as, later, by Blake.

Another important component of Berkeley's philosophy is his theory
of meaning. Concentrating on perception, Berkeley concentrates on
vision: "Visible ideas . . . signify . . . after the same manner that words
of any language suggest the ideas they are made to stand for" (par. 43).
This theory, elaborated "in *Sect.* 147 and elsewhere of the essay con-
cerning vision" (par. 44), also by Berkeley, defines vehicle and tenor as

ideal entities: "The connection of ideas does not imply the relation of *cause* and *effect,* but only of a mark or *sign* with the thing *signified*" (par. 65). Sensible imagery, accordingly, is significative; and the terms and process implied are mental. This is a system of signification that, mounted on an ideal ontology and implying a process of correspondence between sensible and intellectual, not only converts vision to a metaphor of intellection, as Locke had done, but goes on to define the process of vision itself as a metaphorical act. For writers after Berkeley, this theory of signification affects not only models of vision; by fusing optics with metaphor, Berkeley has injected the metaphorical process itself with ontological validity and importance. When nonverbal reality itself is perceived as symbolic, then the symbol-making process, understood as a microcosmic repetition of the act of cosmic creation, has more than merely verbal significance.

As I shall be arguing again below, a similar theory of meaning appears in eighteenth-century literature on biblical prophecy. William Jones, for example, points out the Bible's "application of all visible objects to a figurative use."[29] Leslie Tannenbaum has observed that Jones's principles go back to Saint Augustine, citing "Augustine's idea that through the Incarnation the objects of sense are transformed into signs."[30] Thus, in his *Explanatory Notes upon the New Testament*, John Wesley cites Martin Luther: "Divinity is nothing but a grammar of the language of the Holy Ghost."[31] Like Augustine and Jones, Berkeley argues that sensible objects form a signifying alphabet and grammar, since *all* visible things "signify . . . after the same manner that words of any language suggest the ideas they are made to stand for."

It is Berkeley himself who points us to the relevant system of verbal symbolism, urging that his immaterialism is consistent with scripture (par. 82). Similarly, in an openly theological argument, Henry More had written of "the Existence of God, and of things Incorporeal" that "a greater Certainty, even of these things, is to be drawn from the Scriptures rightly and compleatly understood, than from the clearest Fountains of Philosophy."[32] It is significant that the same argument appears thus in empirical philosophy and in theological commentaries on the Bible: these systems of thought penetrate one another, offering what Blake and Shelley were to find so useful—authority for an idealism that is at once literary and philosophical.

Finally, the force and nature of Berkeley's influence depend on an understanding of the way in which Berkeley viewed his own methods and aims. He explicitly circumscribes all his tools, procedures, and purposes with a statement of moral intention that declares the teleology of mental revolution: "To recreate and exalt the mind" (par. 109). That is the clearest statement possible of the governing purpose of a spiritual revolutionary.

A pattern appears within and among all the philosophers whom I have considered so far: each trims some elements from his predecessors' philosophy. Descartes began his method by eliminating as much as he thought possible from the circle of claimed knowledge, doubting whatever he could; what he was able to construct was a three-term ontology of mind, matter, and a correlating divinity. Descartes was able to construct so much largely by means of his innate ideas. Locke carried on Descartes' own process, doubting and eliminating principles from his philosophy by removing those innate ideas. Locke thereby reduced the known even further than he was prepared to admit; nevertheless, he offered some version of the same three ontological terms. Berkeley, then, was even more thorough and consistent in removing superfluities: he showed matter to be an unnecessary and in fact unintelligible part of his predecessors' theories, and cut it away. The perceiving mind and its ideational activities remain, and with them a few ontological dogmas. Chief among these is Berkeley's self-assurance concerning transcendentals, and these do not go unchallenged for long.

Therefore, when Sir Leslie Stephen writes that "the influence, indeed, of Hume's teaching is the more obscure because chiefly negative," he identifies a characteristic of Hume that, paradoxically, lodges him in a continuous tradition.[33] It is precisely this process of transforming a predecessor's philosophy, by applying further his own procedures, that defines the intellectual tradition of which Hume is a member.

Hume's place in that tradition is defined by his writings on three subjects: philosophy, history, and religion. I shall concentrate on his philosophical work, because it is most pertinent here, and also because literary scholars already have such a solid understanding of Hume's historical and religious tendencies.[34] The complicated epistemological and ontological principles on which these are based deserve whatever attention and clarification we can give them, because they affect the form and substance, positively and negatively, of his successors' work. In Hume's case, as in Berkeley's, method and conclusions are closely related, and so both require attention.

The most convenient synopsis of Hume's philosophy is Stephen's:

> The "substance" in which the qualities of the phenomenal world are thought to inhere is a concept emptied of all contents, and a word without a meaning. The external world, which supports the phenomena, is but a "fiction" of the mind; the mind, which in the same way affords a substratum for the impressions, is itself a fiction; and the divine substance, which, according to the Cartesians, causes the correlation between these two fictions, must—that is the natural inference—be equally a fiction.[35]

These doctrines are also Shelley's: "A catalogue of all the thoughts of the mind, and of all their possible modifications, is a cyclopedic history of the Universe" (*Prose*, 7:59). For Hume and for Shelley, "beyond the limits of perception and of thought nothing can exist" (*Prose*, 7:59). The external world, Shelley says, "is 'such stuff as dreams are made of'" and he denies personal identity (see *Prose*, 6:194– 96).

Shelley is obviously following Hume, but Hume's rationale is more explicit.[36] To follow his argument is, therefore, to explicate these parts of Shelley's thought; it is also, simultaneously, to locate Shelley's position in a coherent tradition of British philosophy, because Hume indicates his own departure from his predecessors, Locke and Berkeley.

Hume begins with an epistemological premise that is consistent with the first principles of Locke and Berkeley: "'Tis impossible for us so much as to conceive or form an idea of anything specifically different from ideas and impressions."[37] That is a methodological statement, about how one can form ideas; but, just as Berkeley had done, Hume modulates his methodological statement into an ontological principle. He even uses Berkeley's example: "That table, which just now appears to me, is only a perception, and all its qualities are qualities of a perception" (p. 239).

Shelley repeats this argument, precisely. "It is an axiom in mental philosophy, that we can think of nothing which we have not perceived," Shelley says, beginning (like Hume) with a methodological statement. Quickly, however, this axiom changes to an ontological principle: "Beyond the limits of perception and of thought nothing can exist" (*Prose*, 7:59). For Shelley as for Hume, the final authority is concrete perception. As a result, the idea of substance is rejected: it is but an idea that, as Hume says, "the imagination is apt to feign" (p. 220). Only mental events remain.

As the list of Hume's rejections grows, his departure from Berkeley can be perceived more clearly as a continuation of the process that reduces certainty and, for the philosopher, reality, to mental events. This is precisely the process to which Hume subjects cause and effect: those are terms applied by the mind to a mental phenomenon. The impression antecedent to the idea of cause is internally conditioned; Hume argues that there are mental events—including internal dispositions such as that which we call cause. Thus we do not perceive *cause* as an *object;* we perceive only our own internal disposition (pp. 155–66). Here again, Shelley was later to agree: "Cause is only a word expressing a certain state of the human mind" (*Prose,* 6:197). That is also the process to which Hume subjects time and space: first Hume shows that their infinite divisibility is a function of the mind; then he shows that time and space are themselves functions of the mind. They are never perceived—they are fictional constructs (pp. 26–39).

Hume does not stop with these impressive reductions, but goes on to define the doctrine of mental event even more sharply. In a carefully worded passage that makes use of a now familiar metaphor, Hume differs from Berkeley concerning the mind itself. Mind is an ontological ground that Berkeley himself did not want shaken; but an epistemological problem that Berkeley solved by an appeal to etymology recurs in Hume, who rejects the device that saved mind from Berkeley's negative procedures.

Berkeley had observed that mind, being active, cannot be represented by an idea, which is passive (par. 27). As soon as the mental representation of an activity freezes into a static object, it is no longer an accurate representation of the activity. But Berkeley needs to save the ontological status of mind, though he needs so little else, and he does so by introducing a new word, *notion.* This is not a bare trick of word-play or double-talk: the word, in accordance with its Latin meaning, refers to an act of coming to know, whereas *idea* denotes, for Berkeley, the known.

When Hume analyzes the ontological status of mind, he implicitly invokes Berkeley to transcend him in negation: "The mind is a kind of theatre, where several perceptions successively make their appearance; pass, re-pass, glide away and mingle in an infinite variety of postures and situations. There is properly no *simplicity* in it at one time, nor *identity* in different; whatever natural propension we may have to imagine that simplicity and identity" (p. 253). Hume certainly knew the history and implications of the metaphor of the theater of the mind; implying art and imagination, for example, it was regularly applied by other writers to visionary art. As Hume continues the passage, it will appear that he qualifies the relevance of the metaphor, but before he does, he packs his sentence with five active verbs. The philosophical relevance of all that verbal activity should be obvious: he is writing about that which is by definition—by Berkeley's definition—active in essence. Then Hume swiftly refutes the two traditional philosophical supports of the idea of personality, and he accounts for their popularity. He assigns the terms and their use to imagination. Thus he draws together two strands from the foregoing sentences, imagination and mental activity, and he quietly advances a theory of mental behavior.

That is a great deal to achieve in so short a passage, but Hume, not yet finished, continues: "The comparison of the theatre must not mislead us. They are the successive perceptions only, that constitute the mind; nor have we the most distant notion of the place, where these scenes are represented, or of the materials, of which it is compos'd" (p. 253). Here Hume has achieved a remarkable definition of the mind: it is "successive perceptions only." However consistent with the principles of empiricism, this definition is new to the tradition. In offering it, Hume specifically denies the mind exactly what Berkeley had granted it; he rejects the usage of *notion* to save the mind as known and real.

Hume has completely replaced the idea of personal identity, or self, with a newer, scantier model; as a result he leaves to reality even fewer terms than his predecessors had left. "Mankind," he writes, "are nothing but a bundle or collection of different perceptions, which succeed each other with an inconceivable rapidity, and are in a perpetual flux and movement" (p. 252). This is empirical extremism. Nothing but mind remains; and nothing remains even of mind but those events which Hume calls perceptions. Such a philosophy upsets the security of virtually every idea it is possible to have, other than perception itself.

One threatened idea particularly requires mention: God. In his analysis of cause, Hume has shown that we have no idea of power, because it does not arise from any impression whatever. Later, he is explicit about the implications of this claim with regard to the idea of God: "We have no idea of a being endow'd with any power, much less of one endow'd with infinite power" (p. 248). Hume does not assert atheism openly, but even where he asserts a belief in God, he undermines his own statement by concluding it with a reminder that we have no idea of any such thing (p. 633 n.). Here again, Shelley was to follow Hume: "For when we use the words *principle, power, cause*, &c., we mean to express no real being" (*Prose*, 6:208).

Descartes, who started this process of doubting, might have been alarmed at its results; Hume, in fact, attacks Descartes' argument for God specifically (p. 160). The line proceeding to Hume, however, involves Descartes' own method, though the bulk of the work was done by British philosophers. All of them began with mind; as a group, they ended there. Fewer and fewer terms remained impervious to the doubt that, after Descartes, became a moral obligation and a revolutionary creed.

Hume's writing on historical subjects was also influential, primarily because of two characteristics that are identified by Carl Becker.[38] In terms of method, Hume's work is characterized by a pull toward universality: Becker reminds us of Hume's observation that "history informs us of nothing new or strange. . . . Its chief use is only to discover the constant and universal principles of human nature" (p. 95). In terms of ideology, Hume and his followers were radical. As Becker puts it, "The eighteenth-century Philosophers were not primarily interested in stabilizing society, but in changing it" (p. 97). Hume also restores the center of religious interest to a humanized context. This is Becker's thesis: "The new heaven had to be located somewhere within the confines of the earthly life, since it was an article of philosophical faith that the end of life is life itself, the perfected temporal life of man. . . . The salvation of mankind must be attained, not by some outside, miraculous, catastrophic agency (God or the philosopher-king), but by man himself" (p. 129). Significantly, Becker takes the phrase "new heaven" not from the eighteenth-century philosophers but from the Book of Revelation. That book had special relevance to events of eighteenth-century political history. That relevance was not a matter of religious dogma but rather of revolution, and the distinctly intellectual character of that revolution involves the philosophical insurrections of Hume. The humanization of final values, the correlative reduction of reality to perceived mental events, and the dynamic perception of all that remains in this humanized version of the world—these are characteristics of Hume's work which contribute to the apocalyptic temper of the period. These intellectual developments, and Hume's work in general, are signs of the times.

A related body of doctrine also appears, later, in the Romantic writers. This is the doctrine of monistic materialism as it was expounded by Enlightenment philosophers of the revolutionary period, chiefly by Joseph Priestley in the *Disquisitions Relating to Matter and Spirit* and by Holbach in *System of Nature*. This is a related body of doctrine for two reasons: it attempts to solve the same Cartesian dilemma that Berkeley and Hume attempt to solve, and it offers a dynamic view of the world as active process. The Cartesian problem, as both of these materialist philosophers state it, is this: given matter and mind, essentially different and sharing no common property, how could those two entities ever act upon one another in such a way as to produce knowledge? One solution—the one that we have seen—is to eliminate matter from the scheme; but the other, represented by Holbach and Priestley, is to reduce mind to a material function: "Those who have supposed in man an immaterial substance, distinguished from his body, have not thoroughly understood themselves; indeed they have done nothing more than imagined a negative quality of which they cannot have any correct idea: matter alone is capable of acting on our senses, and without this action nothing would be capable of making itself known to us."[39] Priestley agrees, and employs a common topic to argue on the point, though the same evidence is used by Berkeley to argue for the opposite case: "The notion of two substances that have no common property, and yet are capable of intimate connection and mutual action, is both absurd and modern; a substance without extension or relation to place being unknown both in the Scriptures, and to all antiquity."[40]

Clearly, Priestley and Holbach are using the same methods that the immaterialists had used. They appeal to the possibilities of knowledge to solve the same problem—dualism—and yet they reach the opposite conclusion: they write of "the uniform composition of man," arguing that "what we call mind, or the principle of perception and thought, is not a substance distinct from the body, but the result of corporeal organization."[41] As Holbach puts the case, man's "soul, or the moving principle that acts within him . . . is only the body itself considered relatively with some of its functions, or with those faculties of which its nature and its peculiar organization renders it susceptible."[42]

Holbach's stress on activity represents the second point of similarity between these materialists and the immaterialists Berkeley and Hume: they are ontological activists. Holbach writes that everything which Nature "contains necessarily conspires to perpetuate her active existence."[43] These two principles, then—the repudiation of dualism for epistemological reasons and the postulation of universal activity—show these contrary philosophers to be at work in the same context, the same intellectual culture. So too does the revolutionary tenor of Holbach's philosophy, and of Priestley's.[44]

Blake and Shelley both were to recognize that revolutionary tendency and four other major principles of this philosophical tradition. Those principles, to recapitulate, include the priority of perspective or point of view, increasingly exclusive focus on the activities of the perceiving mind, an idealistic theory of meaning, and a process philosophy of mind and being. And, as Becker has shown, these humanistic philosophical principles entered religious writing: the effect (again) was to relocate the new heaven within the present and earthly life of man. This common ground of secular and religious writing helps to explain what has bewildered students of eighteenth-century philosophy, as Stephen J. Stein has pointed out: apocalyptic speculation goes hand in hand with rigorous professional and natural philosophy.[45]

In fact, major philosophers of the period were also commentators on prophecy—Henry More, Sir Isaac Newton, and Joseph Priestley, for example, all devoted volumes to the interpretation of the Apocalypse, the culmination of biblical prophecy. As Christopher Hill writes, "It was in a *scientific* spirit that scholars approached Biblical prophecy," and Hill names Napier, Brightman, Mede, Ussher, and Newton.[46] In Newton's case, as I have argued, science and philosophy were the same; and so they were for those "English scholars, trained in biblical learning and the new sciences, who had become fascinated with the prospect of coordinating scriptural prophecy with the new theories about the universe," scholars whom Stein cites.[47]

This fusion of philosophy, science, and apocalypticism is also Tuveson's subject, in his *Millennium and Utopia*: "The religious concept of the millennium was transformed, even by supposedly orthodox theologians. Gradually the role of Providence was transferred to 'natural laws.'"[48] Tuveson shows persuasively that the philosophy and science of the eighteenth century were fused with the teleology of biblical prophecy.[49] The effects of this fusion were, first, to place the philosophies of

More and Newton in a biblical framework and then, second, to endow biblical prophecy with new and earthly applications.

Newton, for example, wrote several influential commentaries on the Book of Revelation, and all of them belong to a visionary tradition that recognized in prophecy a language of symbols, and then assigned to this figurative technique a philosophical purpose. Newton's interest in immaterialism is uncertain and arguable; Blake and Shelley interpret Newton differently on this point, and (more recently) so do Carl Grabo and Donald Ault.[50] Newton's ambiguity appears equally in his biblical writings. He recognizes the theories of figurative language on which his predecessors (including Henry More) base their idealistic interpretations of prophecy, but Newton regularly assigns the symbols of prophecy to external and terrestrial points of reference. Materialistic as his readings often are, Newton is, as I shall show, committed to principles of biblical symbolism that locate his work in a coherent tradition of visionary theory. This tradition was later known to the Romantic writers, who made use of its philosophical and aesthetic principles.[51]

Commentators perceive in the Book of Revelation the perfection of visionary art: "There was never any Book penned with that Artifice as this of the *Apocalypse,* as if every word were weighed in a Balance before it was set down."[52] Beyond doctrinal concerns, this prophecy's artistic excellence was widely admired, commentators setting "it down as a fundamental Law in the Interpretation of the Apocalypse, that not a single word is superfluous"[53] and declaring that "the whole may be considered a number of scenic pictures."[54] The form's dominant metaphor, vision, regularly elicited such analogies to visual art: Revelation is "the Theater of Visions."[55] The mind's eye of the visionary (John) has perceived a cosmic spectacle; by means of the visionary book, the mind's eye of his audience perceives such a spectacle too.[56] Like a theatrical performance, visionary art is a composite form: its visions are "written by Characters in letters," but also "painted by certain shapes." In a prophecy, verbal and visual components are "to be joyned together."[57] Dealing with the art of impassioned and imagistic language, "the prophetic office had a most strict connection with the poetic art."[58]

Commentators exhibit widespread agreement about some of prophecy's special characteristics. Lowth, for one, argues that "this species of poetry is more ornamented, more splendid, and more florid than any

other. It abounds more in imagery, at least in that species of imagery
which . . . is transferred from certain and definite objects to express
indefinite and general ideas." More visual than other forms, a prophecy
is also more intellectual in its reference. A related principle exempts a
prophecy from conventional restraints: "Naturally free, and of too
ardent a spirit to be confined by rule, it is usually guided by the nature
of the subject only, and the impulse of divine inspiration."[59]

Noticing that John's words, "come and see," refer to his method as
well as his subject, commentators conventionally perceive the fusion of
form and content that prophecy achieves: it is the art of vision, just as
Enlightenment philosophy became its science. For some commenta-
tors, including Thomas Goodwin, prophecy supplies a mental model.
John's vision was a modification of "his Faculties," and the purpose of
John's book is to enable his readers to model their minds after it— "that
is, to give up our Selves, our Powers and Faculties, to the Spirit's Rule
and Guidance" by submitting to the mental conformations displayed in
Revelation; the prophecy portrays "the Form or Pattern . . . into which
all Saints on Earth should be moulded." For this reason the four beasts
full of eyes, from chapter 4, "have eyes *within* as well as *without,* to see
to their own Hearts, as well as to others." [60] Striving to unfold Revela-
tion as "the true Portrait of the Holy Ghost's Mind," Goodwin internal-
izes the prophecy's purpose and many of its symbols: "The Threat-
enings of the Gospel are *Arrows*, striking secretly, and dartingly, into
Men's Hearts." As clearly as any philosopher, Goodwin implores his
readers to allow Revelation to "raise up your Thoughts higher."[61]

The figurative technique of biblical prophecy embodies a philoso-
phy of mind in eschatological terms. Thus A. C. Charity observes of
biblical language that it "is applied . . . not only *to* the hearer and his
existential understanding, but *in* the actual response of the hearer."
This conception of a mental model is deepened in the prophecies, as
Charity says, by the eschatological act that is known only in the
language of the prophecy.[62]

Just as Locke explains the metaphorical relation between seeing and
understanding, Emanuel Swedenborg explains that in a prophecy, "to
see signifies to understand." Unlike Locke, Swedenborg distinguishes
sharply between material and intellectual vision: "How crass and mate-
rial the Sight of the bodily Eye is," and how inferior "to the Perception
of spiritual Things." Spiritual vision is a purely intellectual act, because
"Spirit signifieth the Mind of Man, and whatever belongeth thereto."[63]

Locke's philosophical predecessor, Henry More—one of the men from whom Newton learned biblical commentary—also applied the analogy between intellectual and bodily sight to visionary art. John wrote when his mind was "vacant from this earthly body, and external senses, and wholly seised by this Divine and Angelical Power, which caused in it the following Visions, and Prophetical Impressions, but as lively and clear as any objects to the outward or corporeal senses."[64] More's statement appears within an aesthetic context, but it posits an epistemological model. Like Locke's, this model is nicely designed to invite an ontological paraphrase: More defines "the spirit of Prophecy, the spirit enabling [men] firmly to believe and declare beyond what flesh and blood can attain to."[65] We have seen that to limit knowledge by the bodily senses is also to limit that which exists. More illustrates an opposite tendency that is common among visionary theorists: to expand perception beyond what the bodily eye can compass is to increase ontological terms.

Because it is founded on an active model of mind, and because its immediate object is art, visionary theory exalts imagination.[66] This faculty becomes increasingly identified with *inspiration* as the prophet's source, and critical attention shifts to the prophet's mental act. Robert Lowth, for example, writes that the Hebrew word that "means *an oracular saying* . . . is no more peculiar to predictions of future events, than to every species of that eloquence which is supposed to come by inspiration." It is derived, Lowth writes, "from *nasa*, he raised, he produced, he spoke . . . not . . . he received."[67] Clearly, that shift in emphasis is consistent with the direction of eighteenth-century philosophy. A visionary is committed to imagination because, as Austin Farrer has pointed out, "the Apocalypse writes of heaven and things to come, that is, of a realm which has no shape at all but that which the images give it." [68] The point is at once aesthetic and ontological: the visionary's images—his ideas—form the reality of which he writes; his symbolic terms recapitulate a symbolic reality, and his imaginative act imitates creation.[69] This principle is exactly the opposite of Locke's and Newton's denigration of imagination; it shares with Berkeley's idealism a recognition that nonverbal reality is itself symbolic. It also shares with Hume a vision of the world as "perpetual flux and movement," a world composed of mind-forged fictions, shifting forever in the shapes of active intellect.

The metaphor that is most commonly used to describe prophecy—

vision—underscores these implications; and so does the metaphor commonly used to interpret prophecy, namely, the metaphor of dreams. Arising both from the oft-interpreted prophecy of Daniel and from the oriental scholarship of Joseph Mede and others, the interpretation of dreams was conventionally identified with the interpretation of prophecy.[70] This technique supplied commentators with a code for interpreting symbols; it also supplied them with an analogy that began to shape their conception of prophecy. Prophecy is understood as literary idealism, if, like a dream, it is composed of images that are to be read as the shapes of ideas. The interpreter, using the *Onirocriticis* of Rigaltius, assumes a consistent symbol-system, and his task, like the prophet's, is to transcend idiolect (or idiosyncratic usage) and apprehend the schema itself (a shared system of meaning); he does so by discerning in the prophet's individual utterances a universal reference. Further, commentators make free use of virtually any other book of the Bible, Old Testament or New, to explicate the Book of Revelation: the interpreter infers a semantic design.[71] Prophecy is a composite form, containing verbal and visual terms, just as a dream combines them; these terms form a language in a semiological sense although they are not limited to a purely verbal language—prophecy includes iconographical units as well.[72] Like a dream, therefore, a prophecy arises within the mind and orders its terms and their reference within the circle of vision.

The analogy with dreams suggests another dimension of prophecy that virtually every commentator takes for granted: the visionary event is a process; the visionary poem, like a dream, consists of ongoing action. Its knowledge is its act of knowing, created by the prophecy and not merely contained in it. This principle brings to aesthetics the Cartesian assumption that being arises from thinking; it recalls More's definition of innate ideas; and it is consistent with Hume's intellectual theater across which perceptions ceaselessly pass. It is also consistent with modern epistemology, which is "tending more and more today to regard knowledge as a process more than a state."[73]

This philosophical tendency enters the specific principles of interpretation, too. Synchronism, for example, is a principle defined by Mede and used after him by such major commentators as More and Sir Isaac Newton; these commentators use synchronism to define both the literary form of prophecy and also its concept of time. Mede explains that in Revelation events that are presented separately should be under-

stood to occur simultaneously;[74] its visions are distinguished spatially
and symbolically, and yet the audience of the prophecy must perceive
their essential unity if that audience is to interpret them.[75] The inter-
preter must rise above the distinctions of time; a lesson in exegesis,
Mede's principle is also a lesson in philosophy. Similarly, Boethius, in
book 5 of his *Consolation of Philosophy,* describes the events of time as if
they formed a tapestry. From the narrow perspective of the temporal
present, events are viewed one after another; from the larger perspec-
tive of an eternal present the entire array can be seen at once. For the
prophet, as for Boethius and Hume, time considered as terrestrial
sequence is a perceptual handicap, a mind-forged manacle from which
the mind is to be liberated; the visionary selects for this liberation the
medium of art.

This vision of essential unity, outside time, endows prophecy with
denser significance than conventional time-sequence could afford:
intellectual value, and not mere chronological order, governs the selec-
tion and distribution of a prophecy's parts: "In the Divine idea . . .
there is no time, but instead of time there is state."[76] To abolish the
restrictions of conventional ideology is to allow access to ideas beyond
that ideology. Prophecy's form and content, therefore, are uniquely
adapted to one another and to the art's guiding purpose: to cleanse the
doors of perception, sweeping the clutter of binding fictions from
before the mind's eye and allowing it to perceive the infinite—the
universal—which was hid.[77]

Throughout biblical aesthetics, issues of art give rise to issues of
doctrine. In the aesthetics of prophecy, an art that abounds in imagery,
the technique of symbolism gives rise to the philosophy of idealism.
More, for example, affirms that "the *Schemes of Speech in Prophets and
men inspired* are usually such as *most powerfully strike the Phansie* and most
strongly beat upon the *Imagination.*" The characteristic exaltation of
imagination includes an equally characteristic notice of the prophets'
"sensible, palpable" imagery. A doctrinal issue arises: some theologians
flatter "*the* External Person *of Christ,*" while others "*will have nothing to
do with his* Person, *but look upon the Mystery of Christianity as a thing wholly
within us*"; the visionary aesthetician, understanding both vehicle and
tenor of prophetic utterance, argues instead for "*the Truth and Necessity
of both* Christ within *and* Christ without."[78]

This use of multiple meanings bridges a traditional ideological gulf:
one tradition of theologians (including Irenaeus) reads biblical proph-

ecy as referring to an earthly millennium; another tradition (exemplified by Origen) rejects earthly chiliasm. Saint Augustine begins to close this ideological gap when he accepts the Apocalypse as prophecy, but interprets it in purely spiritual terms.[79] Henry More's interpretation, in turn accepting both applications of biblical symbolism, is the more common among Protestant exegetes, and it derives from a fourfold interpretation that was dominant in the Middle Ages.[80] More's doctrine is thus both literary and ideological: vehicle and tenor, history and the individual mind, inner and outer revolutions, are brought together in the symbolism of prophecy, which therefore recapitulates the symbolic universe.

Elsewhere, More does affirm that God "is not only *Intellectual,* but that great and *Eternal Intellect.*"[81] More's definitions of this crucial term, *God,* seem equivocal, but they are rendered consistent precisely by his aesthetic theory. He cites Paul's Epistle to the Romans: "For the invisible things of him from the creation of the world are clearly seen, being understood by the things that are made." More elicits from Paul a different formulation of the relation of interiors and exteriors: the Lamp of God is firmly located "in us," but is "fed and nourished from external Objects. . . . This *Light within us . . .* judges and concludes after the Perusal of either the *Volumes* of *Nature* or of *Divine Revelation.*" The emphasis shifts from the world of art to the world of being: in both cases, external objects are fuel that the fire of intellection converts to incorporeal light. Such a formulation translates aesthetics into ontology; thus, it does not matter whether we are considering "the *Volumes* of *Nature* or of *Divine Revelation.*"

Commentators who affirm that "the spiritual sense alone discloses" the meaning of biblical prophecy also affirm idealistic philosophy; they insist that "the Spirit of a Man is his Mind," and so a spiritual reading of prophecy yields intellectual philosophy.[82] Visionary symbolism recapitulates idealist ontology: the tenor of a symbol "does not appear in the sense of the letter; for it is within it, as the soul is in the body." The visionary interpretation of human experience is identical with the visionary interpretation of art: the "Infinite is in finite Things . . . and in Men, as in its Images."[83]

Instructing its readers in the art of interpretation, prophecy conducts them to the perception of the infinite. Its palpable terms have spiritual tenors: the winepress in Revelation, for example, is interpreted as "*pressure* of *conscience.*" The completion of the prophecy is a revolution occurring not only among men's political institutions but "in the inward powers of their minds." The intellectual process of symbolism implies an intellectual plane on which Revelation's action occurs, its figurative terms having ontological correlatives. Thus, the prophecy's wars and slayings are not "*to be brought in by the* Sword, *unless it be by the* Sword *of the* Spirit." Throughout Revelation, there "is no Carnal Warfare" but rather intellectual. More finds in the Apocalypse not a call toward political reorganization merely, but a guide for the souls of the blessed, leading them toward "the renovation of their inward Man."[84] Such a perception results in humanism: nothing is needed "to rouse us effectually out of this carnal drousiness toward the attainment of the dispensation of the Spirit" but individual intellectual revolution.[85] A last judgment occurs whenever a man undergoes such a mental renovation, embracing ontological truth and casting off the corresponding error; this point was Blake's, in *A Vision of the Last Judgment* (*E.*, p. 551), and it was also a traditional perception.

Christian commentators who were also Platonists recognized the similarity of some of Plato's formulations to their own: Plato is of the "best sort" of pagans, for whom sensible images are "significative of that or this Divine Power," and for whom "God is a Mind or Intellect . . . pure from all Matter." Plato was a literary artist, according to this view, "so it is apparent how strange soever the use of these *Images* may seem, that it was no other than that of Books," such images "raising our Minds" to contemplation of intellectual form.[86] Commentators had been conflating pagan and Christian symbolism long before Blake and Shelley did so: perceiving the intellectual kinship of such contrary theologies, Joseph Priestley, for example, writes a book-length comparison of Hebrew, Christian, and Greek theisms.[87] Priestley dedicates this piece of comparative religion to a Catholic and an Anglican, affirming that their differences are slight beside their agreements. Converted to intellectual principles, argues Priestley, like More before him, all religions are one. Inheriting this perception too, both Blake (in *All Religions are One*) and Shelley (in *A Defence of Poetry*) also affirm that the visionary faculty—imagination—is the permanent source of religious forms.

Despite such statements of universal agreement, Christian apocalypticism does not settle into stagnant orthodoxy; controversy does arise. Sir Isaac Newton, for example, deviates markedly in his reading of the Apocalypse from his immediate predecessor and friend, More.

Newton regularly interprets the symbols of biblical prophecy according to worldly politics: the prophet puts "a storm of thunder, lightning, hail, and overflowing rain, for a tempest of war descending from the heavens and clouds politic, on the heads of their enemies." For Newton, the heavens consistently behave in a punitive manner, and this punishment is a signal "of the relation which the Apocalypse of John hath to the Book of the Law of Moses." The God of law and punishment, usually corporal punishment, is one with the God of Revelation, of inspiration. The Old Covenant of Moses and the New Covenant of Jesus are consistent in Newton's view. That consistency is a matter of law enforcement: the writings of the prophets "contain the covenant between God and his people, with instructions for keeping this covenant; instances of God's judgments upon them that break it: and predictions of things to come."[88] After Newton, Blake insists on exactly the opposite interpretation, opposing Jesus Christ to the law absolutely (*M.H.H.*, pl. 23–24); before Newton, More had distinguished just as plainly between the Old and New Covenants, writing of "the *Lowness* of the *Mosaical* dispensation" because it propounded "worldly advantage as a reward of . . . obedience." More and Blake do not disagree with Newton in ethical terms only; the difference is finally one of ontological theory, hinging on the issue of inner and outer, material and mental being:

> Our Conversation under the *Mosaical* Covenant, and our Frame of Spirit there is but an ordinary accustomary Temper or Habit of doing or not doing such and such things; and consequently all that Righteousness but a fleshly rational Fabrick of Mind. . . . But under the Covenant of Christ, nor Fear nor Custom, but an inward Spirit of Life works us into everlasting Holiness and a permanent Renovation of Nature and Regeneration of the hidden Man.

The first point of difference between the two covenants is the difference between materialism and intellectuality; "the second main point wherein the Difference consists" is *"namely Liberty."*[89]

Few commentators produce a reading as materialistic as Newton's or as spiritualistic as Swedenborg's: traditional exegesis perceives several simultaneous levels of meaning in a prophecy, as More does when he interprets *"the minde of Moses, according to a* threefold cabbala."[90] It is in fact worldly revolutions that traditionally excite keen interest in the

Book of Revelation. "The Reformation," writes Hill, "stimulated the spirit of prophecy," and "in England the revolutionary decades gave wide publicity to what was almost a new profession—the prophet."[91] The complexity of the biblical commentators does not express a simple identification of political and prophetic concerns, but, as Hill has shown, the Puritan revolution was widely interpreted in prophetic terms.[92] In the eighteenth century too, temporal focus intensifies commentaries; Thomas Newton's widely read commentary testifies to this fact in its title: *Dissertations on the Prophecies, which have remarkably been fulfilled, and at this time are fulfilling in the world.* Thomas Newton's commentary, like those of his contemporaries, achieves a sense of urgency by thrusting its subject into immediate practical affairs.[93] In this way, Thomas Newton profits from the antagonistic lines of commentary that preceded him, materialist and immaterialist: "That the kingdom of heaven shall be established upon earth, is the plain and express doctrine of Daniel and all the prophets as well as of St. John." He thus brings the literary duality of the symbolic process to a political usage: the affairs of the world will become, in his view, a sort of objective correlative for the city of God, "God dwelling visibly among men."[94] Prophecy effects a revolution of mind, of perception; Thomas Newton understands this revolution as a divine means, effecting in turn a revolution of history. Prophecy renovates the mind, so that the mind can renovate the earth.[95]

This multiplicity of meanings—political, religious, and philosophical—is unique to prophecy because this form of art claims sacred authority for its insights. In another form, however, that multiplicity was conventional in the literature of the period. Dryden's poem, "To My Honor'd Friend, Dr. Charleton," for instance, employs multiple frames of reference, but without such authority. The "tyranny" in the first line of that poem refers to intellectual and religious tyranny, as well as political; biblical exegetes similarly use the term to include all those levels of reference. Dryden's use of *light*, also both literal and metaphorical, represents a method of multiple meaning. But as he does not claim to derive his inspiration from a sacred source, his own imaginative process does not require the kind of reverent attention that the commentators bestow on the prophets. Wasserman's reading of Pope's "Windsor Forest" focuses precisely on this process of multiple meanings, including the political.[96] In Pope's case, as in Dryden's, the

secular poem, claiming no divine origin, does not direct devout atten-
tion to the poet's imaginative process, to inspiration itself.

Another difference arises as well. The poems of Dryden and Pope
manifest conservative ideology. Dryden writes with enthusiasm of
Restoration, not of revolution. Pope's poem celebrates monarchs and
ministers of corporeal war; it does not consign them to the bottomless
abyss. Revelation prophecy, according to many commentators, has a
distinctly radical orientation: "Through his role and his message the
prophet is committed to break with the established order; to this extent
he stands apart in society . . . and is a potential agent of change."[97]
Spenser's use of the Book of Revelation in *The Faerie Queene* is an
apparent exception; more characteristic of prophetic ideology is the
writing of John Milton.[98]

That ideology is radical. Norman Cohn writes that the Book of
Revelation arose under political conditions, as it "was evoked about
A.D. 93 by the experience of persecution under Domitian," but that its
achievement is "an eschatological prophecy of great poetic power"; the
book expresses revolutionary "patterns which in their main outlines
recur again and again" throughout history. Thus, the "Sibylline and
Johannine prophecies deeply affected political attitudes" and the most
influential medieval interpreter, Joachim of Fiore, mounted such a
radical system of thought on the Book of Revelation that "there was
scarcely another intellectual who did so much to shake not only the
structure of orthodox medieval theology but also the assumptions
which must underlie any conceivable Christian faith."[99] The ideology
of prophecy flourished in England during and after the Civil War, and,
as I shall show subsequently, during and after the French Revolution.
Although Tuveson refers chiefly to the idea of progress rather than
political revolution, his remarks are pertinent here: during the Renais-
sance, "interpretations of the Apocalypse centered in the individual
soul," but eventually these interpretations "involved the relations of
classes within the state and the very nature of all authority, whether
ecclesiastical or political." Thus Tuveson argues that "no study of
English thought is complete without an understanding of the part
played by 'prophecy.'"[100]

Historically, interest in prophecy has also involved philosophical
speculation, however, and so interpretation of prophecy is not so simple
as direct conversion to political terms. Instead, a refined aesthetic
arises, able to deal with politics, philosophy, religion, and art at once.[101]

The Romantic writers, in their own time of revolution, inherited this rich legacy and put it to use. Their tool for the construction of prophecy was identical with the traditional tool for its interpretation: symbolism, or the simultaneous multiplicity of meaning.

As Blake and Shelley knew, visionary symbolism had been studied systematically for centuries before they wrote. This art and its aesthetic were known to them, and they employ its tradition. Readers of Romantic prophecies who do not share the poets' knowledge of tradition, nor acknowledge the existence of such a tradition, complain of the poets' obscurity, treating their poems as solipsistic impromptus, originating "in the private emotions and imaginings of their authors." Without reference to the tradition of visionary symbolism, a reader finds that such poems are not "immediately referable . . . to any extrinsic system of beliefs or truths," and so loses patience.[102] Arising from biblical prophecy, and especially from the Book of Revelation, a specific system of symbolism forms a tradition in which the Romantic writers place their visionary poems. Their symbolism is "extrinsic" to the extent that it is traditional, and their calculated semantics are darkened by readers' ignorance rather than by the visionaries' alleged privacy. The aesthetics of prophecy include the assumption that Revelation employs "figurative expressions"; understanding the prophecy depends upon "a right discerning of the meaning of the words and phrase," and that meaning is determined by a traditional symbol-system.[103] Explicating that symbol-system, commentators place it at the disposal of visionary poets.

Commentators recognized and identified this symbolism in secular poems as well as sacred. More, for example, explicates *The Faerie Queene* according to the symbolism of Revelation 12:6: "*Spencer's* description of *Una's* Entertainment by Satyrs in the Desart" depicts "the condition of Christianity since the time that the Church of a Garden became a *Wilderness*. . . . *Una* could beat nothing of the inward *Law of Life* into them, but all was spent in an outward idolatrous flattery, as the Poet complains Stanza 19."[104] In Spenser, as in Revelation, More identifies a symbolic relation and a parallel philosophical one, a relation between inner and outer, material and immaterial; locating the technique in *The Faerie Queene*, he emphasizes the availability of visionary symbolism to secular art.

A basic premise of visionary symbolism is therefore philosophical: all images that make up the literal "sense of the Word . . . correspond to

. . . spiritual and celestial things."[105] The prophecy is a microcosm, its symbols duplicating the objects of nature precisely because they are also symbolic, converting to ideal forms. In this way the prophet repeats the creativity of God, and his art requires readers to lift their minds, by the vehicle of vision, from the perception of sensible to intellectual forms. The referents of visionary symbols are historical as well as ideal, because Revelation is a miniature history of the cosmos "to the end of time" and yet it employs "purely *a language of ideas.*"[106]

Christian incarnation came to be recognized as a paradigm for this duality: using the apparent oxymoron, the Lord's "Divine Human," Swedenborg mounts an aesthetic theory on the assumption that prophecy's task is to bring a first intellectual cause into sensible form, duplicating the act of God. Thus "all things in the Word have also a contrary sense," each image having a literal and figurative meaning, and each object in nature having a natural and an intellectual existence.[107] The task of prophecy is to strip the veil of illusion—literality and materiality—from the intellectual tenor of art and of human life. "The Genius of these *Apocalyptick* Visions" consists in their being made "to seem . . . very complete and articulate in the very outward *Cortex,*" while containing "the History of Truth within." Revelation contains the paradigm of this duality within itself, in the symbol of the book that is written within and without: More "and several others understand this being *written within and on the back-side,* of a *Literal* and *Mystical* Sense."[108] By means of this technique of semantic doubling, prophecy "relates both to *things temporal* and *things spiritual.*"[109]

Prophecy is a self-interpreting artifact: in addition to the book written within and without, Revelation contains a symbol for its own reception, when John is commanded to eat the little book, because "*to eat* a prophecy signifies *to receive and digest it.*" Further, a prophecy contains commentary on other prophecies: "the Prophet [Daniel] and the Apostle [John] seem to be the best commentators upon each other's meaning."[110] This perception indicates the coherence of the line of vision, prophets being a knowing brotherhood of conscious artists. It also recalls the prophet's guiding purpose, enabling his audience to *see* and (what is the same) to understand. For this reason, a prophecy is an "inspired comment" on its predecessors.[111]

The visionary obscurity of which Karl Kroeber complains is in fact a hallmark of this tradition. "What studied Concealments and Obscurities there are in this Book of the Apocalypse," exclaims More.

These obscurities are "purposed, though not invincible": they are
designed "to keep this treasure hid" from those who "are not worthy."[112]
Revelation also contains within itself a symbol for this aspect of proph-
ecy, in the sealed book that is only gradually opened to the eyes of
those chosen to receive it. Lowth explicates this principle with the
metaphor of vision and light, affirming that "prophecy in its very nature
implies some degree of obscurity, and is always, as the Apostle ele-
gantly expresses it, 'like a light glimmering in a dark place, until the
day dawn, and the day-star arise.' "[113]

Another cause of prophecy's obscurity is its complexity. The mind of
Moses is to be interpreted according to a threefold cabbala, as we have
seen, and Revelation also yields three levels of meaning—literal, moral,
and mystical.[114] Swedenborg tirelessly supplies at least two contrary
senses to every symbol that he explicates. Faber insists that Revelation
"is incapable of any other than a *figurative* sense," but observes that the
prophecy's symbols "must be divided into *two grand classes:* the one
typifying *temporal,* and the other *spiritual,* objects."[115] Mede supplies a
detailed explanation of the first six seals of Revelation, referring to
Roman political events; yet he explicates the war in heaven as if it were
psychomachia, occurring within men. The angels put tendencies in
"their minds"; they have an "invisible manner of working" and "they
appear not in a visible shape."[116] Most commentators similarly resist
one-to-one correspondences, preferring to elaborate a symbol-system
that can encompass heaven and earth, the mind and nature, at once.

That figurative system is carefully distinguished from common alle-
gory. In the same passage in which he cites *The Faerie Queene,* More
affirms that "to allegorize away that blessed Immortality promised in
the Gospel is the greatest blasphemy against Christ that can be imag-
ined." He and his successors do not repudiate allegory to embrace a
literal reading that would be inconsistent with the figurative assump-
tions that characterize virtually all commentary; instead, More dis-
tinguishes between *kinds* of figurative systems. The allegorical method
that he repudiates in this passage is specifically defined: it is the
method of interpreting prophecy "in a *Political* sense," converting its
terms to terrestrial meanings. Such a reading is incorrect and ir-
religious for two reasons, according to More: first, the symbols of
prophecy have multiple meanings, and no single perspective will suf-
fice for understanding them. Second, terrestrial "Applications are too
small and petty usually for these Prophecies," which are designed to

address spiritual matters; "the Prophecies themselves, if they had no other Meaning, might very well have been spared." More cites Hugo Grotius as an example of an interpreter guilty of such a narrow political approach, but clearly Grotius was not the last such interpreter. To the present, a class of readers blithely subsumes visionary art under the name of political prophecy, treating each visionary poem as if it were a willfully obscured news announcement. More's arguments supply a richer perspective, insisting that a prophecy includes human history but is not limited to mundane events. This was Blake's perspective when he wrote that "a Prophet is a Seer not an Arbitrary Dictator" (*E.*, p. 607), gifted to perceive and reveal the infinite, not merely the finite future. Shelley repudiates the "gross sense of the word" *prophet* (*Prose*, 7:112), repeating More's claim that the prophet sees not particular events but rather their spirit: prophecy is "rightly understood in a mystical and prophetical sense . . . which was the meaning intended by the Holy Ghost, whatever Apprehensions the private Spirit of Zacharias might entertain thereof."[117]

Thus Thomas Newton, a commentator who is normally intent on the political present, nevertheless writes that "it was not by temporal means or arms that the Christians obtained this victory, (ver. 11.) but by spiritual."[118] He refers to temporal correlatives—identifying this victory with Constantine, for example—but he also internalizes the referents of prophetic symbols. Swedenborg is less equivocal, arguing that "every truly spiritual meaning is abstracted from the idea of persons, places, and times." A characteristic explication from this perspective informs us that "Pharoah and the Egyptian . . . signify the natural man separate from the spiritual."[119] On this point again, as on the issue of the distant God and his punitive code, Sir Isaac Newton reverses the traditional perception, externalizing the prophecy's reference and employing what Blake was later to call single vision. His predecessor insists that Revelation can be best "illustrated and display'd by this *Mystical* way of Exposition"; Isaac Newton prefers to identify the angel of the bottomless pit as "a very fit type of the numerous armies of *Arabians* invading the *Romans*. They began to invade them A.C. 634, and to reign at *Damascus* A.C. 637."[120] Newton knows and advances the historical scholarship of his predecessors at Cambridge, including Mede and More; but his visionary interpretation, like his optical philosophy, locates the object of vision in external space, in a fixed and definite time, and, alongside of the elaborate multiplicity that others unfold, his interpretation deserves to be called single vision.

One tool for the interpretation of prophecy conveniently illustrates Isaac Newton's relation to his tradition. Using the *Onirocriticis* that Mede had applied to Revelation, More compiles "*a compendious Alphabet* of Prophetick Iconisms." More explains that "*Visions* and *Dreams*" are "both fantasms impressed on the Imagination," so his dictionary of symbols can be used to interpret "*Symbolical Visions,* which manifestly are *Prophetick Parables.*" Here as elsewhere, More assigns multiple meanings, literal and figurative, to visionary symbols: blood, for example, "is an Hieroglyphick of *Slaughter*" and "the letting out" of blood signifies death; but "in Analogy, the destroying the Strength of any thing, or that Power or Virtue whereby it is what it is, is the *Death* of that thing, not considering whether it be Animate or Inanimate."[121] After More, Isaac Newton repeats Twisse's insight that "for understanding the Prophecies, we are, in the first place, to acquaint our-selves with the figurative language of the Prophets." Like More, he sets out to accomplish this acquaintance by compiling a dictionary of prophetic symbols. This dictionary represents one of the ways in which, as Frank E. Manuel writes, Newton "would show himself to be a master of the traditional tools of scriptural exegesis." Manuel rightly shows that Newton was such a master, but it is misleading to assert that "the elaboration of a complete lexicon of scriptural prophecy, a dictionary of prophetic symbols . . . was his own achievement." Again, when Manuel writes that "for Newton, this language of prophecy, in which objects beheld in visions stood for political and religious entities, was not a special, coded speech invented by Daniel and John," he implies rightly that prophetic symbols are not peculiar to these writers, but Manuel's idea of code apparently involves idiolect rather than schema, an idiosyncracy rather than a shared semantic design.[122] In linguistic terms, the language of the prophets certainly *does* involve a code, in Newton's view as in Mede's and More's. Newton's lexicon, therefore, and the linguistic assumptions that underlie it are traditional.

Newton's interest in oriental scholarship is traditional as well: Newton understood that the prophets' "hieroglyphic expressions had a resemblance to the system of symbols common to many Eastern nations and to the ancients in general," as Manuel says. It is correct to observe that "Newton was fumbling with an idea that Giambattista Vico was soon to develop, . . . that the earliest peoples expressed

themselves in symbols and poetic speech, not in ordinary prose."[123] It is
also correct, and more to the purpose, to notice that Newton was
fumbling with an idea that had *already* been developed, not by Vico but
by Mede and More, Newton's own predecessors at Cambridge. These
men, like Newton, used such scholarship specifically for the purpose of
interpreting prophecy, and not only for general philosophy of history.
What distinguishes Newton from these commentators, and changes the
history of exegesis, is rather the nature of his interpretations. Newton
considers the first six chapters of Daniel "a collection of historical
papers." He adopts Mede's metaphor of the "apocalyptick Theater,"
but locates that theater solidly in terrestrial space: "The whole scene of
sacred Prophecy is composed of three principal parts: the regions
beyond *Euphrates*, represented by the two first Beasts of *Daniel;* the
Empire of the *Greeks* on this side of *Euphrates*, represented by the
Leopard and by the He-Goat; and the Empire of the *Latins* on this side
of *Greece,* represented by the Beast with ten horns."[124] This naturalized
version of supernaturalism is very different, obviously, from More's, and
it is also very different from that which arises later, in the prophecies of
Blake and Shelley. When Blake interprets prophetic beasts, he locates
them "in every Man" (*F.Z.*, 3:4), not in exterior geography; for
Shelley, as well, distinctions of time and space are irrelevant to inspired
and visionary art (*Prose*, 7:112).

More isolates other figures of speech besides iconisms, and he uses
them to demonstrate again that a prophecy's images "signifie merely
symbolically"; these figures also illustrate Newton's deviation from
tradition. Whereas Newton assigns symbols a definite referent outside
the mind, More interprets their very definiteness in terms of the mind
itself. *Hylasmus*, for example, is the technique of "exhibiting crass and
palpable objects" because such images "more strongly strike the
Fancy"; nevertheless, in prophecy they "are *Mystical* or *Spiritual Symbols*
of quite another thing." Whereas Newton assigns prophetic scenes to
specific times and places, More argues that in prophecy "diverse
Events, and distinguished by Distant Times, are signifyed by one
Prophetical Type," and he places this figure within the class
henopoeia.[125] This theory is far closer to Blake's and Shelley's than
Newton's; according to it, a prophet strives for universality, transcend-
ing time and space. It is a theory that is congenial with the idealism of
More, Blake, or Shelley; its alliance with philosophy constructs a

radical humanism according to which, as D. H. Lawrence has written, "we can drop or rise to another level, and be in a new world at once."[126]

Another visionary device for transcending time and space is typology, especially the form of typology that Henry More calls *Israelismus:* "a Prophetick scheme," frequent especially in the Apocalypse, "which is a speaking of the Affairs of the Christian Church under the Names and with Allusion to such Places, or Persons, or Things, as did of old concern the Israelites." This scheme employs imagery of the Israelites "in a mystical or spiritual Meaning." More lists as examples the "*Mystical Egypt*" and "*Spiritual Sodom*" of Revelation 11:8, the brazen serpent erected in the Israelites' camp, which "was . . . a Type of Christ's Hanging on the Cross," and the manna which the children of Israel ate in the wilderness— "a Type of . . . the daily Food of the Faithful."[127]

Milton uses this kind of typology in *Areopagitica*, where he treats England as a new Israel and "a nation of prophets."[128] So too, in *Jerusalem*, Blake uses this sort of Israelism repeatedly, but in all these cases the device does more than to identify two literal places or peoples—it subordinates both places and peoples to a universal idea, to be found in the present.[129] As Tannenbaum points out, this typology is based on a concept of history which "juxtaposes events, things, or persons from different time periods in order to relate them to a central theme or paradigm that transcends the world of time and causality."[130] In this sense, John Wesley's interpretation of the Great Red Dragon (Rev. 12:9) is typological: this dragon is the serpent who deceived Eve, but "he has *deceived the whole world*—Not only in their first parents, but through all ages and in all countries, into unbelief and all wickedness, into the hating and persecuting faith and all goodness."[131]

In one sense, *typology* refers to the technique of reading Old Testament figures as foreshadowings of Christ; in a larger sense, it refers to an allusive or allegorical use of imagery from the biblical past.[132] As a literary structure, biblical typology (including Israelism) presents archetypal stories, with two related ideological results. The significance of the story is universalized, because it is intellectualized:

> What was once "history," whether in the Bible, Homer, or Virgil, has now entered memory, has been detemporalized, and is relived as fictional event in the actions of the protagonist, and as spiritual event in the consciousness of the reader. Allegory thus takes account of the historicity of the paradigmatic story, its repeatability as a fiction set in a

new time and place, and the significance of the history and its corre-
sponding fiction for an analogous spiritual or psychological event taking
place in the consciousness of the reader.[133]

Like synchronism, then, biblical typology or Israelism transforms a
concrete diversity (different places, or things) into an intellectual unity
(a common idea or theme). For commentators such as Henry More,
other interpretive tools also reveal a collapse of multeity into unity.

When commentators invoke "the Sense of the ancient *Cabbala*," for
example, they do so to universalize the meaning of a prophecy: "*For
Seven we substitute* All . . . *the* Septenary *Number with the* Cabbalists
signifying Universality."[134] A. B. Peganius uses cabbalistic terminology
to express the presence of the invisible in the visible, in what amounts
to a sort of pre-Christian incarnation theory: "God in the ordering of
the heavenly Schechinah, in a certain manner and form shews his
Face." Peganius uses that cabbalistic concept to expound a cosmic
interpretation of Revelation, converting its tangibles to infinite signifi-
cance: "The Divine Essence is incorporeal, invisible, and in itself
incomprehensible; and . . . no finite thing can comprehend an In-
finite. . . . Therefore the whole Divine Essence . . . can communi-
cate itself . . . to no finite Eye or understanding." For that reason, God
bestows upon his prophets "a voluntary Representation and Exhibition,
which may well be call'd the Divine *Schechinah* or Cohabitation."[135]
This theory liberates the visionary from time, enabling him to perceive
the infinite which was invisible. Visionary theorists use cabbalism to
unfold meanings that are unlimited by terrestrial space and time, quite
unlike Sir Isaac Newton's Arabian troops at Damascus in A.C. 637.

The common topic of etymology is also incorporated into visionary
theory. One example is "Asia, *in allusion to the Hebrew word* . . .
signifying Fundamentum." More expounds the term further, finding
another word "*of a like nearness of sound*" that denotes "*the lowest of those
four worlds notoriously known amongst the* Cabbalists, Aziluth, Briah,
Jetzirah, Asia, *of which last the lowest part is this Earth we tread upon.*"[136]
This reading is the reverse of Newton's, which *ended* in geography.
Swedenborg similarly reverses Newton's terrestrial interpretation,
when he explains that "the inhabitants of Asia are not here meant, but
all, wheresoever they are, who are in the spiritual light of intel-
ligence."[137] Clearly different from More's definition, Swedenborg's
nonetheless shares with it and with the tradition to which both writers

belong a strong pull toward universality, from finite terms to infinite significance. The names of the seven churches in Asia, according to this view, "may be applicable to this or that state of any particular Church of Christ, in any particular Place or Age of the World."[138]

Nevertheless, some places and ages of the world are more likely to prompt apocalyptic speculation than others: when reigning ideologies are overthrown by revolution, British poets tend toward apocalyptic diction and form. The French Revolution animated apocalyptic feeling in the Romantic writers, who perceived Liberty as a "holy flame" by which France was "delivered."[139] Thus Harrison writes that "the French Revolution excited a spate of interpretations [of biblical prophecies] on both sides of the Atlantic designed to show that the world was entering upon the last days." Among these interpretations, says Harrison, "there was constant reference back to the prophetic studies of Sir Isaac Newton, Joseph Mede, and William Whiston."[140] E. P. Thompson writes that "it was in the immediate aftermath of the French Revolution that the millennarial current, so long underground, burst into the open with unexpected force."[141] The generalizations of these historians should provide fertile suggestions for literary scholars, because, throughout the Romantic period, scholars such as Faber wrote commentaries on the Book of Revelation and poets such as Shelley communicated with these commentators. F. B. Curtis has observed that "over eighty separate works on the prophecies and the Book of Revelation were written and published between 1792 and 1818" and that Blake worked for many of these booksellers in this period.[142] We know that Blake personally exchanged ideas with leading intellectuals of this publishing circle, including such visionary theorists as Priestley.[143] We should not be surprised, then, that the poets knew and used both Revelation and the commentary that was published on it. William F. Halloran has shown that the French Revolution called forth Blake's apocalyptic art.[144] Criticism has been slower to perceive the same truth in connection with Shelley, who names Jesus Christ the "great Reformer" and who pairs Christ's passion with the French Revolution (*Prose*, 7:5; *P.U.*, 1:567–615).

Literary culture of the Romantic period reflects all the elements of visionary tradition—ontological, epistemological, and aesthetic. The political excitement that characterizes the spirit of the age in fact intensifies these interests. The sort of political discussion in which these writers engaged "penetrates more profoundly into the existential foundation of thinking than the kind of discussion which thinks only in terms of a few selected 'points of view.'"[145] Visionary writers and theorists of the Romantic period use both philosophical and prophetic tradition to penetrate to the process of vision itself, shaking the very foundations of thought. Their interests in imagination, philosophy, and apocalypse are therefore identical.

Thus Faber can argue that prophecies are written in a "language of ideas" and also that they comprise a "prospective detail of successive future events." His visionary aesthetic is specifically designed to allow perception of the universal in the particular. "*Antichrist . . .* is a sort of generic name, including all persons who answer to the several parts of the ample description, which is given of the character of that monster," and yet Faber and his contemporaries do not hesitate to find temporal correlatives for this universal idea in the history of their own time. Writing with a view to "recent transactions," Faber and other commentators point to the French Revolution and to French philosophy in order to interpret the scriptural prophecy. Thus, Faber writes: "The *year* 1789 . . . in which the French revolution broke out, a revolution big with misery to the whole of Europe, perfectly corresponds with the predicted chronological commencement of *the third woe*. . . . At the sounding of *the seventh trumpet*, a revolution, unequalled in its horrors and unparalleled in its consequences, has suddenly burst upon an astonished world."[146] Joseph Priestley also writes that the political revolutions of the period were "distinctly and repeatedly foretold in many prophecies, delivered more than two thousand years ago." Like Blake and Shelley, Priestley views these revolutions more cheerfully than Faber, because they "make a totally new, a most wonderful, and important, aera in the history of mankind. It is . . . a change from darkness to light . . . a liberating of all the powers of man."[147]

Commentators disagree in interpreting the revolution, some execrating it like Faber, some blessing it like Priestley; but they agree about its prophetic significance: "History no where informs us of any event so extraordinary as the late revolution in France." For all who consider that revolution, "it must surely excite the greatest astonishment." It is an event of religious importance, because, as James Bicheno explains,

"those who have been used to unite in their minds the providence of God with human occurrences (whether they approve of this great change or not) cannot help enquiring, Is this from men, or is it from God? *Is it one of those*

commotions produced by the conflicting passions of men, that rise and sink,
and are soon forgotten; or, is it one of those events which mark the great aeras
of time, and from which originate new orders of things?—If the latter, it is
undoubtedly the theme of prophecy.

Bicheno concludes that "the French revolution then may be of God,
and designed to issue in good,"[148] but another commentator of the
period, Charles Walmesley, wrote rather to "awaken a thoughtless and
criminal Generation to the great and awful Truths and salutary terrors
of Religion."[149]

Just as prophecy interprets itself, so the visionary theorists of this
period interpret their predecessors. The anonymous editor of *Prophetic
Conjectures on the French Revolution,* for example, writes of commentators
long dead that they themselves "predict a grand and important REVOLU-
TION IN FRANCE," and that they do so "on the authority of certain
passages of scripture." Observing that most of these authors "wrote
either during times of persecution, or in the immediate prospect of
them," this author voices the radical ideology of his tradition: this
revolution will be "fatal to popery and tyranny, but friendly to the
liberty, peace, and happiness of mankind."[150]

Prophecy is an art of multiple perspectives, its synchronized visions
providing different ways of viewing one event or idea. The cultural
upheaval that all these writers mention, to celebrate or to damn it,
multiplies perspectives and causes writers to consider the different
ways of seeing, and not only the objects seen. To see is to know;
epistemology, then, is a science that grows in periods of widespread
disagreement. Furthermore, the violence of Revelation's imagery, the
martial force of its cosmic regeneration, renders that book uniquely
attractive to the dispossessed; the prophecy's art is revolutionary.[151] To
perceive the relation of intellectual philosophy and political revolution
is to understand the special appeal that the prophetic form had for the
Romantic writers: if, in their prophetic works, "the external means was
replaced by an internal means for transforming the world,"[152] it should
be no surprise. Both internal and external apocalypse, and their dialec-
tic, were known to the poets through English tradition.

Aesthetic elements of the prophetic paradigm were equally insepara-
ble from this political element. Just as Sir Isaac Newton understood
that a prophecy "consists of two parts, an introductory Prophecy, and
an Interpretation thereof,"[153] commentators of this later revolutionary

period understood that prophecy combines vision and interpretation. They also used the metaphor of theater and dramatic scenes, as well as analogies with the visual arts; and they understood synchronism, according to which prophecy consists of "visions . . . variegated, for our instruction."[154] These writers' use of art, philosophy, politics, and religion should remind us of what More made so explicit: a prophecy is a work of art that has multiple levels of meaning. By means of this art, men can and do interpret their own times and, simultaneously, eternity.

Prophecy thus supplied the Romantic writers with a literary form and tradition whose subjects included both political revolution and what Mannheim has called "preformed patterns of thought."[155] This art is concerned with spirit, a synonym for *mind;* its final cause is intellectual revolution, and this revolution, like God, shall become manifest in history. The efficient causes of prophecy include, first, inspiration—imagination—and a traditional symbolism. Repeating the incarnation, these symbols convert idea to visible form, leading their readers' minds on an intellectual journey whose end is the mind's discovery of itself and its power. To enhance its audience's perception a prophecy employs the composite form of drama, picture, poem, and dream. It sets in motion, in the mind of its recipient, a revolution whose historical equivalent is the political liberation of mankind. Thus, a prophecy is art and history in one: "History treats of things and persons which have been in actual existence; the subjects of Poetry are infinite and universal."[156] The moral and perceptual subjects of visionary art connect its methods and concerns with philosophy. Thus the Christian visionary and the atheist Holbach can both demand release for the human mind; they both appeal to a universal energy that will at last liberate humanity from the mind-forged manacles in which they find it enslaved. Those contrary bodies of thought, religious and secular, therefore share much; in the greatest works of the greatest Romantic writers, they finally lock arms, "to walk forward thro' Eternity" (*M.,* 22:5).

TWO

"Humanity Divine":
Blake's *Jerusalem*

Jerusalem begins by recalling the primeval state in which Wisdom, Art, and Science were unified; it ends by bringing together these branches of knowledge and also "All Human Forms" (99:1). And yet these statements imply a simplicity that at first does not appear: *Jerusalem* is perhaps the most complex work of all Romantic art. This poem is difficult because its author wishes to exercise his readers' minds, to rouse their faculties to activity. Such arousal is common to all prophecies; Blake calls it mental war. Visionary aestheticians had supplied specific strategies for achieving this goal, and Blake adopts these strategies as well. One is calculated obscurity, and so Blake has locked his vision in dense and difficult form. Another strategy is multiplicity of perspectives, and so Blake supplements text with design, presents dramatic encounters, and recasts episodes in different parts of his poem. A third strategy is "multifarious Allusiveness,"[1] and almost every plate of *Jerusalem* alludes to the Bible—most often the prophecies—and also to British writers on mind and nature. This tangle of difficulties perplexes interpretation until we perceive the common aim of these strategies: the liberation of the human mind. Here the purposes of prophecy and philosophy converge, tending toward the center from which they both arose: "The Primeval State of Man, was Wisdom, Art, and Science" (*J.*, pl. 3, *E.*, p. 144). In one of the greatest philosophical poems, they are the systems with which Blake strives in order to deliver us.

Accordingly, the problem of *Jerusalem* is precisely the problem of context. To perceive its use of philosophy is not impertinently to invoke one's "outside reading," as E. B. Murray pretends;[2] rather, it is to understand the cornerstone and creed of Blake's career: "All sects of

59

Philosophy are from the Poetic Genius" (*A.R.O., E.*, p. 2). To direct us
to philosophy, as *Jerusalem* does, is not to deviate from strictly poetic
aims, but to achieve them. To see deeply into religion, philosophy, and
art is to perceive the burning fountain from which they came, which
Blake names "the Spirit of Prophecy" (*A.R.O., E.*, p. 2). As early as
1788, then, Blake had stated his goals and embraced the literary genre
best adapted to them. To cause his reader to perceive the unity of all
mental endeavor is to lead him in at heaven's gate, studiously built in
Jerusalem's wall. It is for this reason that *Jerusalem* ends where the
universe begins, in mental unity. In the light of vision all beings and
forms—material and ideal, historical and moral—are revealed as multi-
ples of an imagining mind. *Jerusalem*'s diverse techniques, gleaned
from visionary tradition, tend toward its unifying end. Its philosophical
purpose is symbolized in text and design by the cosmic get-together at
the end of the poem, depicting the mental state that at once subsumes
all wisdom, art, and science (see Fig. 33).

Like Revelation, *Jerusalem* consists of vision and interpretation, both
prophecies establishing continuity with their predecessors but also
modifying tradition by interpreting and supplementing them. Further,
each prophecy contains commentary on itself. One result of this dual
purpose is a matter of form: the prophet presents a symbolic vision and
a discursive commentary on it. John's tool for transmitting both compo-
nents was language; Blake, a professional illustrator of the Bible,
learned another method, counterpointing visual and verbal compo-
nents. Illustrations can interpret verbal art, as Blake's illustrations to
Milton's poems do (see, e.g., Fig. 20); but in the opening of *Jerusalem*,
as in Blake's other re-creation of Revelation, his "Vision of the Last
Judgment," his language explicates his visual symbols.[3] Like his col-
leagues in commentary, Blake converts these symbols to ideas, and
more explicitly than any of them he spells out the resulting relationship
between visionary art and philosophies of mind.

Jerusalem can be understood in two ways: its conflicts and themes
can be perceived in almost every plate, condensed into minute particu-
lars; or, once read, the entire poem can be perceived as a unit. A third
possibility, reading the poem as a narrative progression, will not work
for *Jerusalem*, as I shall argue later. Instead, it is necessary to study
carefully individual plates—the poem's visionary moments—and only
later assemble their meanings into the larger vision. The poem's first
five plates are especially useful for this purpose of close reading,

because they encapsulate the poem. They also indicate why narrative structure is irrelevant to *Jerusalem*, and so their minutiae make a fit approach to the poem and a useful preliminary to general discussion.

Apart from deleted inscriptions, the frontispiece to *Jerusalem* is a symbolic design unaccompanied by text (see Fig. 9).[4] To interpret the picture requires description of what Blake incised on copper, and then of what he added later by color-wash, producing what must be considered the final state (see Fig. 10). Then, placing the picture in its widening contexts can unfold its multiple meanings.

The plate, in its original state, depicts a male form, bending slightly and stepping over the threshold of a dark room. This room is labeled "a Void, outside of Existence" by an inscription, in an early state of the plate, on the arch of the door-frame (1:1), but when Blake added color to the plate he deleted the inscription completely—though it is still partially legible in the posthumous copy, I. In the original state of the plate, the door is suggested only in outline, by thin white lines marking its top portion; beyond this door and the male's right leg, nothing is visible inside the room. The globe in the figure's right hand emits some thin white lines that do not intrude into the room; when the plate was colored, these rays of light became larger and brighter. The male's left leg, hat, hair, and coat, all of them on our side of the doorway, are lighted; his right leg is visible, stepping into the room, but his foot is past the threshold and blocked from our view. As yet, the area "outside of Existence" is not lighted or revealed, but remains, pictorially, "a Void." Whether Blake wished to erase the meaning of this inscription when he deleted it by pouring black over it (copy A) or dark brown (copy E), or whether he was merely obscuring that meaning, is unclear. He preserved the emptiness of the room in the final colored copy, by permitting no light to enter it, though he splashed light liberally on our side of the door. Blake has added an intense eye, in that copy, and an arched brow, so that we know that he was attending to minute details. The threshold and the figure's leg crossing it are both more clearly defined, too, but the interior of the room remains "outside of Existence," or at least outside our field of vision.

The textual gloss to this picture appears on plate 45 of the poem:

Fearing that Albion should turn his back against the Divine Vision
Los took his globe of fire to search the interiors of Albions
Bosom, in all the terrors of friendship, entering the caves

Of despair & death, to search the tempters out, walking among
Albions rocks & precipices! caves of solitude & dark despair,
And saw every Minute Particular of Albion degraded & murderd
But saw not by whom.

(45:2–8)

The dislocation of the illustration and its verbal gloss amounts to a
strategy: Blake "considerd what is not too Explicit as the fittest for
Instruction because it rouzes the faculties to act" (*E.*, p. 676). Else-
where in *Jerusalem* Blake again separates text from gloss, and even splits
an episode in the middle, to deprive the poem of the clarity that
continuity could supply. Earlier, he had used this strategy of disloca-
tion in *Milton*, where he moved the illustration to plate 24, placing it as
plate 47 in the later two copies of that poem. This strategy may also
account for the removal of the explanatory inscription on the fron-
tispiece to *Jerusalem*. Its effect is to force intellectual effort.

Once located, the gloss explains some details of the design. The
words "murderd" and "death" account for the tomblike trappings of the
picture, and the phrase "saw not by whom" accounts for the darkness
and the troubled ignorance of the figure who we now know is Los.
Blake and Los had previously been identified as one man on the
dislocated plate 47 of *Milton;* and a glance at portraits of Blake reveals a
hat, coat, and in some cases hair much like that of Los on the fron-
tispiece. Aptly, Blake and Los, the spirit of prophecy, together charged
with the care of the "Divine Vision in time of trouble" (95:20), conduct
us into the poem and into the sleep of death that this poem proposes to
explore. Tonal ambiguities, arising from luminous and sinister elements
in the design itself, receive a partial gloss on plate 45: the spirit of
prophecy appears in a saving mission, but its locus is the tomb of the
dead.

A slightly wider context illuminates other particulars and preserves
the tonal ambiguity. "Death's Door," for example, which appears in a
unique print but also, variously, in *America*, *The Grave*, and *The Gates of
Paradise*, reveals important similarities (see figs. 11–14). The state of
the *Gates of Paradise* that is entitled "For the Sexes" is closest to
Jerusalem chronologically; there, we recognize the bent male as a dying
man, and the room he enters is obviously a tomb. Differences arise,
however, as the frontispiece reverses elements in "Death's Door."

Naturally enough, the wind ruffling the dying man's hair and garment blows into the tomb; unnaturally enough, its direction is reversed in the *Jerusalem* frontispiece, the wind originating in the tomb. "Death's Door" is hinged page right; the frontispiece door is hinged page left. "Death's Door" depicts an old and bearded man; the frontispiece depicts a young and beardless one, though his body is also ominously bent. The dying man looks page left; Los or Blake depicts a reversed perspective, looking page right. Irene Chayes has pointed out that in *Jerusalem* the right side of the page seems to belong to the goats (see Fig. 21), and she has noted the foreboding suggestions of a rightward-gazing figure elsewhere in the poem.[5] Even without extrapolating to Chayes's theory, however, we may notice that Blake has imported and reversed elements from the "Death's Door" design. The resulting ambiguity is consistent with other pictorial allusions on the frontispiece.

Plate 45 defines Los's lighted disc as a "globe of fire," a phrase that Blake has imported from the *Book of Urizen* (20:48), where the globe illumines another fearful journey. There, however, it is Urizen who carries the "globe of fire," and not Los (see Fig. 15). The fullest text of Urizen exploring his dens appears in the *Four Zoas:* "Los brooded on the darkness, nor saw Urizen with a Globe of fire / Lighting his dismal journey thro the pathless world of death" (70:1–2). In *Jerusalem*, Los is again unable to see an antagonist, and there too the globe of fire is associated with death. To understand Blake's choice and use of the globe of fire, we must widen our context a little further.

Used as a lamp, the globe of fire symbolizes the prophet.[6] A commentator on Revelation whom we know Blake to have admired writes that a lamp symbolizes heaven or the truth of the Word.[7] But Los's lamp, though a little brighter than Urizen's (Fig. 15), fails to illuminate the interior of the tomb or even the area touching its own surface. This failure is significant because "to have a lamp is not enough: one must . . . have heavenly light, if his goal is to enter Jerusalem."[8] The door is a biblical symbol of induction;[9] but in Revelation John was able to say "I saw" when the door was opened, and the prophet on the frontispiece "saw not" what he desired. Again, as in the borrowings from his own work, Blake adopts symbolic elements but makes his design ambiguous by complicating their values.

The globe of fire is complicated by its proximity to death and by the inadequate light that it emits, but also by other allusions that Blake has in mind. The God of Job, for example, whom Blake and the Bible agree in depicting as capable of malice, gives his death-dealing beast Leviathan "burning lamps" (41:19). Los with the fire in his hand, looking at the dead, also recalls Abraham who, ready to slay his son, "took the fire in his hand" (Gen. 22:6). The image is specifically associated with the fallen condition of Jerusalem in 1 Kings 15:4, where the wicked Abijam reigns over Judah: "Nevertheless for David's sake did the Lord his God give him a lamp in Jerusalem." Again, the angry God of Ezekiel manifests himself as lamps (1:13), in the living creatures to whom Blake alludes repeatedly in *Jerusalem*. Further meanings of the symbol become apparent when we recall the explanation given in Proverbs 6:23: "The commandment is a lamp; and the law is light." Blake regularly ascribes destructiveness to the law and commandments; they are suggested on the frontispiece amid deathly detail. He has introduced the theme of death and specifically sacrifice, a theme that will recur in the poem. He will make much more of Ezekiel's angry God, in chapter 1; and the fallen condition of Jerusalem, invoked here pictorially, is the subject of the poem. It is also significant that the harsh ambiguities—the symbols' contrary sense, as Swedenborg would have it—can be perceived along the lines of Old and New Testament: insofar as Los resembles John with his lights at the door of heaven, the frontispiece strikes an optimistic note as it conveys us into Blake's vision. Insofar as he recalls Old Testament antecedents, of which Blake was equally aware, the frontispiece is a dark design of death.

Blake's Old Testament context also clarifies the curious detail of the impossible wind that blows weirdly from an enclosure outward. Unless the wind is a backlash thrown by the doorway, or unless it is caused by Los's forward motion, it is a phenomenal absurdity; it forces us to find a symbolic explanation, and not a naturalistic one. A clue appears in the partially deleted inscription that labels the tomb "a Void." Blake's antecedent here, in the coupling of wind and void, is Isaiah 41:29, literally translated: "Behold they are all iniquity, their works are nothing; their molten images are wind and a void."[10] Isaiah is railing at fallen Jerusalem; in Blake's poem, we encounter those molten images on plate 67, where the inhabitants of Albion are seen producing them. London is identified as the fallen Jerusalem in the lament that concludes chapter 1; there and on the frontispiece, Jerusalem's fall and redemption are simultaneously invoked.

These allusions contradict the picture's cheerful Christian elements, and so do some other facts. Los entering the tomb is sometimes compared to "Christ descending into the Grave," from the *Grave* illustrations. Analogies obtain between the pictures, but if we attend to detail—and Blake demands that we do so—important differences also appear, which prevent the mistake of identifying the figure on the frontispiece with Christ. First, Los is evidently ignorant of what is ahead: he peers into the dark, using a lamp. Christ, disdaining borrowed light, shines with his own internal light, as Blake says everything in eternity does. Inside and outside, or inner and outer, form a dialectic that is almost a diagrammatic key to the values in *Jerusalem*. When Christ appears on plate 76 (see Fig. 32), his own head is his source of light, just as it is in the *Grave* illustration, and as Milton's is on plate 16 of *Milton* (see Fig. 16); this fact distinguishes Blake's emblems of inspiration from Los on the *Jerusalem* frontispiece. Another distinction is posture: Los looks sideways; Christ, upright, strides forward, his arms outstretched. So too does Milton, on plate 16 of *Milton*. Milton stands straight on plate 1 of that poem, and on plate 2 he is a shining star. By his use of light and posture, then, Blake stops us short of an identification that other details invite; the frontispiece invokes and yet contradicts the salvation promised by the New Testament.

Another *Grave* illustration supplies other analogies. "The Soul exploring the recesses of the Grave" also carries an external light into a tomb, bent exactly as Los is on the *Jerusalem* frontispiece. This figure, though, is plainly female; the crescent moon over her head—a major symbol in subsequent designs—recalls "The Creation of Eve" (Fig. 20), a watercolor illustration for *Paradise Lost*, where it also highlights the dire female will.[11] The *Grave* figure exhibits the same stern face as Los, and, more obviously, comes to peer at the dead, not to upraise him. Blake has evidently assimilated elements from previous designs that had contrary significance; combining them on the frontispiece, he presents a deliberately complex and disturbingly ambiguous picture.

The density of biblical allusion on the frontispiece should surprise no reader of *Jerusalem*: this poem is a prophecy, and Blake intends that his reader apprehend its exegetical dimension. Blake, like previous prophets, was a scholar of scripture, but he had other knowledge as well, and he is also writing a commentary on British philosophy. His allusions to Bacon, Newton, and Locke appear in both designs and text. On the frontispiece, these allusions add to its complexity and make it a fit induction to Blake's philosophical poem. The void that is named in the deleted inscription refers to Isaiah, but it also refers to the philosophy of Newton and Locke, which leaves a void where substance should be. "Abstract" and "void" are concomitants in Blake's view; Locke's and Newton's philosophies depend on abstraction, and so Blake calls them "abstract Voids" (13:37). Repeatedly, he uses the term to refer to the impenetrable abyss that Locke and Newton posit between the mind and its objects of knowledge: Locke wrote that one sees images but not their cause, and Blake depicts this pattern on plate 45.

Seen from one perspective, then, the frontispiece portrays Locke's model of mind, a *camera obscura:* "External and internal sensation are the only passages I can find of knowledge to the understanding. These alone . . . are the windows by which light is let into this *dark room.* . . . The understanding is not much unlike a closet wholly shut from light, with only some little openings left, to let in external visible resemblances of things without."[12] Blake had read this book in his youth, annotating it heavily; now in *Jerusalem* he mentions Locke seven times. The frontispiece is a visual rendition of Locke's "dark room."

Blake regularly links Newton with Locke, and correctly. In his *Opticks* Newton refers more than a dozen times to "the sun shining into a dark chamber through a little round hole."[13] His obsessive repetition of the phrase suggests a fondness for Locke's metaphor; Blake found it in both writers, and highlights its aptness to *Jerusalem* by quoting it pictorially on the frontispiece. The allusion darkens Blake's design, because he perceives Newton's as a philosophy of death. It also adds another context to Blake's art.

Plate 2, the title-page of *Jerusalem* (figs. 17 and 18), draws on identical contexts and is equally complex. Its major symbols—and only two change significantly when Blake adds color-wash—also suggest both death and rebirth. Like plate 1, the title-page pits New Testament idealism first against the Old Testament's wrathful God and then against materialist philosophy. The tonal changes that accompany color are also identical with those on plate 1: the color imparts cheer and light, and actually submerges grim implications. These latter persist, though muted. In the plate's earlier state, it is a dark page, white lined; in the later state it is rainbow-colored and dazzling. Similarly, in *Milton,* Blake depicts a rainbow occasionally by its shape (as on plate 10 of copy B), but more generally by its color alone; employing this strategy on the title-page of *Jerusalem,* he introduces a major symbol that combines in itself Blake's contrary contexts. Certainly, not all many-colored designs are implicit rainbows; but here Blake's strategy is obvious, because he surrounds the full spectrum with other allusions, including (as I shall show) allusions to Newton's work on the rainbow, and allusions to biblical usages of the symbol.

It is called "a Bow of Mercy" on plate 97; Noah's ark on plate 44 of copy E may remind us of the cosmic optimism that the biblical image suggests. Blake also would have known its usage in the prophecy that he is rewriting, Revelation 4:3 and 10:1. Swedenborg explicates the rainbow as "Divine truth,"[14] and in Blake's poem about the Divine Vision, the allusion is obvious. Still, sinister connotations are not far away.

The angry God who poured the man-killing flood is not absent from *Jerusalem:* his flood, a symbol of materialism, appears on plate 57. There, Blake underscores the rainbow's contrary sense: "Albion fled from the Divine Vision" (57:13) that elsewhere the rainbow symbolizes. Again, on plate 14 (Fig. 24), Albion is depicted turning his back on the Divine Vision, arched by a full-color rainbow. On that plate he reposes by an ocean: the rainbow and the flood are never far removed, the signal of the promise regularly accompanied by the material destruction over which it rises. Clearly, Blake has again invoked an Old Testament vision of a wrathful God and, simultaneously, a merciful contrary from the New Testament.

Another contrary context of the rainbow is equally evident. It is inconceivable that a writer who knew Newton's work as well as Blake did could fail to see the rainbow scientifically;[15] Newton's theory of light, on which Blake comments explicitly, is an attempt to explain the colors of the rainbow.[16] Both Newton and Blake are careful to include the complete seven-color spectrum in their presentations, both treat it as a key to the process of vision, and both were scholars of its biblical usage. The conflation of sacred and profane contexts may in fact have been hinted by Newton. Importing the doctrine of vengeance into Revelation, Newton morally identifies the God of the flood and the God of apocalypse; God's prominent symbol, the rainbow, becomes the focus for Newton's study of vision, the *Opticks*. Blake invokes Newton for a complex of reasons: he attacks equally Newton's theology of vengeance, rooted in the Old Testament God of wrath, and Newton's materialism, evident both in his historical research and his natural science.

Other elements in the design on plate 2 support the contraries suggested by the rainbow. The beautifully colored female flying across the top of the page is insect-winged. Page left of the name *Jerusalem* floats a green-winged and leaflike figure with antennae, perhaps a butterfly. She has been given less obviously human features, but the brilliant colors of both these figures can hardly fail to gladden the viewer. The smaller figures "cheering our way along the title" include a fly, a moth, and a bat.[17] Every figure on the page is winged: an apparently mournful female with bat-wings crouches page left; a feathery female hides her face in her hands page right. The obvious center of attention is the supine female with butterfly-wings who sprawls across the bottom of the page. Everyone else is staring at her, except the leaflike reader of the word *Jerusalem,* and she elicits visible grief. Her brilliant wings and bright flesh-tones are cheerful, but her evident unconsciousness introduces another major symbol of materialism, sleep.

As on the frontispiece, Blake's addition of color introduces optimistic tones, in the rainbow and the beautiful wings, and it also obscures grim suggestions. Starry-sky symbols regularly accompany Newtonian philosophy in *Jerusalem,* and the wings of the supine sprawler (Jerusalem herself, apparently) as well as those of her mourners contain stars and the crescent moon. The color-wash has softened the pessimism that these symbols suggest; they now glitter. Spheres in Jerusalem's top two wings are obscured, and the feathery female's stars have become small spots of gold. Their presence, though, together with the wholly female population of the plate, hints disaster: specifically, they suggest the female will, a version of materialism that is most fully developed in chapter 3. Thus, on the title-page symbols of death and materialism are contiguous with symbols of spiritual rebirth.

Blake's reasons for assigning materialism to the female will, a pattern that is continuous in his poems since *Europe,* will need to be explained more fully later, but I shall briefly indicate them here. A conventional interpretation explains materialism as a consequence of the fall from grace. Elsewhere I have argued that Blake adopts this fiction in the *Four Zoas,* and that he may have found it in Henry More.[18] When Blake writes of Los that "Enitharmon like a faint rainbow waved before him" (86:50), as he does twice in *Jerusalem* (cf. 83:67), he imports from the *Four Zoas* a recasting of the story from Genesis which, like Henry More's, ascribes materialism to the creation of a sensual female. Blake's illustrations of the episode of Adam and Eve—including the "Creation of Eve" (Fig. 20)—repeat the idea, placing a crescent moon over Eve's head. Material philosophy, as Blake knew, is also abstract philosophy, and the crescent moon over the female symbolizes both. This mix of biblical myth and philosophy helps to explain Blake's treatment of Newton, in *Europe* as in *Jerusalem:* his fortunes run parallel with those of the female will. Both imply an indifferent world separate from man, both advocate doctrines of punishment, and both employ abstraction— a word whose literal sense, "to take away," would not have escaped either Newton or Blake. In the large color-print, "Newton," Blake employs the same cluster of visual symbols that he uses repeatedly in *Jerusalem:* every color of the rainbow appears in the rock on which Newton sits, and a bluish watery tint covers the print—again both rainbow and flood are suggested. The Tate Gallery's print of "Newton" bears a watermark of 1804, the date that also appears on the title-page of *Jerusalem*; as Blake's etched dates are more likely to be conceptual rather than factual, the coincidence of dates suggests shared concerns of these works.[19]

Another element on the title-page, also borrowed from Blake's de- pictions of the fall from grace, becomes yet another pictorial theme. The supine figure at the bottom of the page recalls "Adam and Eve Sleeping," as well as the "Creation of Eve" (Fig. 20). Henry More associates the material world with the sleep of Adam; so does Blake, as we shall see.[20] On the title-page, Blake quotes himself pictorially to suggest this sleep, the ugly effects of which are made even plainer by another design for Genesis, "Elohim Creating Adam" (Fig. 6). The supine posture's deathly denotation is established unmistakably by the lurid "House of Death" (Fig. 1). The ambiguous quality of the supine female on the title-page—part human, part insect or leaf—is also stated pictorially on the frontispiece of the *Gates of Paradise* (Fig. 19), in the form of another sleeper. The motive grows ghastly on plate 33 (Fig. 25), and becomes downright horrible on plate 58 (Fig. 29), which in turn recalls the color-print, "Satan Exulting Over Eve" (Fig. 7).

It should be obvious now that dense allusiveness makes it impossible to simplify Blake's meaning, and so do tonal ambiguities. Brightness and dark, living and dead, mingle often on one plate, as Blake portrays a simultaneous presence of contraries, which he has already marshalled for the poem's intellectual war. The theologies of vengeance and mercy, their respective biblical canons, and sacred and profane models

of mind all clash at the prophecy's outset. Already their vehicles exhibit
a density of suggestion that Blake's visionary predecessors had em-
braced for centuries. Almost all of *Jerusalem*'s plates employ yet another
complexity that we have yet to approach, the composite art of picture
and poem. Before entering the entangled texture of the poem proper, it
will be well to mark closely the words of Blake's argument to the poem,
which occupies plates 3–5. There, he encapsulates in language the
themes and purposes of his art, as he had encapsulated them first in
visual designs. These verbal components will help to define the field of
Blake's intellectual war.

Blake's address "To the Public" defines his poem's purpose and
its context as Blake perceived it. Significantly, "the Enthusiasm of
the following Poem" stands out from a deleted passage, remaining,
ungrammatically, quite plain (see Fig. 21). Boasting of his enthusi-
asm, Blake invokes the tradition of inspiration, and immediately he
names Jesus, defining him as "the God [*of Fire*] and Lord [*of Love*],"
the object of prophecy: "The Ancients look'd and saw his day afar
off." Narrowing his context, Blake differentiates his theology from that
of the more ancient prophets, including Ezekiel and Isaiah: "The
Spirit of Jesus is continual forgiveness of Sin." To say that this is the
moral theme of *Jerusalem* is to overlook the poem's repudiation of all
moral forms; but when this repudiation is perceived here, in Blake's
argument, then his theme and its context—Christian prophecy—be-
come apparent.

Next, a poem in meter and rhyme precedes a repudiation of meter
and rhyme. No poet of Blake's time knew Revelation and its literature
better than Blake did, and that literature's stress on composite form
precipitates a formal fact about *Jerusalem*. Subsequently the poem
ranges from epic to dramatic to elegiac devices. When the final para-
graph of "To the Public" claims that in Blake's prophecy "every word
and every letter is studied and put into its fit place," Blake is deliber-
ately echoing *Paradise Lost*, but also previous commentary on Revela-
tion, to claim for his poem what Joseph Mede and almost every
subsequent commentator claimed for John's prophecy. He insists that
we perceive *Jerusalem* as he did, as Revelation's successor. Other sug-
gestions of this role include his claim that "this Verse was . . . dictated
to me," a claim that recalls *Paradise Lost* but also goes beyond that poem
to recall the Ur-poem of his genre—the Book of Revelation.

Like plates 1 and 2, plate 3 conflates this Christian context with a philosophical one, and, at the same time, defines the intellectual reference of Blake's art. The small poem in rhymed couplets refers to "God from whom [*all books are given*] / Who in mysterious Sinais awful cave / To Man the wond'rous art of writing gave." This passage is stranger than it seems. Blake says that his "Reader! [*lover*] of books!" is also a "lover" of this God, and yet there are important indications that Blake himself is not. "Mystery" is destroyed at the poem's rhapsodic conclusion. That "awful cave" is more likely to remind us of the gloomy hole on the frontispiece than an inspiration to be celebrated. Blake refers specifically here to the giving of the Ten Commandments, thereby introducing another terrible enemy to be put off by his poem. Under the symbolism of the Ten Commandments and their tablets, this moral law darkens designs and texts throughout Blake's career. In another commentary on Revelation, Blake writes that "in Paradise they have no Corporeal <& Mortal> Body" (*V.L.J.*, *E.*, p. 554). Knowledge of good and evil is regularly identified with materialism, from the episode of the apple tree onward. In this way, the expulsion from Eden and the flight from Egypt are symbolic reproductions of the same story: "The Creator of this World is a very Cruel Being" (see Fig. 6; cf. Fig. 1). In contrast, Blake is "a Worshipper of Christ" (*V.L.J.*, *E.*, p. 555). Here Blake distinguishes his theology from Milton's in *Paradise Lost*, where the creation of this world was given to Christ. Instead, Blake considers that he who jailed man in a tomb of flesh also bound him with an annotated law code. Jesus Christ comes precisely to overthrow both morality and materialism. This dialectical theology allows Blake to conflate two contexts, ethical and ontological, and it gives him a set of symbols and a theory of symbolism, both appearing on plate 3.

Blake mixes his theory of art with his philosophy when he discusses the "art of writing." His antecedents here have not, as far as I know, been identified previously, and so they deserve some attention. Gershom G. Scholem's summary of a cabbalistic principle applies equally to Blake's theology: "The Tree of Knowledge became the tree of restrictions, prohibitions, and delimitations, whereas the Tree of Life was the tree of freedom, symbolic of an age when the dualism of good and evil was not yet (or no longer) conceivable, and everything bore witness to the unity of divine life, as yet untouched by any restrictions, by the power of death, or any of the other negative aspects of life, which made their appearance only after the fall of man."[21] It is difficult to find a clearer summary of *Jerusalem*'s themes. Scholem goes on to summa-

rize a corollary principle to which Blake may be alluding when he
writes that "the art of writing" originated in Sinai.[22] Talmudic tradition
distinguishes between two Torahs or Words of God, the oral and the
written: "The first tablets contained a revelation . . . in keeping with
the original state of man, . . . a truly spiritual Torah," but "on the
second tablets the Torah appears in a historical garment and as a
historical power," a truly material Torah.[23] The awful tones of God's
literary bequest accordingly signal a fall from spiritual to material
vision.[24] The art of writing is a perfect means of conceiving the
process: "The old prophetic word," as W. W. Baudissin says, "has . . .
perished in and through this fixation in writing."[25] Later, this Talmudic
conception entered Christian apocalypticism. More's *Conjectura Cab-
balistica* is only one example of such an interpenetration of cabbalistic
and Christian thought, many commentaries on Revelation also citing
cabbalistic theory. One result of this interpenetration is the analogy
between the book of nature and the book of divine revelation: "Invisi-
ble things . . . are clearly seen, being understood by the things that are
made" (Rom. 1:20).[26] A material form in nature is a manifestation of an
idea; so is a literary symbol. Recurring as Swedenborg's theory of
correspondence, and as Blake's theory that "it is impossible to think
without images of somewhat on earth" (*E.,* p. 590), this link of
aesthetics and ontology is a commonplace of visionary thought, as we
have seen. In *Jerusalem*, the theory offers contrary perspectives—fall
from idea to matter, or ascent from matter to idea—and the ambivalent
tones of the verse passage on plate 3 result from these contrary
perspectives.

Blake's theory of allegory also features dual perspectives, material
and ideal, which Blake respectively damns and blesses. When conver-
sion is perceived as upward into eternity, the allegory is sublime; when
the conversion is downward into history, for Blake as for the cabbalists,
the original fall is repeated.[27] Blake's invocation of the theory on plate 3
is prudently placed: embarking on his re-vision of Revelation, he
ensconces his theory in the idealist line, converting the famous symbols
of biblical prophecy not into historical equivalents but upward, into
ideas: "Thunder" is to be read "Thought," and "flames" are "fierce
desire." Blake's exegesis is traditional, but still controversial; Isaac
Newton's interpretations of prophecy's symbols regularly refer to cor-
poreal war, and so here, too, Blake is engaged in intellectual conflict.

The sentence that follows Blake's poem on plate 3 shifts the conflict from its biblical context to a philosophical one. When Blake writes that "every thing is conducted by Spirits, no less than Digestion or Sleep," he alludes to a theory that Isaac Newton also entertains and that Newton is likely to have learned from Henry More, his senior colleague at Cambridge. More expounded a theory of spiritual causation in his work on natural philosophy,[28] and Newton speculates that "we might add something concerning a certain most subtle spirit which pervades and lies hid in all gross bodies" and which causes all attraction and sensation. But Newton is not "furnished with that sufficiency of experiments which is required to an accurate determination and demonstration of the laws by which this . . . spirit operates."[29] When the fallen Albion asserts that "by demonstration, man alone can live, and not by faith" (4:28), he repeats Newton's refusal. The doctrine of spiritual causation entered Revelation commentary, as Blake knew. Exploiting its history in theology and in science, Blake suggests an intellectual unity from which man has evidently fallen. From *The Marriage of Heaven and Hell* onward, Blake's art attempts this restoration of vision: "Heaven, Earth & Hell, henceforth shall live in harmony." For reasons at once epistemological and theological, this achievement will be a return: Blake ends his address "To the Public" by reminding us that "the Primeval State of Man, was Wisdom, Art, and Science."

But the fall has split this primeval state; and so on plate 3, the pictures as well as the text symbolize contrary states (see Fig. 21). The "Sheep" and the "Goats" are split by the page's width. On the "Sheep" side, a figure, part human and part insect or vegetable, floats. On the "Goats" side float two similar figures, visibly more insect- or plantlike. Their rise or fall is ambiguous. Enclosing two paragraphs in clouds, Blake alludes pictorially to the same theory of language that his poem adumbrates: "Bright clouds are the Divine Truth veiled over . . . such as the Word is in the letter."[30] Blake portrays the conversion of language upward into ideas by a human figure flying upward from "heaven"; he portrays the conversion of language downward, into material forms, by vegetable appendages growing from words on the bottom half of the page. Having conflated his contexts, his contrary tones, and his conflicting perspectives, in text and in design, Blake's introduction is complete.

The first page of the first chapter of *Jerusalem* confronts the viewer with a vision of contraries before he begins to read the text (see Fig. 22). The cloud enclosing the title is bright, like other instances of

"Divine truth in ultimates," but only between its letters; above them stretch "dark clouds, the Divine Truth covered over with fallacies" of materialism, "such as the Word is in the letter with those who are in falsities."[31] Immediately beneath "Jerusalem," a hooded figure separates two perspectives, to the left and to the right. The man gazing goatward sits on dark rock, while the man gazing sheepward sits on a green and gold hill, directing his energies upward to "Μονος ο Ιεσους." That phrase is enclosed by a crescent moon in a starry sky. Below the man on his cliffs—Albion's cliffs of death—falls a Web of Religion. "Implied is the birth of Adam into the material world," as Erdman has suggested.[32] Right and left male, upward and downward sequences, and materialism (with its moral law) and spiritual rebirth are all set in clear contrast, before the poem even begins.

The first two lines of the epic prophecy state its theme, which should already be obvious from the designs: "Of the Sleep of Ulro! and of the passage through / Eternal Death! and of the awaking to Eternal Life." The sleep of Ulro is what the figure enters, with his goatward gaze, on the frontispiece; it is a condition suggested by the supine nude on the title-page. Its relations with "Eternal Death" recall the "House of Death" design (Fig. 1) and look forward to the supine dead on plates 33 and 58 (figs. 25 and 29). The kinetic thrust of "passage" through this sleep and the upward motion of "awaking" are ends to which Blake commits his poem.

Jerusalem begins exactly as Revelation does, the Savior dictating to the prophet. The Savior's song itself repeats themes and symbols from the address "To the Public," defining the poem's normative theology. "Awake! awake O sleeper of the land of shadows"—this line recalls the traditional association of fallen man (Adam or Albion) with both sleep and shadow,[33] as Jesus calls man to waken from the dream of material life. When the Savior reports that "a black water accumulates" (4:10), he describes the sleep of Ulro with one of its major biblical symbols, the flood. When he complains that "the Divine Vision is darkend" (4:13), he repeats verbally the significance of the dark clouds above the text; he also brings the blackness of the flood—an Old Testament symbol— against the New Testament's vision of Christ. That vision he explicates, further, according to its salient intellectual features: interiority and its consequence, unity. "I am in you," he says, "and you in me" (4:7). A theological key to *Jerusalem* appears when Christ says, "I am not a God afar off," and he immediately presents the idea in terms of the dialectic of inside and outside: "Within your bosoms I reside" (4:18–19). This locus of God, in the human breast, was already stated in *The Marriage of Heaven and Hell;* here, Christ tells Blake and mankind at once that the radically human origin of God is a specifically Christian vision. Earlier, Blake had conflated the unity in Christ that John had preached with his own philosophical idealism, when he glossed his line about the "Mighty Ones" who "are in every Man" by citing John 17:21–23 (*F.Z., E.,* p. 297). The same absolute humanism opens *Jerusalem.*

Already, Christ's speech has defined *Jerusalem*'s continuity with bib-lical prophecies and also its distinction from them. God had appeared to Isaiah at the opening of that prophecy, as Christ appears to Blake here; but in Isaiah, God spoke of what his "soul hateth" (1:14) and the destruction that He was eager to enact: "I will ease me of mine adversaries, and avenge me of mine enemies" (1:24). It is with just such a tone that Blake illustrates Isaiah, in a drawing on wood block that was the basis for an engraving: the design is "Isaiah Foretelling the De-struction of Jerusalem," and—drawn ca. 1821—it is a useful gloss for *Jerusalem* because of its themes and its composition (see Fig. 4).[34] The sharp divisions of left and right suggest the divisions of plate 3; the forcibly contrasted directions of gaze, upward to vision and downward to the letter of the law, repeat the motif from many plates, including plate 33 (Fig. 25); and the fastening of Isaiah's hand on the written law recalls the prose of "To the Public" and the design for plate 37 (Fig. 26). One of the central recurring devices in the visionary designs of *Jerusalem* is also repeated in the drawing for Isaiah: the vision of the visionary is delineated above his head, exteriorized both spatially and conceptually, but clearly dramatizing the prophet's *own* mental act, his attribution; the device is repeated in the illustrations for Job (see Fig. 3) and, over and over again, in *Jerusalem* (see, e.g., figs. 23, 24, 25, and 32). Isaiah's vision is of vengeance and destruction, and the prophet's act is thus an exteriorizing; the vision of the Savior is its contrary, displaying both interiority (4:18–19) and forgiveness (4:20)—*not* vengeance.

In *The Marriage of Heaven and Hell,* Blake had already called attention to Isaiah 34, "the day of the Lord's vengeance," and he knew this God's antagonism toward His own people. Thus Ezekiel's God opens with the statement that the children of Israel are a rebellious nation and that therefore "I will cause my fury to rest upon them . . . moreover I will make thee waste, and . . . I shall execute judgments in thee in anger

and in fury and in fierce rebukes" (5:13–15). Blake, like Isaac New-
ton, knew the violent ways of this God; compare his expressive design,
"Ezekiel" (Fig. 2), with "The House of Death" (Fig. 1) and with the
design inscribed "Does thy God O Priest take such vengeance as this?"
(Fig. 5). The analogies are obvious, and so is the implication—this part
of the vision of Ezekiel is the vision of death. Unlike Newton, Blake
did not find the doctrines of this God espoused equally in the New
Testament prophecy, Revelation. There, the God who dictates the
vision is ambivalent emotionally: His epistles to the churches include
grievances, because every prophecy is a call to people who have fallen
from grace, but His anger is carefully balanced in those epistles by His
approval, and he stops short there of the virulent invective of the Old
Testament God. Newton, however, and other commentators in his line
view the prophecy as an expression of divine wrath. Blake, for whom
"the Spirit of Jesus is continual forgiveness of Sin," sees exactly the
opposite: purging John's vision of threat, Blake's Savior sings a "mild
song" (4:5), not of foreheads hardened against one another (see Ezek.
3:8), but of God and man "mutual in love divine" (4:7). So doing, he
not only separates the Old Testament God from his own; he advances
beyond Revelation. Every prophet, as we have seen, collects parts of
his predecessors' visions, purging them of the dross. He must do so
because the purpose of prophecy is to extend the divine vision to a
people who are in a time of trouble. Blake, knowing this pattern,
engages in commentary, creating by re-creating the vision of God. The
absolute forgiveness that Blake celebrates arises from a philosophical
principle: interiority. Jesus—another name for human imagination—is
"in" men because he is a mental faculty; in fact, he is the origin of
mental life. Converting theological unities into epistemological unities
is exactly the process that enables Blake to purge the prophetic stance
of its violence and wrath.

   This softer, milder song of *Jerusalem* amounts to a reinterpretation of
the Book of Revelation. Florence Sandler has seen that *Milton* also
changes the vision of John: "In the Apocalypse of St. John, the fate of
the Two Witnesses provokes the elders in heaven to call for Justice, and
for the destruction of those who destroy the earth," but Blake's Spirit of
Prophecy urges patience and mercy.[35] This same critique of John is
expressed in *Milton* and in *Jerusalem,* and also, pictorially, in illustra-
tions for the Book of Revelation. In his description of his painting of the
Last Judgment, Blake states that a last judgment begins with the

casting off of "Questions concerning Good & Evil," not with the adjudication of sins (*V.L.J.*, *E.*, p. 544). This judgment will not consist of corporal punishment, but of "throwing off the Temporal that the Eternal might be Establishd" (p. 545). In Blake's design, Moses is depicted "casting his tables of stone into the deeps" (p. 546); the old covenant of law is cast off, replaced by the new covenant of mercy. Blake's language similarly separates the two testaments, and associates his vision with the ethos of forgiveness. He portrays "three fiery fiends" engaged in wrathful scourges; these figures represent, not a wrathful God, but "Clergymen in the Pulpit Scourging Sin instead of Forgiving it" (p. 547). In Blake's vision, it is not God who calumniates and murders "under Pretence of Holiness & Justice": it is Pilate and Caiaphas (p. 547). Blake assigns the "book of Accusations" not to the Lord sitting in judgment but to Satan and the Great Red Dragon (p. 548). The blessed are accompanied by "Divine Providence as opposd to & distinct from divine vengeance represented by three Aged men on the side of the Picture among the Wicked with scourges of fire" (p. 549).

This theological inversion of John's prophecy has a philosophical cause. It is not behavioral obedience but "Contemplative Thought" that will enable a man to "arise from his Grave" and "meet the Lord in the Air" (p. 550). Heaven arises from within humanity: "What are all the Gifts of the Spirit but Mental Gifts whenever any Individual Rejects Error & Embraces Truth a Last Judgment passes upon that Individual" (p. 551). The saved are not corporeally transplanted at a later date; they are intellectually changed at any moment, "Conversing with Eternal Realities as they Exist in the Human Imagination" (p. 552). This internalization alters John's vision: in Revelation 20 it is God who acts, casting the devil, death, hell, and "whosoever was not found written in the book of life" into the lake of fire; the damned themselves are all described in the passive voice. In Blake's account, this situation is reversed: it is the damned themselves who act, "howling & . . . dragging each other into Hell & . . . contending in fighting with each other" (p. 543). The blessed also act: they "embrace & arise together & in exulting attitudes of great joy tell each other that the New Jerusalem is ready to descend" (p. 543). Salvation and damnation— and in fact all eternal creation—flow directly from humanity, not from an exterior agent.

Blake's pictures display this theology in visual detail. His watercolor,

"The Great Red Dragon and the Woman Clothed in the Sun" (Fig. 8), an illustration for Revelation 12, shows us that woman with the moon at her feet, wrapped in a shape that is at once the sun, angels' wings, and a human heart. She is diaphanous and light; her persecutor, the dragon accuser, looms over her, massive and solid. His material bulk and downward gaze—like those of the spectre on *Jerusalem* plate 6 (Fig. 23) and the bat on *Jerusalem* plate 33 (Fig. 25)—exactly reverse the luminous and upward-gazing woman. The bottom right corner of the picture shows human faces arising from—or turning into—stone or cloud, in torment: whichever image is suggested, the symbolic implications of wrath and materialism are identical. These stonelike forms or cloud-shapes are part of the error to be cast off. Gazing at the dragon, they assume his stony form; at the time of judgment, this error will roll away (p. 543). Blake's additions to the imagery of Revelation reinforce his humanized vision, according to which an infernal fall or blessed ascent is, like a tear, "an Intellectual thing" (*J.* 52:25). The upward gaze of the woman and the downward gaze of the condemning dragon symbolize those figures' intellectual tendencies; these gazes are made possible only by Blake's additions to John's prophecy, where the dragon was not above the woman but "before" her (12:4). Blake humanizes apocalypse: he gives the woman the red color and the form of a human heart, of which there is no suggestion in Revelation. The God who presides over the last judgment is not an external power seated on a throne above us—it is the divine humanity itself (*V.L.J., E.,* p. 551).

On plate 4 of *Jerusalem,* Man responds to this milder message from the divine voice by turning away and fleeing. His short speech identifies the context that he represents. He declares, *"We are not One: we are Many"* (4:23), repudiating the principle of intellectual unity that Blake, following John, expresses: "All of us on earth are united in thought" (*E.,* p. 590). Albion calls Christ a "Phantom of the over heated brain" (4:24), citing Locke's opinion of enthusiasm: "fancies of a man's own brain."[36] He repeats Newton's value, "demonstration" (4:28), and he declares his intention to "build my Laws of Moral Virtue!" (4:31). Thus, he has assembled the same principles and contexts that Christ had assembled above, but in reverse perspective; in this way, the text of plate 4 reproduces the patterns of contraries and reversal that characterize the preceding designs.

The first paragraph on the next plate introduces two visionary techniques into the poem, both of which we have already isolated in visionary tradition. In line 3 Blake lists "Cambridge & Oxford & London," which he says "are driven among the starry Wheels." We have met those stars and their "Void" (5:3) already, in the designs; they function as imagistic connections among the plates. In the same paragraph in which he adds British place-names to their context, Blake cites for the first time "Moab & Ammon & Amalek & Canaan & Egypt & Aram" (5:14), names we shall encounter again and again. These words are all names of biblical places whose peoples oppose the children of Israel en route to the promised land, but they are used here in a completely figurative sense. They name essentially the same idea, just as in Revelation commentary, Egypt, Babylon, and Rome name the same idea, "including all persons who answer to the . . . ample description."[37] They engage in "sacrifices and the delights of cruelty" (5:15), in their idolatry worshipping gods of this material world.

The paragraph that begins with British place-names ends with biblical place-names. Northrop Frye has studied Blake's technique of conflating the two sets of place-names, and the technique itself needs no demonstration here.[38] This passage is one of the first examples in the poem of the calculated technique of Israelism, or Anglo-Israelite typology, whereby biblical place-names symbolize contemporary intellectual conflicts. A consequence of this technique that Blake, like his predecessors, deliberately exploits is its tendency to extrapolate the concerns of his narrative to universal dimensions. This universality results from the terms' conversion to ideas rather than to physical places; the gaps of time and space are obliterated. As John Howard has argued in connection with *Milton*, Blake's habit of jamming irreconcilable spaces and times together forces the reader to seek intellectual rather than natural meanings.[39]

Then, Blake withdraws from his vision into comment upon it, restating his theme and reminding us of the visionary process. "I rest not from my great task!" he declares (5:17), reminding us, as John did, that the vision is being mediated through the prophet. The prophet is therefore engaged in a rhetorical effort, which Blake defines in the following terms: "To open the Eternal Worlds, to open the immortal Eyes / Of Man inwards into the Worlds of Thought" (5:18–19). This definition of the prophetic task makes its affinity with commentary plain: the two acts are really one. Another affinity, though, is a matter of exegetical history; Blake enters the conflict, still current, between those commentators who read Revelation outward, converting its terms into history, and those who perceive its sublime allegory, unfolding its spiritual or intellectual sense. Accordingly, Blake equates absolutely "the Bosom of God" and "the Human Imagination" (5:20), and says that "Imagination / . . . is the Divine Body of the Lord Jesus" (5:58–59). The Book of Revelation also repeats itself. Both there and in *Jerusalem*, the device underscores important lines: this one is crucial to Blake's theology.

Two elements here, the apotheosis of imagination and the stress on interiority, signal Blake's combative stance. Naming both Newton's and Locke's universities on plate 5, Blake also contradicts their doctrine. Locke's famous distrust of imagination, which I have already cited at length, is subjected to Blake's inversional transformation.[40] Newton's equally famous outward gaze into the world of nature rather than "the Worlds of Thought" is ascribed on plate 4 to fallen or falling Man. Within a Christian context, too, both Locke, seeking to demonstrate "the reasonableness of Christianity," and Newton, compiling his mundane histories to explain Revelation, are equally under attack. Blake's principles are clear, and so are the identities of his antagonists. They are, precisely, philosophies, intellectual perspectives. Revelation's diverse symbolism of a single idea, a device noted by almost all commentators, is carried to even greater lengths in *Jerusalem* than in the Bible. The meanings of those diverse symbols, though, like the meanings of the diverse systems Blake attacks, resolve at last into an intellectual unity. Now, his principles and his contexts established, major symbols already introduced, and the lineaments of *Jerusalem* already set forth, Blake's narrative—if it is a narrative—resumes.

It is misleading to call *Jerusalem* a narrative, however, because evidence suggests that Blake deliberately broke whatever continuity the poem once displayed. Blake shuffled plates, without any effort to adapt them to their new context; the poem contains obvious insertions, mismatched catchwords, and illustrations widely separated from their texts. The resulting structure has elicited prodigious and brilliant explanations, inviting us to perceive various organizational analogies: Ezekiel, the four gospels, *Paradise Regained;* biblical history, the ages of man, four zoas, four seasons, four times of day.[41] One commentator has suggested that the best method of perceiving the poem's structure is to ignore much of the poem,[42] while one of the most complex essays on *Jerusalem* suggests seven simultaneous structures, built on twos, threes, fours, and sixes.[43] Despite their disagreements, all of these commentators remind us of the important fact that *Jerusalem* does not exhibit a mad lack of form, but rather a form that many readers are simply not trained to perceive. While its structural antecedent remains in the dark, its principles of order or disorder, however hotly debated, are likely to go unnoticed.

Jerusalem consists, not of events in order, but of symbolic variations on a theme.[44] Its events are mental ones, elicited in its audience; *Jerusalem* is designed to produce vision, not to imitate earthly sequence. Blake employs the form of Revelation, presenting one symbolic vision after another. According to the principles of classical narrative, what should be events in sequence are, in prophecy, symbolic recastings of an original unitary vision.[45] The plot of *Jerusalem* or of Revelation is the audience's progress from darkness to light, gradually apprehending thematic coherence amid narrative discontinuity. Plate-shuffling does not defeat this end; it helps to achieve it. As theorists from More to Lowth would have reminded Blake, obscurity is a technique designed to elicit the labors of thought, a means of entangling the audience of a prophecy in an intellectual struggle whose outcome is mental revolution. In the case of *Jerusalem,* Blake forces his reader to undergo an effort of cognitive unification. He deliberately acquaints readers with their own mental powers; by inducing acts of intellection, he teaches his reader about them. To search for the structure of *Jerusalem* is, finally, to earn a perception of intellectual unity. That unity is the subject of the poem.

Therefore the plates of *Jerusalem* possess the coherence of pictures in a gallery, not episodes in a prose narrative.[46] The eye passes from vision to vision, and thus the mind actively perceives a unity. The most important visual motif in *Jerusalem* binds its parts, though narrative is violently disrupted: to study in sequence plates 6, 14, 33, and 76 (figs. 23, 24, 25, and 32) is to perceive contrary visions of God. In each instance, one figure looks upward at another—that is, one figure has a vision of another—and throughout the sequence particular elements help to interpret each vision and invite comparisons. Thus the bat-winged figure with a human head (plate 6) turns entirely animal (plate 33); he who has the vision is horizontal and "miserable"[47] (plate 14); then another horizontal figure is evidently dead, evidently becoming inanimate material (plate 33); but when at last the visionary is vertical, upright, it is a different and brilliant God that he sees.

That fact that *Jerusalem* is modeled after biblical prophecy has become the subject of a theory by Harold Bloom, from which I had better distinguish my own reading at once. In *Ringers in the Tower*, Bloom writes that in *Jerusalem* "Blake goes at last for prophetic form to a prophet, to the priestly orator, Ezekiel, whose situation and sorrow most closely resemble his own" (p. 65). Yet in his attempt to argue in support of the similarity of the two prophecies, Bloom unwittingly highlights the opposite, compiling a series of statements as self-defeating as that one, which invites us to consider Blake as a priest. Bloom does use the term *prophet* repeatedly, saying that "from Ezekiel in particular Blake learned the true meaning of prophet, visionary orator, honest man who speaks into the heart of a situation to warn: if you go on so, the result is so; or as Blake said, a seer and not an arbitrary dictator" (p. 66). But the odd use of the term *priestly* remains to trouble Bloom's argument with inappropriate ideology. When Blake uses the term *priest*, he often couples it with *king*, and the two are pejorative.

More pertinently, J. F. C. Harrison writes that the prophet inevitably "finds himself in opposition to the priesthood." The prophet challenges and changes established orders of belief, and he challenges his precursors: "Like Jesus he can but repeat, 'It is written . . . , but I say unto you.'"[48] Precisely because his art is prophecy, Blake inverts Ezekiel; he does not repeat him. "God made Ezekiel as hard as adamant. . . . Blake knew he had to be even harder," writes Bloom (p. 66), ignoring the fact that Blake's God is the Savior of the "mild song." Arguing that Blake, like the author of Revelation, went straight to Ezekiel for a precursor, Bloom misses the true sequence, that *includes* Revelation, as Blake's more immediate model; he also misses the poem's radical Christianity. Thus, "Blake's God, like Ezekiel's, sends a 'watchman' to admonish individuals," claims Bloom (p. 73); but "admonish" is at once too gentle to describe Ezekiel's God and too stern to describe Blake's, the former setting head against head and the latter softly singing, "I am in you and you in me mutual in love divine." Ezekiel and his God are invoked in *Jerusalem*, not because Blake's situation and theology resemble Ezekiel's, but precisely because they are different, Blake reversing the wrathful vision at every point. Ignoring this fact, Bloom arrives at what are clearly misreadings, including his misunderstanding of the Spectre's famous speech, and Los's answer, in chapter 1. Bloom rejoices that "a passage from solipsism to otherness is made" and yet reads that sequence as solipsism, translating theological tones into Blake's anxieties (p. 69).

When he does observe that Blake's vision swerves from Ezekiel, Bloom claims that Blake chose "a darker emphasis" (p. 77). This contention Bloom fails to support, adducing only one argument, and that one based on the implausible assumption that in *Jerusalem* events are arranged in chronological order. Briefly, Blake's relation to Ezekiel involves radical transformations. They are based, however, not on a shrinking anxiety neurosis but on a contrary vision of God. In *Jerusalem* Blake does not cringe with nervousness; he openly engages in mental fight.

When Bloom refers to "the theater of mind," he does so only to belittle the concept that Blake and his visionary tradition exalt; without citing the relevant philosophical tradition *or* the relevant visionary theorists, Bloom does not recognize the epistemological importance of this concept, instead reducing it to what is merely trivial and personal (p. 69). Neither Blake, Shelley, Hume, Mede, More, nor Isaac Newton would accept Bloom's flat distinction between "the theater of mind" and "the orator's theater of action" (p. 75); it had been the philosophical project of centuries to relate these levels of reference, and it is a part of Blake's project even utterly to identify them.

Usefully correcting Bloom, and helping to focus the issues, Randel Helms has seen that "Ezekiel's righteous condemnation of Jerusalem becomes in Blake an ironic condemnation of the accusers themselves," and he points rightly to some parallels in plot. [49] Insisting that "Ezekiel's accusations of whoredom are accurate" may be misleading, however; and the related question of whether chapter 3 is about "war on earth" or some other kind of war remains to be asked. [50] Its answer conducts us to *Jerusalem*'s form and meaning: the poem is a specifically Christian prophecy, subverting and recasting its precursors to achieve its end, which is liberation from the tyrannies of time, space, matter, and moral law. *Jerusalem* contrasts two kinds of Gods, throughout all of its various symbolic scenes: one is a tyrant, maker of matter and of law, both of which He imposes from without; the other is the Divine Vision, or human imagination. [51]

One of Blake's repeatedly stated aims is to annihilate the forms of time and space, revealing them as products of the mind and not its governors. The two major structural principles of *Jerusalem* are specifically designed to force the reader toward this perception; both principles Blake derived from Revelation, whose interpreters—unlike

Blake's—uniformly understood them. The first, a method of annihilat-
ing time, is synchronism; the second, annihilating space, is Israelism.

Stuart Curran has pointed out that in each of the first three chapters
Luvah is slain and Albion dies. "Only by stretching the meaning of the
word beyond its customary associations can such a pattern be called
narrative."[52] Yet that pattern perfectly reproduces a different conven-
tion, synchronism, a technique that I have discussed and that is sum-
marized by Wittreich: "Each vision looks back to and epitomizes what
precedes it, with the result that certain motifs are tenaciously re-
peated."[53] The device pervades *Jerusalem:* Jerusalem turns into a cloud
and bends eastward on plate 5, and then again on plate 15; Tyburn's
tree shoots up on plate 12 and then again on plate 28; Golgonooza is
built on plate 12, but on plate 53 Los is at work building it. In his
authorial intrusion on plate 74, Blake comments on his poem's anti-
chronological sequence: "I walk up and down in Six Thousand Years:
their Events are present before me" (74:19). From a perspective that
transcends time, the order of events is subject to intellectual control,
the mind free to rearrange or repeat them. When we encounter the
ringing shout that "Time was Finished" (94:18) at the poem's close, we
are only hearing of what we must have noticed all along. Thus, synchro-
nism serves a philosophical purpose here just as it does in other Revela-
tion commentary. Like Archimedes and the earth, we require a spot
outside time in order to control time; synchronism supplies the need.
All times, like all religions, are one. We are free to replace the exterior
order of chronology with a mind-made order according to meaning.
Doing so, our intellects discover themselves and their power.[54]

As I have argued in the preceding chapter, Israelism (or Anglo-
Israelite typology) is the similar conflation of spaces. An obvious
example appears on plates 16 and 72, where Blake identifies bib-
lical with British place-names, but this device is pervasive:
"Reuben is Merlin" (32:41), for example, Schofield is Adam (7:25),
and Tyburn is Calvary and Golgotha (12:26–28). Blake identifies the
purpose of this device when he interprets the four faces seen by
Ezekiel: they are "in every Man" (12:58). Israelism universalizes
meaning, as Blake indicates on plate 16; there, he follows his conflations
of Bible and Britain by stating that visionary art depicts "all things
acted on Earth" (16:61), collapsing the multiplicity of experience into a
symbolic center.

All that can happen to Man in his pilgrimage of seventy years
Such is the Divine Written Law of Horeb & Sinai:
And such the Holy Gospel of Mount Olivet & Calvary.

(16:67–70)

The reference of biblical terms, accordingly, is not to particular persons or places, but rather to universal ideas: "The Return of Israel is a Return to Mental Sacrifice & War" (*J.*, pl. 27, *E.*, p. 172).[55]

Like other prophets, Blake is his own best exegete, isolating and explaining his own devices. A third such device, his doctrine of states, though less obviously traditional than synchronism and Israelism, points equally to his poem's mental reference. Blake explains that "as the Pilgrim passes while the Country permanent remains / So Men pass on: but States remain permanent for ever" (73:44–45). His example on this plate is the symbolic identity of "all the Kings & Nobles of the Earth" (73:38), to which biblical exegetes had traditionally pointed. On plate 31, Blake uses this doctrine of states to explicate his ambiguous frontispiece design: the Divine Vision says that "Albion goes to Eternal Death: In Me all Eternity. / Must pass thro' condemnation, and awake beyond the Grave!" (31:9–10). He goes forth to create states, to lift men's vision from the particular to the universal. The dark reminders of moral law on plate 1, the ambiguous cheer imparted by the light-bearer, and his multiple identity are referable to the fact that the picture symbolizes a universal event "in every Man." On plate 31 the Christian Divine Vision goes forth to reverse the Mosaic Moral Law, precisely by replacing individual and mundane vision with the intellectual perspective, or the doctrine of states.

Blake supplies other indicators too of the mental reference of his symbols. When Golgonooza is being built, Blake tells us that "the stones are pity, and the bricks, well wrought affections" (12:30), providing mental correlatives for the sensible images. One is less likely to lament the stiffness of the allegory when its relations to Blake's philosophy are clear, and they become clearer on plate 34. There London speaks, saying, "My Streets are my, Ideas of Imagination," and "My Houses are Thoughts" (34: 31, 33). Blake converts not only metaphors but also places and objects to ideas. When he writes that "the Walls of Babylon are Souls of Men" (24:31) he uses several of these techniques at once. The identity of London and Babylon, to which I have referred earlier, is an Israelism; it also implies the doctrine of states, London converting to Babylon just when it lapses into the state of fallen vision.

Another technique also sublimates Blake's allegory. Golgonooza, described on plates 12–13, cannot be visually imagined; its dimensions contradict the demands of physical space. One example will suffice: "West, the Circumference: South, the Zenith: North, / the Nadir: East, the Center" (12:55–56). Blake has simply substituted one set of spatial coordinates for another with which it is incompatible. He forces a symbolic reading by preventing a literal one. This device recurs, as when Ireland's counties are said to "center in London & in Golgonooza, from whence / They are Created continually East & West & North & South" (72:28–29). This arrangement is obviously a spatial impossibility, and can only refer to an intellectual meaning; such a conclusion is reinforced when these same counties of Ireland, impossibly centered in London, are sprayed across "all the Nations of the Earth" in the next line of the poem.

When Blake declares that "Devils are False Religions" (J., pl. 77, E., p. 229), his interpretation is traditional. His conversion of the term, from symbol to mental condition, is also conventional, and it is consistent with the final cause of prophecy as he states it on plate 92, "that we may Foresee & Avoid / The terrors of Creation & Redemption & Judgment" as we have seen them displayed in "Visionary forms dramatic" (92:19–20; 98:28). The subjects of prophecy are therefore not particular events of history, but rather their spiritual causes. *Jerusalem* is about the intellectual forms that are variously manifest in the Bible, Blake's biography, biblical Egypt and Palestine, and "War on the Rhine & Danube" (47:9). Erdman has explicated *Jerusalem* according to the theme of vengeance as that idea pertains to the European wars of Blake's time, and so he has enriched our understanding of the poem.[56] Such insights, however, are most valuable when they are understood to enrich the poem's manifold meanings, not to comprise them; the poem's final subject, the mind of man, is the unity to which the various symbols, including those drawn from history, refer.[57] Whatever corporeal disasters man beholds emanate from their spiritual cause, "from within his witherd breast" (19:9). Toward this vision all of Blake's visionary aesthetics contribute. His rare moments of explicitness are also designed to make his directions unmistakable: his Zoas, the faces seen by Ezekiel, and his own titular subject, Jerusalem, are "in every individual Man" (39:39); and so he demands of his reader: "Turn your eyes inward" to see (39:41).

One of the most important recurring visions in *Jerusalem* is presented verbally in the dialogue between Los and his Spectre in chapter 1. The Spectre speaks to Los in much the same way that God speaks to Ezekiel: he complains of the faithlessness of Albion and his sons (7:10), just as God complained of the children of Israel; he speaks of shame and sins (10:37), of what "the Law of God commands" (10:38), of sacrifices upon the altar (10:39), of a "Righteous" God who "is not a Being of Pity & Compassion" (10:47). This God delights "in cries & tears" (10:49), and in the voice of the Spectre he demands redress of grievances. As we have seen, these are the hallmarks of the Old Testament God, particularly Ezekiel's, as Blake perceived them (see Fig. 2); this is he who "comes with a Thump on the Head" (*V.L.J.*, *E.*, p. 555). In Blake's theology, the contrary is Christ, whose "mild song" opens *Jerusalem:* after the angry God thumps one's head, "then Jesus Christ comes with a balm to heal it." It is significant that this last statement was made in Blake's commentary on Revelation; in *Jerusalem* he repeats the dialectic. In the dialogue between Los and his Spectre, Los responds, not by agreeing to violence and wrath, but rather by urging mercy: "They have divided themselves by Wrath. they must be united by / Pity" (7:57–58). He wishes to "abstain from wrath" (7:59), embracing instead the mercy of the Lamb of God (7:59–70). Clearly the Spectre dictating to Los is a dark parody of the Savior dictating to the prophet on plate 4. *That* God did not complain of Man's sins, instead "forgiving all Evil" (4:20). To understand Blake's relation to Ezekiel requires that we first perceive the similarity between the Spectre and Ezekiel's God, both hovering over the prophet to speak of sin and wrath. Then we must notice a difference: Ezekiel, accepting the authority of the wrathful God and believing that God's accusations are righteous, relays his moral railing to the people of Israel. Los, Blake's prophet-figure in *Jerusalem*, breaks the sequence and silences the voice of the wrathful God by repudiating his demands for law and vengeance, embracing the doctrine of mercy, and, like the God of Revelation, wiping away tears from the sufferer's eyes (10:61; Rev. 7:17, 21:4).

Blake's designs repeat the antithetical conception of God. Plate 6 (Fig. 23) depicts the Spectre hovering over Los, stretching his dark bat-wings over Los's head. This vision locates God—or here, a parody of Ezekiel's God—outside the prophet, where Jesus says He is not. It also sets God and Man in exact opposition: their spines are perfectly perpendicular to one another. This design is repeated on plates 33 (Fig. 25) and 58 (Fig. 29), the hovering bat growing less and less evidently human and the poor mortal growing more and more evidently dead. The contrary vision is depicted on plate 76 (Fig. 32), where the higher figure is not dark but luminous. In place of the ugly bat-wings, Man sees God's outstretched arms. The Spectre's God plainly resented his grievances; this God forgives those who know not what they do. The figure below Him, recipient of vision, is becoming one with Him, literally incorporating the Divine Vision. The implied movement is upward, to the source of light. On plate 58 the implied movement is downward, toward the dead stuck to the bottom of the page. On plate 33, both contraries are evident: the bat-over-the-dead design occupies the lower portion of the page, and its lines move downward. In the upper portion of the page is a luminous *Pietà*, a figure of mercy lifting the stricken body upward. These elements are simultaneously present on plate 6 too, where the Spectre's gaze and wings are aimed downward and the prophet, refusing his vision, is looking up.

These contrary visions of God amount to a unifying theme in *Jerusalem.* Blake not only depicts the contrary Gods and gives them dialogue, but he also explains their origin. Fallen Albion is "self-exiled from the face of light" (19:13); the threatening God is his own projection. Man's trumpet and harp, symbols of prophecy, are silent; he simply has ceased to exercise his faculties of vision, and in that respite or sleep the external and loveless God arises. These same symbols are repeated in the Job illustrations, where the trumpet and harp are silent (p. 1) and where Job exiles himself from the face of light (p. 2). Blake describes the process; the appearance of God above Man is "a Shadow from his wearied intellect" (43:37) and nothing more. Worshipping this projection as if it were external, Man is "idolatrous to his own Shadow" (43:46). It is precisely when Man envisions God as external to himself that he begins to suffer judgment and anger (43:37). He becomes obsessed with sin: "These hills & valleys are accursed witnesses of Sin" (28:9). Then he converts to materialism: "I therefore condense them into solid rocks" (28:10), referring to Newton's materialism, "demonstrative truth" (28:11), and also to the God of the Old Testament. This God is both materialism and moral law: "He is the Rock . . . all his ways are judgment" (Deut. 32:4). So, on plate 37 (Fig. 26), Man is depicted as a victim of this vision. In an early state of the design (Fig. 27), he is surrounded by rocks; in the finished state the rocks are replaced by scrolls or tablets of the written law. As those laws were first issued on stones, the two symbols are interchangeable. The contrary is expressed on plate 54, where Blake replaces law with liberty and an external God with internal light (54:1–5).

This vision takes another recurrent shape in *Jerusalem,* in Blake's account of the creation of the material world. On plate 17, its four elements—fire, water, earth, and air—are the work of the Spectre, Blake's Elohim. Immediately a religion arises around the "Creator of this World," who is "a very Cruel Being" (*V.L.J.*, *E.*, p. 555):

> Calling that Holy Love: which is Envy Revenge & Cruelty
> Which separated the stars from the mountains: the mountains
>   from Man
> And left Man, a little grovelling Root, outside of Himself.
>
>   (17:30–32)

The jealous God, His vengeance, and His materialism are all involved in this religion. On plate 30, the issues are raised again; the stars are said to flee Man's members again, but this catastrophe follows the creation of "a Female Will" (30:31). This female will is a projection of Man's mind; exteriorized, her role is reversed, and she seems to be "Mother of all" (30:9). She is Vala or material nature (30:29). According to this account, the material world arises when Man exteriorizes his ideas, and then beholds what is within as if it were without. The female and the entire universe are then perceived as "outside of Himself."

The same vision takes the shape of a commentary on Genesis:

> And Enitharmon like a faint rainbow waved before him
> Filling with Fibres from his loins which reddend with desire
> Into a Globe of blood beneath his bosom trembling in darkness
> Of Albions clouds. he fed it, with his tears & bitter groans
> Hiding his Spectre in invisibility from the timorous Shade
> Till it became a separated cloud of beauty grace & love
> Among the darkness of his Furnaces dividing asunder till
> She separated stood before him a lovely Female weeping
> Even Enitharmon separated outside, & his Loins closed
> And heal'd after the separation: his pains he soon forgot:

Lured by her beauty outside of himself in shadowy grief.
Two Wills they had; Two Intellects: & not as in times of old.

(86:50–61)

Here Blake, like Henry More before him, interprets the creation of Eve
as a separation of a feminine portion from a prior and masculine
character; both writers emphasize the male's delight in her beauty; and
both use her to connect him with the external and material world. The
"masculine Adam . . . consists in pure subtile Intellectual Knowl-
edge," according to More, whereas the "Feminine part" that separates
from his breast "is that Vital principle that joins the Soul to the Matter of
the Universe."[58] More and Blake explain the sequence of sleep, divi-
sion, and materialism: only after Man's sleep—the sleep of death that
Blake describes—does he assume a material body. "*Adam*'s Soul de-
scended into the prepared Matter of the Earth, and, in due process of
time, Adam appear'd cloth'd in the skins of beasts; that is, he became a
down-right Terrestrial Animal, and a mortal creature upon Earth"
(3:16). The resulting mortality explains why Man's sleep is the sleep of
death; the fact that the feminine portion lured Man *outside* of himself
accounts for the creation of the material world; and the opposition of
her will to his, also explained by More (3:6), disbands the intellectual
unity that Blake ascribes to paradise (86:61).

On plate 32 the same vision appears, but in a different symbolic
shape, this one a commentary on Joshua's crossing of the Jordan. Here
again Man "sees the Elements divide before his face" (32:27), here
again matter is made from a rib (32:4), and here again it is precisely the
process of division that precipitates dire events (32:3). Los folds Reu-
ben's tongue "between Lips of mire & clay" (32:6), just as in the *Four
Zoas* he fabricates men's bodily forms (103:32–37); to understand why
this function falls to the spirit of prophecy, we have only to notice that,
as More explains, Man was incorporated to allow for his eventual
redemption, generation being the image of regeneration. Throughout
Jerusalem Blake uses the biblical trope that More had called *henopoeia*,
Reuben's name representing all of the tribes of Israel: he crosses the
Jordan, just as the tribes did under Joshua; in Blake's version he imparts
his material form to everyone who sees him, as "they became what they
beheld" (32:9). Next, Los materializes Reuben's ear, bending it "out-
ward," and sends him over Jordan again (32:13). Once more the effect is

to propagate materialism, all who see him becoming what they behold (32:14). Thus, Blake interprets Joshua's march toward the promised land, with its "Patriarchal pomp & cruelty" (83:4), as a sublime allegory, addressing men's intellectual powers: "The Four Eternal Senses of Man / Became Four Elements separating from the limbs" of Man (32:31–32). To understand *Jerusalem* is to understand Blake's reading of the Bible,[59] and we find an important signal of that reading when we recognize that for Blake Genesis and Joshua tell the same story. That story is of the creation of the material world, a fall from vision that amounts to no more, in either case, than a failure of Man's intellectual faculties.

All religions are one; pagan religion also lodges man in a material world, and so Blake ascribes similar effects to heathenism. When moral virtues are repudiated at the poem's climax, they are attributed not to the religion of Moses, but to heathenism (98:46). In the symbolism of moral law Moses and Priam are stand-ins for one another. Blake recognized a similar treatment of paganism in *Paradise Regained,* where the four elements—"fire, air, flood, and . . . earth"—and their knowledge, which is pagan wisdom, are ascribed to Satan.[60] More and Priestley also ascribed dangerous worldliness to the pagans, and so Blake's conflation of Hebrew and pagan gods of this world should not surprise us.[61]

Blake's Christian vision can be only heuristically separated from his philosophical context; now we must reentangle them, as Blake has done. In the passage on plate 30 in which he laments the creation of the female will and the material world, Blake describes the result of these catastrophes: the female will is "to / Converse concerning Weight & Distance in the Wilds of Newton & Locke" (30:40). Albion's Spectre is at once the rock-god whom we have seen so often and also "Bacon & Newton & Locke" (54:17). He, Satan, and Newtonian philosophy are absolutely identified when he, like the wrathful God, damns a "Rebel against my Laws" (54:19), when he utters Satan's speech on turning stone to bread (54:21), and when he discusses that episode in terms of Newtonian science (54:22).[62]

Blake adopts various biblical symbols for Newton and Locke: their philosophy performs the crucifixion (24:55); their abstraction is Daniel's "Abomination of Desolation" (10:16); their reasonings, natural religion, and natural morality cause the cruelty of sacrifice (66:1–15); their philosophy of reflection is ascribed to the Antichrist (89:10–15). To interpret various biblical symbols as figures for one idea is, as we have seen, traditional; Blake is not the only commentator on Revelation to assign the Dragon to the philosophy of the material body.[63] Plate 88, immediately preceding Blake's revelation of the Antichrist, accounts for his identification. Los, the spirit of prophecy, praises minglings in "thunders of Intellect" (88:7). Blake recapitulates this idea here because it serves to introduce the identification of Antichrist. The demonstrative science of Newton and Locke posits, as we have seen, a division of mind and universe. It posits a passive model of mind, also suggested by Blake's sleep of death, in which impressions originate in a cold inanimate world without; the origin of ideas is inhuman. When Los praises minglings in intellect, he is urging man's recovery of the mental universe, his own creation; this will be the recovery of paradise. The philosophy of Newton and Locke is the Covering Cherub standing between Man and this paradise.

Thus Blake's prophetic mission is exactly the release of his readers from the philosophy of externally imposed matter and morality. The biblical symbols of this philosophy include the Dragon, the Whore of Babylon, Antichrist, and the Abomination of Desolation. Blake adds Rahab, a harlot from the Book of Joshua whom he identifies with Babylon (75:1) and who is moral virtue (35:10) and Vala or material nature (70:31). To shift to a philosophical vocabulary, this same system of ideas is also named Bacon, Newton, and Locke; and so Blake defines his task:

> O Divine Spirit sustain me on thy wings!
> That I may awake Albion from his long & cold repose,
> For Bacon & Newton sheathd in dismal steel, their terrors hang
> Like iron scourges over Albion.
>
> (15:9–12)

Blake's visionary eye sees all the biblical figures that John saw, including the seven-headed dragon (plate 50; Fig. 28); it also beholds the "Loom of Locke" and the "Water-wheels of Newton" (15:15–16). Like every true prophet, Blake has brought vision to his own cultural matrix and supplied a commentary, interpreting his symbols. He allows us to perceive that revelation is an ongoing and eternal process, its coordinates the sleeping or waking faculties of its audience's minds. The philosophy of Locke places an insuperable flood between the mind and its objects of knowledge, but "those in Great Eternity" (32:50) assert, like Berkeley, an absolute identity between them.[64]

The new paradise is the reawakened mind. No longer beholding *without* that which is *within*, the mind creates the objects of its perception, "creating exemplars of Memory and of Intellect / Creating Space, Creating Time according to the wonders Divine / Of Human Imagination" (98:30–32). The perception that imagination is the principle of *all* intellection assimilates poets and philosophers: "And Bacon & Newton & Locke, & Milton & Shakespear & Chaucer" (98:9) voyage through strange skies of thought together.

Earlier in the poem, when Albion sees "the Elements divide before his face" (32:27), another division had also occurred: "England who is Brittannia divided into Jerusalem & Vala" (32:28). But then, where the mind and its objects are again unified, near the poem's close, a unity is restored with this complex feminine figure: "England who is Brittannia" repents for her murder of Albion "in Stone-henge" (94:22–24). This language reinterprets a passage from chapter 3:

> . . . Vala the Wife of Albion, who is the Daughter of Luvah
> Took vengeance Twelve-fold among the Chaotic Rocks of the Druids
> Where the Human Victims howl.
>
> (63:7–9)

Thus England or Brittannia includes *both* Vala and Jerusalem; it is as Vala that she murders, but it is as Jerusalem that she returns to Albion, restoring to Albion the Divine Vision:

> England who is Brittannia entered Albions bosom rejoicing
>
> Then Jesus appeared standing by Albion as the Good Shepherd
> By the lost Sheep that he hath found & Albion knew that it
> Was the Lord the Universal Humanity, & Albion saw his Form
> A Man. & they conversed as Man with Man, in Ages of Eternity.
>
> (96:2–6)

Thus, one of the unifications that Blake portrays is the unification of mind and object; another is the unification of Albion with England or Brittannia, who acts, thus, as Jerusalem:

> In Great Eternity, every particular Form gives forth or Emanates
> Its own peculiar Light, & the Form is the Divine Vision
> And the Light is his Garment. This is Jerusalem in every Man.
>
> (54:1– 3)

Brittannia's entrance into Albion, near the end of the poem, restores this paradigm whereby Jerusalem is both in every Man and also associated with the Divine Vision. Further, Brittannia had divided into Vala and Jerusalem (plate 32); opposition, symbolized by the murder at Stonehenge, ends when Albion's emanation is restored to him (plates 95 and 96).

Another identity—of the antithetical women of Revelation, the Whore and the Bride—was already hinted on plate 61 where the Divine Voice denies the virgin birth. To reveal that the Whore and the Bride are one is only to clarify what has been implicit from the beginning: Babylon, "the City of Vala" (18:29), is Jerusalem, seen from a reversed perspective, and in another state. The multiplicity and contradictions among the visions of God resolve themselves in the poem's climax into this principle of mental unification: plate 99 (Fig. 33) portrays a diety who displays the love and light of Christ and who also resembles the old man God of the Old Testament as He appears in *Job* and "Elohim Creating Adam" (figs. 3 and 6). As we see Revelation ending with the marriage of Christ and His Bride, Jerusalem, so we recognize that marriage here in the obviously sexual union of God and woman. The text over their heads reminds us of their meaning: "All Human Forms identified" (99:1), Man reclaims to his bosom that which originally emanated from within him. He reclaims the universe.

Thus the ending of *Jerusalem* returns us to its middle. The vision of unity that concludes the poem suggests at once a unity of mind and object, God and humanity, and vision with vision. *Jerusalem*'s structure only gradually reveals this last kind of unity—intellectual coherence among its parts—but two more continually recurring visions are now susceptible of interpretation, as symbolic variants of the theme. These two—the visions of the serpent and the crucifixion—are also retellings of biblical episodes, and they also conflate the Bible with British philosophy. The vision of the serpent is the pictorial subject of plates 63 and 75 (figs. 30 and 31), and it appears also on plate 72. In the first instance, the crescent moon presides over a serpent-wrapped naked female who is suffering, much like Laocoön. To perceive the Laocoön analogy is to recognize important contexts: "The Gods of Priam are the Cherubim of Moses & Solomon" (*E.*, p. 271), writes Blake, explicating the conflation of Moses and Priam which he uses again in *Jerusalem.* The victim of the serpent "is only The Natural Man & not the Soul or Imagination." The meaning of the serpent is judgment: "Good & Evil are / Riches & Poverty a Tree of Misery / propagating Generation & Death" (*E.*, pp. 270–71). It is in the nature of aphorisms to condense much meaning, and these aphorisms condense Blake's multiple contexts, as he conflates moral law, the God of punishment, and material generation. Further, the *Jerusalem* design refers to contemporary politics, the naked female representing France under allied attack;[65] but the design also depicts material nature, because "the Goddess Nature is War" (*E.*, p. 270). In the person of Vala, both levels of reference coalesce.

Plate 72 clarifies other implications. The serpent stretching across the bottom of the page presents, in the shape of his coils, the doctrine of female will that Blake elicited from the story of Eve: "Women the Comforters of Men become the Tormentors & Punishers." Aptly, this statement about reversed perspective is etched in reversed writing. The serpent, regularly associated with the female will, represents a philosophy that moves counter to the current of creation; he symbolizes moral law and material nature, which Blake has identified as the subject of Genesis. Plate 75 shifts the symbol from the beginning of the Bible to its end, portraying the serpent as the seven-headed dragon of Revelation. Again the serpent is twined with a female, the "hidden Harlot" (75:20), whose other name is Vala and whose philosophy is material nature. Again Blake identifies her with war (75:20). Another textual gloss on the design, characteristically removed from it, appears on plate 43. Blake recapitulates the story of Los and Reuben, substituting the names of Albion and Luvah:

> I will turn the volutions of your ears outward, and bend your nostrils
> Downward, and your fluxile eyes englob'd roll round in fear:
> Your withring lips and tongue shrink up into a narrow circle,
> Till into narrow forms you creep.
>
> (43:67–70)

Immediately Blake juxtaposes his variant account of material creation, the separation of male from female in paradise: "And the vast form of Nature like a serpent rolld between" (43:80). Here Blake has drawn many visions together into one in order to display the unity of their multiple meanings. What Erdman observes of the Laocoön aphorisms is equally applicable to the visions contained in *Jerusalem*: "There is no right way to read them—except all at once" (*E.*, p. 735).

Nature is a philosophical problem for Blake, representing a gulf between the mind and its objects of perception. Newton's study of corporeal vision approaches only those forms of light that "depend not on the Power of Imagination," offering purely mechanical analogies and examining dead organs, because he wants only natural explanations.[66] Blake wants "Art deliverd from Nature" (*E.*, p. 272), claiming that "the Eternal Body of Man is The Imagination" (p. 271). Blake knew that his vision inverted Newton's, the materialist believing that "every Point of the Object shall illuminate a correspondent Point of the Picture, and thereby make a Picture like the Object in Shape and Colour, this only excepted, that the Picture shall be inverted."[67] The inversion of vision that materialism implies is exactly Blake's subject in *Jerusalem*, and it accounts for many of the poem's techniques. But nature is also a political problem, being identical with war; it is a religious problem, being another name for our lusterless habitat outside paradise; and it is an aesthetic problem, Blake wishing to liberate art from the imitation of nature. In the form of the serpent, these various contexts spread across the pages of Blake's prophecy.

The sacrifice of Luvah is another recurring vision in *Jerusalem* that assimilates these same contexts. The crucifixion of Luvah is the work of Urizen and his sons (65:12, 66:4); as the Zoas are in every man, this conflict, first mentioned on plate 16, is intrapsychic. It is delineated more thoroughly in the *Four Zoas*, following a pattern from the "Philosophick Cabbala," as I have argued elsewhere.[68] According to More, a "Concupiscible" faculty displaces "Reason," and the fall from grace follows. In the *Four Zoas*, Luvah—called "Love," "his place the place of seed" (126:7−8)—displaces Urizen, whose place is the brain (23:12); the fall from grace follows. According to Blake and to More, then, a mental conflict causes the fall. Here in *Jerusalem* Blake portrays that same mental conflict again, but he transposes the strife between "Urizen, cold & scientific" and "Luvah, pitying & weeping" (38:2) from an Old Testament context to a New Testament one, the crucifixion of Christ.

The crucifixion of Luvah repeats the contrary theologies of vengeance and mercy. Luvah's persecutors try "to decide Two Worlds with a great decision: a World of Mercy, and / A World of Justice" (65:1–2). Those who perform the sacrifice inhabit "a wondrous rocky World of cruel destiny" (66:6). This world incorporates Old Testament images of the wrathful God, whose domain is equally in evidence when the inhabitants of Albion flee over rocks, their brains turning to bone (58:9); when they pile rocks on rocks to reach the stars (66:7); and when the two stone tablets of the commandments are presented as "two frowning Rocks" (66:13). These rocks are also Voltaire and Rousseau, whom Blake calls sons of Bacon, Newton, and Locke (66:12–14). As always, Blake has assimilated his contrary contexts. The place of sacrifice is at once British and Druidical and also biblical and Mosaic; its walls are codes of law enforced by a tyrannical God and they are also Enlightenment philosophers. The conflict between mental faculties is also a conflict between contrary Gods. It is also a division of the mind from its objects of knowledge: Newtonian reasoning and demonstration, natural morality, and the philosophers themselves are again identified with the intrapsychic and religious antagonists (66:3–14).

The conflict is also international, "for Luvah is France: the Victim of the Spectres of Albion" (66:15). Blake is certainly referring to contemporary war, and perhaps to the battle of Waterloo, and yet his political allusion is hardly so simple. The revolution in France, which degenerated into the European wars, was from the first a partly philosophical event. Not only Voltaire and Rousseau, but also Holbach and the other Encyclopedists applied principles of natural philosophy and law to political matters. Blake saw those principles in Bacon, Newton, and Locke, and evidently understood that the revolution in France depended in part on a foundation of insidious and English principles. When Holbach writes that "those terrible convulsions that sometimes agitate political societies, shake their foundations, and frequently produce the overthrow of an empire" manifest the "irresistible power" of the same "general energy" that also operates *within* man, he presents a multiple vision that Blake might approve. When Holbach argues that "man's imagination has laboured to form an idea of the energies of that nature he has personified and distinguished from herself," Blake might approve again. But when Holbach insists that humanity is wholly material and "nothing more than a passive instrument in the hands of necessity," he moves Blake to intellectual war.[69] Materialism, necessity, and a passive model of mind enslave mankind to matter, nature, and law; Blake believed that these principles derived from Bacon, Newton, and Locke. Paradoxically, the philosophy of liberation was thus a philosophy of enslavement. Holbach's aeolian harp, stupidly obeying material winds, is quite as dead a thing as Locke's tablet of wax, or the eyeball of the corpse mentioned by Newton. Considering only natural causes (as Newton had considered only natural causes) the French philosopher soon demands dumb obedience to nature's immutable rules.[70] The French wars mentioned on plate 66, then, are not only those fought with swords; the weapons, as always in Blake, include ideas.

The contexts that are separated into sheep and goats at the poem's beginning are fused into an apparition of the One Mind at the poem's end; but that impulse toward unity is visible on earlier plates, and an examination of those preceding marriages can help us to interpret the poem's conclusion. The God on plate 99 who comprises Christ and the Father and who retrieves the universe to himself is anticipated on plate 48. There the contrary theologies that Blake's designs and texts have set against one another from the poem's beginning are married into one vision, which Blake names "Spiritual Verse" (48:8). On plate 48 he marries the testaments of vengeance and mercy. In both cases the means of unifying contraries is imagination, all alike resolving themselves into intellect. Using this principle of interiority, Blake fuses into one vision

> The Five books of the Decalogue, the books of Joshua & Judges,
> Samuel, a double book & Kings, a double book, the Psalms & Prophets
> The Four-fold Gospel, and the Revelations everlasting.
>
> (48:9–11)

The contrary visions of these books can be perceived as one in the same light that shows all religions to be one. These are exactly the books of the Bible that Blake approved as having an "internal or spiritual sense" that regards not empire nor the material life, but rather human "interiors."[71] As prophet and as commentator on the Bible, Blake's task is to turn his readers' eyes inward, opening worlds of thought. To discard the veil that separates person from person, God from humanity, and the universe from both, is to shed the cloak of matter that shrouds intellectual truth. Just as he colored the cloud, symbol of literal interpretation, onto the pages of his prophecy, now Blake rolls it back, to let the inner light of eternal things shine forth. As Swedenborg labored to explain, the principle is at once aesthetic and ontological: the things of the earth—rocks, clouds, or the war with France—and the symbols in a prophecy are seen rightly only when they are seen through, as shrouds over spiritual truth. The restoration of vision is achieved when history, matter, and the symbols of poems fold back to their mental origin and move onward to their mental ends.

Reason and passion, the mind and its objects, the two testaments, England and France, and tenor and vehicle all ascend to unity, then, in the poem's closing pages. *Jerusalem*'s ending is precisely the same, symbolically, as Revelation's. Blake's poem thus begins and ends with signals of its visionary context, the Revelation of Saint John; but throughout, Blake's poem brings this visionary light to bear on the new shapes of crisis in his age—war and the philosophy that separates mind from matter. Blake's apocalypse, like John's, explodes the fallen universe and calls an end to corporeal creation, not with literal fire and war, but with an intellectual revolution that occurs, at any time, in the human mind. That locus has always been the battleground of these contrary contexts, whose marriage is Blake's symbolic art. Its terms are wisdom, art, and science; Blake has told us that these three goals, like heaven and hell, like all religion, like all the visions of all the prophets, and all that was and is and is to come, are one in the bosom of God—the human imagination.

100

Figure 1. House of Death (color print).
(The Tate Gallery, London)

Figure 2. Ezekiel (line engraving).
(Reproduced by permission of the Trustees
of the British Museum)

Figure 3. *Illustrations of the Book of Job*, no. 13.
(By permission of the British Library)

102

Figure 4. Isaiah Foretelling the Destruction
of Jerusalem (drawing on wood block).
(Reproduced by permission of the
Trustees of the British Museum)

Figure 5. Plate 12 of *For the Sexes:*
The Gates of Paradise.
(By permission of the British Library)

104

Figure 6. Elohim Creating Adam (color print).
(The Tate Gallery, London)

Figure 7. Satan Exulting Over Eve (color print).
(The Tate Gallery, London)

Figure 8. The Great Red Dragon and the
Woman Clothed in the Sun (watercolor).
(Rosenwald Collection,
National Gallery of Art, Washington, D.C.)

106

Figure 9. Plate 1 of *Jerusalem*, copy A.
(Reproduced by permission of the
Trustees of the British Museum)

Figure 10. Plate 1 of *Jerusalem*, copy E.
(From the Collection of Paul Mellon)

Figure 11. Plate 12 of *America*.
(Reproduced by permission of
the Trustees of the British Museum)

Figure 12. Death's Door (white-line engraving).
(Mrs. Charles J. Rosenbloom.
Photograph by Larry Ostrom, Art Gallery of Ontario, Toronto)

110

Figure 13. Plate 15 of *For the Sexes:*
The Gates of Paradise.
(By permission of the British Library)

Figure 14. Illustration for *The Grave*, no. 11
(designed by Blake and engraved
by Louis Schiavonetti).
(Reproduced by permission of the Trustees
of the British Museum)

112

Figure 15. Plate 24 of *The Book of Urizen*, copy B.
(The Pierpont Morgan Library)

Figure 16. Plate 13 of *Milton*, copy A.
(Reproduced by permission of the
Trustees of the British Museum)

114

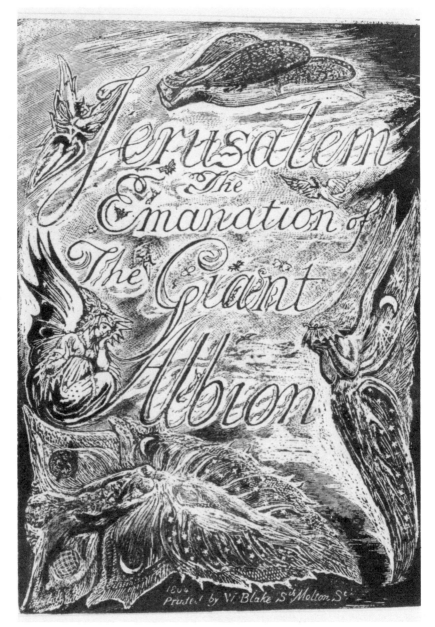

Figure 17. Plate 2 of *Jerusalem*, copy A.
(Reproduced by permission of the
Trustees of the British Museum)

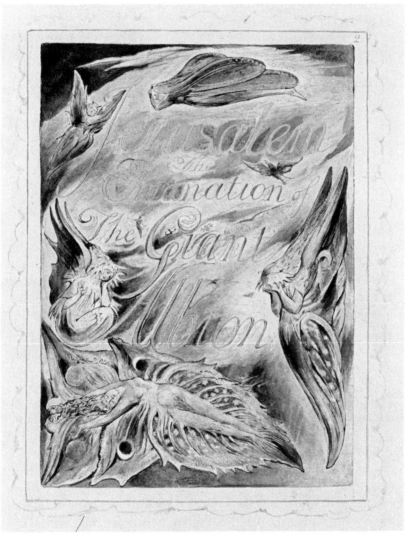

Figure 18. Plate 2 of *Jerusalem*, copy E.
(From the Collection of Paul Mellon)

Figure 19. Frontispiece of *For the Sexes:*
The Gates of Paradise.
(By permission of the British Library)

117

Figure 20. *Paradise Lost*.
The Creation of Eve (watercolor).
(The Huntington Library, San Marino, California)

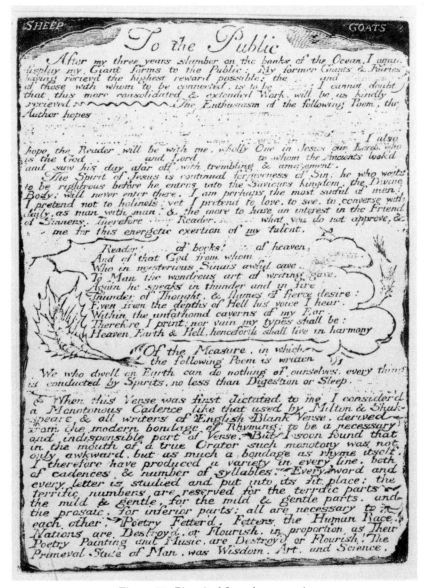

Figure 21. Plate 3 of *Jerusalem*, copy A.
(Reproduced by permission of the
Trustees of the British Museum)

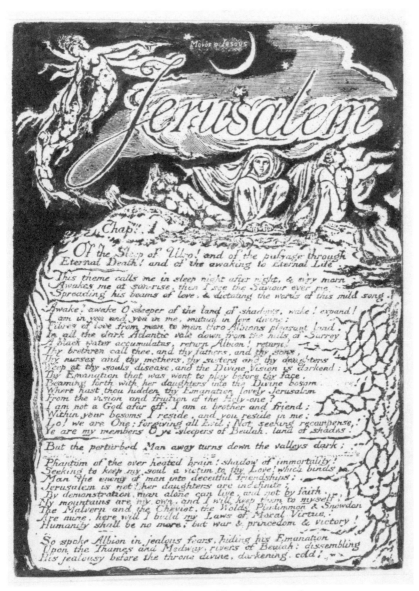

Figure 22. Plate 4 of *Jerusalem*, copy A.
(Reproduced by permission of the
Trustees of the British Museum)

120

His Spectre driven by the Starry Wheels of Albions sons. black and
Opake divided from his back; he labours and he mourns:

For as his Emanation divided, his Spectre also divided
In terror of those starry wheels; and the Spectre stood over Los
Howling in pain: a blackning Shadow, blackning dark & opake
Cursing the terrible Los: bitterly cursing him for his friendship
To Albion: suggesting murderous thoughts against Albion.

Los rag'd and stamp'd the earth in his might & terrible wrath!
He stood and stamp'd the earth; then he threw down his hammer in rage &
In fury; then he sat down and wept, terrified! Then arose
And chaunted his song, labouring with the tongs and hammer:
But still the Spectre divided, and still his pain increas'd!

In pain the Spectre divided: in pain of hunger and thirst:
To devour Los's Human Perfection, but when he saw that Los

Figure 23. Plate 6 of *Jerusalem*, copy A.
(Reproduced by permission of the
Trustees of the British Museum)

One hair nor particle of dust, not one can pass away.
He views the Cherub at the Tree of Life also the Serpent,
Orc the first born coiled in the south: the Dragon Urizen;
Tharmas, the Vegetated Tongue even the Devouring Tongue:
A threefold region, a false brain: a false heart:
And false bowels: altogether composing the False Tongue,
Beneath Beulah: as a watry flame revolving every way
And as dark roots and stems: a Forest of affliction, growing
In seas of sorrow. Los also views the Four Females:
Ahania, and Enion, and Vala, and Enitharmon lovely.
And from them all the lovely beaming Daughters of Albion.
Ahania & Enion & Vala are three evanescent shades:
Enitharmon is a vegetated mortal Wife of Los:
His Emanation, yet his Wife till the sleep of death is past.
Such are the Buildings of Los: & such are the Works of Enitharmon:

And Los beheld his Sons, and he beheld his Daughters:
Every one a translucent Wonder: a Universe within,
Increasing inwards, into length and breadth, and heighth:
Starry & glorious: and they every one in their bright loins
Have a beautiful golden Gate which opens into the vegetative world:
And every one a gate of rubies & all sorts of precious stones
In their translucent hearts, which opens into the vegetive world:
And every one a gate of iron dreadful and wonderful.
In their translucent heads, which opens into the vegetive world
And every one has the three regions Childhood: Manhood & Age:
But the gate of the tongue: the western gate in them is closed,
Having a wall builded against it: and thereby the gates
Eastward & Southward & Northward, are incircled with flaming fires.
And the North is Breadth, the South is Heighth & Depth:
The East is Inwards: & the West is Outwards every way.

And Los beheld the mild Emanation Jerusalem eastward bending
Her revolutions toward the Starry Wheels in maternal anguish
Like a pale cloud arising from the arms of Beulahs Daughters:
In Entuthon Benythons deep Vales beneath Golgonooza.

Figure 24. Plate 14 of *Jerusalem*, copy A.
(Reproduced by permission of the
Trustees of the British Museum)

122

Figure 25. Plate 33 of *Jerusalem*, copy A.
(Reproduced by permission of the

Figure 26. Plate 37 of *Jerusalem*, copy A.
(Reproduced by permission of the
Trustees of the British Museum)

124

Figure 27. Pencil drawing for Plate 37 of *Jerusalem*.
(Lessing J. Rosenwald Collection,
Library of Congress, Washington, D.C.)

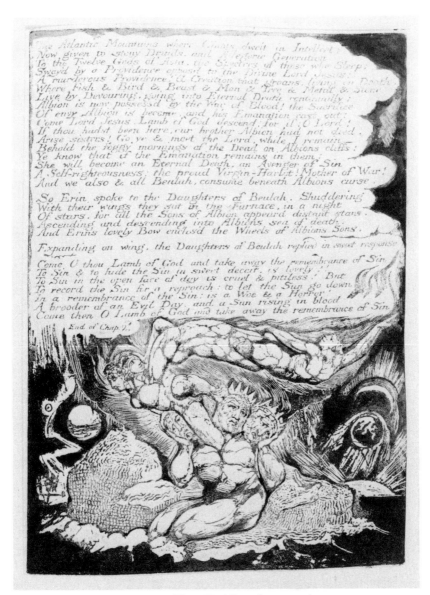

Figure 28. Plate 50 of *Jerusalem*, copy A.
(Reproduced by permission of the
Trustees of the British Museum)

Figure 29. Plate 58 of *Jerusalem*, copy A.
(Reproduced by permission of the
Trustees of the British Museum)

Figure 30. Plate 63 of *Jerusalem*, copy A.
(Reproduced by permission of the
Trustees of the British Museum)

128

Figure 31. Plate 75 of *Jerusalem*, copy A.
(Reproduced by permission of the
Trustees of the British Museum)

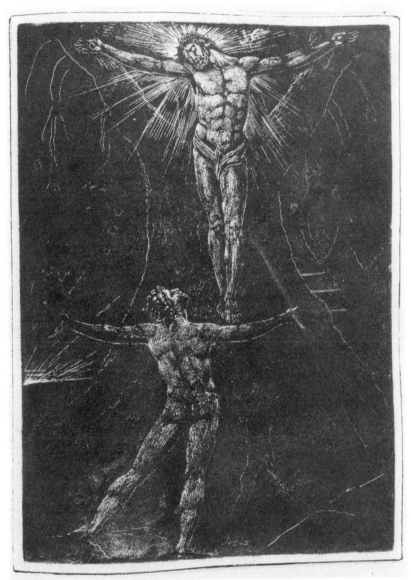

Figure 32. Plate 76 of *Jerusalem*, copy A.
(Reproduced by permission of the
Trustees of the British Museum)

130

Figure 33. Plate 99 of *Jerusalem*, copy A.
(Reproduced by permission of
the Trustees of the British Museum)

THREE

"The Prophecy Which
Begins and Ends in Thee":
Shelley's *Prometheus Unbound*

S helley called *Prometheus Unbound* "a poem in my best style, what-
ever that may amount to," but his modesty should not mislead us:
he recognized that "it is the most perfect of my productions" (*Letters*,
2:127). It is also the poem of Shelley's that most clearly deserves to be
ranked among the great epics, poems bearing "a defined and intelligi-
ble relation to the knowledge and sentiment and religion and political
conditions of the age" in which he lived (*Prose*, 7:130). The vehicle that
Shelley chose for this synthesis is not epic, however, but lyrical drama.
"Composed in dialogue," poems in this form present multiple view-
points, "exhibiting a series of lyric pictures." The form was to be
characterized by Shelley himself as "visionary" (preface to *Hellas*). His
"best style," then, achieves multiple levels of reference by assuming the
form of prophecy: in his lyrical drama Shelley embodies his intellectual
philosophy in "the Theater of Visions."

Thus, Shelley calls attention to the fact that his poetic technique
itself arises from his intellectual philosophy: "The imagery which I
have employed will be found, in many instances, to have been drawn
from the operations of the human mind, or from those external actions
by which they are expressed" (*P.U.*, preface, p. 37). At once, Shelley
attributes this technique to his poetic precursors, including Dante,
Shakespeare, and "the Greek poets," among whom he has already
named Aeschylus as providing a context for his lyrical drama. In this
way Shelley implies a traditional union of poetry and the philosophy of
mind.

Shelley also cites "the sacred Milton," further to define his literary context. In Milton's poetry, like that of Dante, Shakespeare, and the Greek poets, Shelley perceives the union of poetry and intellectual philosophy; thus, he adapts a line from *Paradise Lost* to serve as a gloss on the philosophy of Berkeley and Hume: "All things exist as they are perceived; at least in relation to the percipient. 'The mind is its own place, and of itself can make a Heaven of Hell, a Hell of Heaven'" (*Prose*, 7:137).

In his preface to *Prometheus Unbound*, Shelley goes on from the union of poetry with philosophy to claim even more: religion and politics are to be subsumed with poetry and philosophy. Shelley argues that religion and politics are, historically, related to the others: "We owe the great writers of the golden age of our literature to that fervid awakening of the public mind which shook to dust the oldest and most oppressive form of the Christian Religion" (preface, p. 39).[1] Milton is Shelley's exemplar of this intellectual synthesis: "The sacred Milton was . . . a republican, and a bold enquirer into morals and religion" (preface, pp. 39–41). To say that much was also to say that Milton studied metaphysics, because metaphysics and the study of morals are closely related as two aspects of the one "great science which regards the nature and the operations of the human mind" (*Prose*, 7:71). Thus, in his preface, Shelley indicates several levels of reference that he intends his poem to address simultaneously: philosophy of mind, morals, politics, and religion.[2]

He also makes plain his reason for unifying these contexts within his poem: poetry itself, he writes, "has some intelligible and beautiful analogy" with mind and nature, the sources of emotion and thought (preface, p. 41); poetry's ideal forms, Shelley implies, subsume into apprehensible unity the previously discrete data of mental and natural life. Repeatedly, Shelley stresses this unity of fields of thought: political revolution arises, according to the poet's formulation, from intellectual revolution. Shelley does *not* subordinate psychology to politics, as it has often been alleged that he does; nor does he subordinate politics to psychology, religion, or morals: his statement about Milton stresses the fact that the poet studied *all* these subjects.[3] This same unity of fields of thought is stressed again in Shelley's statement that "poets and philosophers are the unacknowledged legislators of the world" (*Prose*, 7:20). This unification, including poetic, philosophical, and political forms, is a premise of *Prometheus Unbound*. It is also a traditional premise of visionary poetics.

A related principle is also common to Shelley's preface and the previous literature of prophecy: history is an intellectual cause. The Protestant Reformation and, implicitly, the English Revolution, are attributable to a "fervid awakening of the public mind" rather than to material causes; and "the great writers of the golden age of our literature" are, in turn, attributable to the historical fact of religious revolution. Art gathers the lines of influence whose interplay characterizes human history; art conditions political reality and is reciprocally conditioned by it. "Poets, not otherwise than philosophers, painters, sculptors and musicians, are in one sense the creators, and in another the creations, of their age" (preface, p. 41). Shelley is not merely protecting himself from the charge of imitation;[4] he is instructing us in the reading of his poem, by articulating a premise of prophetic art: such art is a comprehensive symbol of history but also a creative agent acting upon history.

Shelley repeats the pattern of unification on other levels; he is not *merely* concerned with political history, but would simultaneously dramatize "the operations of the human mind." These operations also exhibit the paradigm of interpenetration: "A poet is the combined product of such internal powers as modify the nature of others, and of such external influences as excite and sustain these powers; he is not one, but both" (preface, p. 41). This statement transposes the pattern of unification from historical to intellectual terms. This interweaving of internal and external is a philosophical formulation; it is also an aesthetic technique. In *Prometheus Unbound* it is both theme and method.

Shelley's poem is further complicated by his almost constant inversions of tradition. His epigraph, a line from Aeschylus's *Epigoni*, is presented as a taunt "to the Ghost of Aeschylus": the line by Aeschylus is turned against Aeschylus. The epigraph embodies in miniature the pattern of Shelley's use of the Greek poet's material: he borrows to transform.[5] To make this fact even more apparent, Shelley elaborates in his preface: "I was averse from a catastrophe so feeble as that of reconciling the Champion with the Oppressor of mankind" (p. 35). That statement repudiates the supposed resolution of Aeschylus's lost *Prometheus Unbound*, and thus alerts Shelley's readers to his inversional pattern. Shelley defines his relation to Milton, too, by deliberate inversion; he writes that "the only imaginary being resembling in any degree Prometheus, is Satan," but he distinguishes Prometheus from Satan, "the hero of *Paradise Lost*" and repudiates the "pernicious casuistry" that *Paradise Lost* engenders in its reader's mind (preface, pp. 35–37). Shelley writes that Milton's "notions of invisible things" are "distorted" (*Prose*, 7:129), and in the preface to *Prometheus Unbound* he distinguishes himself from "those who consider that magnificent fiction [*Paradise Lost*] with a religious feeling" (p. 37). Instead, he considers it as an exemplum of the intellectual philosophy, a philosophy that he quotes the poem to illustrate. He invokes the religions of Aeschylus, Dante, and Milton only to convert theology to the metaphysics of mind. His art treats of revolution not only in political terms; Shelley transposes the pattern of revolution from politics to poetic tradition, constantly inverting the forms of his predecessors. In this way as well—using the pattern of revolution in poetical as well as political history—*Prometheus Unbound* weaves different forms of thought together.

Later, Shelley was to argue that such close relations had always subsisted between the different forms of human thought: in the *Defence of Poetry* he writes that "poetry is connate with the origin of man" (*Prose*, 7:109), and is in turn the origin of law, philosophy, and social organization. "The drama at Athens . . . coexisted with the moral and intellectual greatness of the age" (*Prose*, 7:121), because poetry participates immediately in the imaginative causes of a culture's thought-forms. Shelley agrees here with other prophetic theorists: Robert Lowth, for example, had written that Aeschylus was a philosopher as well as a poetic dramatist and that in his plays "the allurements of Poetry afforded some accession to the empire of Philosophy."[6]

Shelley's preface reveals his understanding of the form and purposes of poetic prophecy. He projects, for example, a prose work that will articulate principles that are embodied in his visionary poem, and his contrast of these forms—poetic prophecy and discursive prose—includes this important distinction: "My purpose has hitherto [i.e., in the lyrical drama] been simply to familiarize the highly refined imagination of the more select classes of poetical readers with beautiful idealisms of moral excellence" (preface, p. 43). Poetry, Shelley writes elsewhere, is "the expression of the imagination" (*Prose*, 7:109); his argument is that poetry supplies the mind with forms of thought. This ambition differs from that of discursive prose, but such prose depends upon it, because "we can think of nothing which we have not perceived" (*Prose*, 7:59). *Imagination* provides forms on which *thought* can operate and from which *history* will take its shape. To renovate thus the forms of human life has always been the goal of visionary art. "Ethical science arranges the elements which poetry has created," but "poetry acts in another and diviner manner. It awakens and enlarges the mind itself." Thus Shelley explains the metaphor of *apocalypse*: "Poetry lifts the veil from the hidden beauty of the world" (*Prose*, 7:117).

The renovation of political life through mental revolution is the theme of many of Shelley's favorite works of philosophy: it is to be found in the New Testament—which Shelley read as a book of philosophy[7]—and it is recurrent in William Godwin's *Political Justice*. Shelley's particular purpose— "to awaken and enlarge the mind itself," by supplying imaginative forms—is perhaps closer to the purpose of his visionary predecessors. As Thomas Goodwin writes of the prophet John, the poetic vision is a modification of the prophet's "Faculties," and its purpose is to display "the Form . . . into which all Saints on Earth should be moulded."[8]

In a letter to Peacock, Shelley is more explicit about the projected prose work: "My 1st Act of Prometheus is complete, & I think you wd. like it.— I consider Poetry very subordinate to moral & political science, & if I were well, certainly I should aspire to the latter; for I can conceive a great work, embodying the discoveries of all ages, & harmonizing the contending creeds by which mankind have been ruled" (*Letters*, 2:70–71). In fact, the first act of his lyrical drama, already written, *is* a synthesis of "contending creeds" and of other conflicting fields of thought. Its multidimensional art is so complex that it can modify the minds of only "the more select class of poetical readers," and "administers to the effect [history] by acting upon the cause [imagination]" (*Prose*, 7:118). The aims of such poetry Shelley distinguishes sharply from the aims of prose: "Nothing can be equally well expressed in prose that is not tedious and supererogatory in verse" (preface, p. 43); and yet it is simply not credible that Shelley wrote one of the greatest of poetic prophecies because he was too ill to write prose. It may be more probable that he expressed himself thus for the benefit of his reader, Peacock, who was, in this same month, leaving the world of poetry for the world of practical business. Ten days before Shelley's letter, Peacock was writing to Shelley that "I now pass every morning at the India House from half-past ten to half-past four, studying Indian affairs."[9] Working at India House, Peacock was soon to write that "intellectual power and intellectual acquisition have turned themselves into other and better channels, and have abandoned the cultivation and the fate of poetry." Peacock thus advocates withdrawal of attention from poetry to "moral and political knowledge";[10] Shelley writes to Peacock that poetry is "very subordinate to moral & political science," but Shelley then announces—not to Peacock, but to the world—that poetry is "the root and blossom of all other systems of thought" (*Prose*, 7:135).

This ambition of Shelley's—to harmonize contending creeds of religion and to unify religion with other forms of thought—had long been evident. In 1812 he declared his hope that "the time is rapidly approaching . . . when the Mahometan, the Jew, the Christian, the Deist, and the Atheist will live together in one community . . . united" (*Prose*, 5:294); he explicitly compared Christian doctrine with the worship of Jupiter (*Prose*, 5:290), Jesus Christ with Socrates (*Prose*, 5:292), and both Galileo and Voltaire with the Apostles (*Prose*, 5:285–86). In the *Essay on Christianity* Shelley identifies the doctrines of Jesus with those of Plato and Diogenes (*Prose*, 5:284). He thus resolves contending creeds into unity, in this way: he raises each system of belief to a level of universal principle. To do so reduces each mythic framework to its basis, and that basis is a thought-form.

Shelley unifies religion with other forms of thought, employing the same technique with which he unifies conflicting religions. Jesus Christ preached "a system of liberty and equality"; political freedom generates "superiority . . . in literature and the arts" (*Prose*, 7:5); at the Reformation, "the exposition of a certain portion of religious imposture drew with it an enquiry into political imposture, and was attended with an extraordinary exertion of the energies of intellectual power" (*Prose*, 7:7). Shelley argues that "all the powers of man" arise from a "condition of the intellect," and consequently that mechanical arts, equally with metaphysics, proceed from mental forms (*Prose*, 7:10). Similarly, a political revolution embodies and follows a prior configuration of mind (*Prose*, 7:13).

To study Shelley's prose is to multiply examples of such statements: "The creative faculty . . . is the basis of all knowledge" (*Prose*, 7:134), and so "the materials of external life" must be assimilated "to the internal laws of human nature" (*Prose*, 7:135). It is to these *internal* principles—not to material things or external orders of material things—that Shelley devotes his poem. A similar tendency—to unify conflicting systems of belief by referring them all to universal principles—is common in the eighteenth century: Joseph Priestley's study,

The Doctrines of Heathen Philosophy Compared with Those of Revelation, for example, includes classical poets in its design. Priestley's study leads him to the ideas which he calls "universal" and which underlie contending creeds; specifically, he compares the theologies of Jupiter and Hebrew theism, as Shelley does in *Prometheus Unbound*. Lowth also assembles poetic, philosophical, and theological principles into one aesthetic structure, in his *Lectures on the Sacred Poetry of the Hebrews*, a book that (as I shall subsequently show) offers impressive analogies with Shelley's aesthetics. Stuart Curran has studied Shelley's possible use of other religious writers, and concludes that Shelley's art assembles multiple contexts, precisely for the purpose of molding an essential unity from such diversity: in this way Shelley's "dramatic framework" in *Prometheus Unbound* reveals the "theatrics of the mind."[11]

In fact, that metaphor, which rightly describes the poem's focus, also suggests its contexts. Hume had written that "the mind is a kind of theatre," and it is in this theater that the lyrical drama takes place; but that metaphor was also an apocalyptic commonplace, as we have seen. The marriage of East and West, which Curran finds symbolized by the union of Prometheus and Asia,[12] was also a commonplace among writers on prophecy: commentators on the biblical prophecies commonly adduce oriental wisdom to explicate occidental works. Thus Mede applies the oriental *Onirocriticis* to the Bible, and More adds cabbalistic thought; Peganius begins his commentary with an essay on the theater of visions and brings together oriental, Egyptian, and Hebrew philosophy and art.

Shelley's traditions also informed him that, just as conflicting religions can be harmonized, so too can religion itself be harmonized with other contexts. Godwin's secular philosophy is closely related to Calvinism, as Basil Willey has observed, and Godwin's political theory is founded on metaphysics and epistemology.[13] "Lord Bacon was a poet," writes Shelley (*Prose*, 7:114), and Bacon himself writes that his intention is "to write an apocalypse."[14] Surely Shelley would have understood that word's root meaning— "to lift the veil."

Shelley's perception of these multiple contexts arises, thus, from his tradition; the perception leads him further and further into intellectual space, where contrary creeds and contrary forms of thought come together. In the *Defence of Poetry*, Shelley expresses his multidimensional vision—not of art alone, but also of life—and he identifies the "unchangeable forms of human nature," into which contending creeds resolve themselves, as the guiding forms of poetry (*Prose*, 7:115). The forms of art and the forms of social life, he argues, both arise from the human creative faculty—the imagination (*Prose*, 7:125).

Shelley's preface thus indicates the poem's multiple contexts, but so does the subject that he chose for the lyrical drama. Many subjects collapse into this one: the roughly cruciform Prometheus, suffering under the afflictions of a wrathful God above him, obviously recalls Christ; he recalls Job too, a figure about whom Shelley intended to write a drama.[15] Using the language of Milton's Samson, Prometheus has obvious analogies with that figure as well. He has been likened to Jehovah,[16] and Shelley himself compares Prometheus with Satan. The embodiment of so many figures in one enables Shelley to superimpose various mythic forms onto one another, rendering visible the universal pattern that all such forms embody.[17]

Blake of course had used this same technique, as W. J. T. Mitchell has shown. In *The Book of Urizen*, Blake's Los plays "the roles of Abraham, Laius, and Jupiter to Orc's Isaac, Oedipus, and Prometheus."[18] In Shelley's case as in Blake's, this device serves to embody "prophetic vision, the perception of the infinite in all things through an understanding of the interconnectedness of past, present, and future."[19]

One attraction, therefore, of the Prometheus myth is its ready submission to prophetic form: *Prometheus* means "foreknowledge," and the poem employs the four major elements of prophetic tradition: an aesthetic based on multiple imagery, an ethos whose points of reference are vengeance and mercy, a mental ontology that informs both those elements, and, for a final purpose, creation of a new heaven and earth. Shelley could have learned these elements from the Bible itself, which he studied constantly and whose poetry "filled him with delight."[20] More probably, this knowledge was supplemented by his acquaintance with the enormous body of writing on the prophecies that had arisen in London. Much of this aesthetic theory was available to him in the work of George Stanley Faber. For example, he could have read there that such images as *sun* and *earthquake* regularly appear in prophetic poetry to convey political and mental ideas simultaneously, just as they do in *Prometheus Unbound*; he could have learned that his own technique of mixing imagery with the operations of the human mind was a prophetic commonplace; he could have read a concise explanation of the Antichrist's multiple significance, which closely resembles the multiple significance of his own character, Jupiter; and he could have found poetry and philosophy joined as vehicle and tenor, just as he joins them in *Prometheus Unbound*.[21] Visionary aesthetics may have shown Shelley both a literary context within which paradise is a state of knowledge, and also a symbolism according to which nations are at once within and without the human mind;[22] these are among the major premises of Shelley's aesthetics.

Another context—Enlightenment philosophy—approaches that same multiplicity from a different perspective. Holbach writes of "the identity of the soul with the body,"[23] and Shelley's notes to *Queen Mab* indicate that this materialism supplied him with a pattern, universal in scope, for the unification of his art. Godwin adopts that unity from Holbach, and also includes political reality within the same unity, as Shelley knew.[24] The imagistic interfusion of thoughts and things is a philosophical theme that Shelley takes from Berkeley, Hume, and Sir William Drummond, as well as from his sources in symbolic art.[25] The doctrine of imagination as a moral force, invoked in Shelley's preface, draws on another of Shelley's favorite philosophers: Hume sketches a similar theory in his *Treatise of Human Nature*,[26] and Shelley's theme of retribution is as prominent in *Political Justice* as it is in Shelley's Christian sources.[27]

In 1811 Shelley had already written of these two contrary traditions. His ideas changed, certainly, before he wrote *Prometheus Unbound*; his understanding of the philosophical importance of imagination, for example, did not develop until 1819 or later.[28] Already, however, Shelley knew how his contexts related:

> I have long been convinced of the eventual omnipotence of mind over matter; adequacy of motive is sufficient to anything, & *my* golden age is when the present potence will become omnipotence: this will be the millenium of Xtians "when the lion shall lay down with the lamb" tho' neither will it be accomplished to complete a prophesy, or by the intervention of a *miracle*—this has been the favorite idea of all religions, the thesis on which the impassioned & benevolent have delighted to dwell—will it not be the task of human reason, human powers[?]
>
> (*Letters*, 1:152)

In *Prometheus Unbound*, too, Shelley places his millennium in a purely humanistic framework. It is the philosophy of mind that informs Shelley's visionary strategies, and not theological belief.

Thus Shelley's poetic strategies arise from metaphysical principles. Specifically, his *dramatis personae* blend, act, and relate not as distinct persons but as ideal elements. This strategy arises from a philosophical principle: "The words *I, you, they,* are not signs of any actual difference subsisting between the assemblage of thoughts thus indicated, but are merely marks employed to denote the different modifications of the one mind" (*Prose*, 6:196). It may be that Shelley's statement refers to a metaphysical construct distinct from individual cognition;[29] the words *one mind* may refer to a transcending unity to which each human mind belongs. It may be that Shelley's sentence refers instead to the mental experience of an individual, because the "words *I, you, they*" indicate their speaker's thoughts—words can do no more. In either case, it is obvious that Shelley encloses apparent distinctions of person within a single mental frame.[30] Shelley's *metaphysical* principle is consistent with the conditions of *poetic* phenomenology: as a poem is the expression of the imagination, its components are necessarily "modifications of the one mind" within which the poem is born, in composing, or reborn, in reading. This strategy, common to all visionary poems, unifies Shelley's diverse characters: all are modifications of one mind that the poem portrays.

Prometheus, for example, already compared with Satan, describes the god who afflicts him as Satan, using the language of *Paradise Lost*.[31] In that same speech, Prometheus describes Jupiter's weapons as precisely those of the wrathful God of Hebrew prophecy:

> . . . Earthquake-fiends are charged
> To wrench the rivets from my quivering wounds
> When the rocks split and close again behind;
> While, from their loud abysses, howling throng
> The genii of the storm, urging the rage
> Of whirlwind, and afflict me with keen hail.
>
> (1.38–43)

This passage combines imagery from Aeschylus's Zeus and the Old Testament God: the splitting and closing rocks are from Aeschylus, but the earthquake recalls more precisely the Book of Isaiah, one of Shelley's favorite prophecies: "Thou shalt be visited of the Lord of hosts with thunder, and with earthquake, and great noise, with storm and tempest, and the flame of devouring fire."[32] That language is from God's judgment upon Jerusalem. The same image is used in Revelation, where it is combined with that of the splitting rocks: "There was a great earthquake. . . . [Men] hid themselves in the dens and in the rocks of the mountains; and said to the mountains and rocks, Fall on us and hide us from the face of him that sitteth on the throne."[33] The throngs from the abyss recall Revelation 9:2–3. The whirlwind is the Hebrews' angry God, when, through the medium of Hebrew prophets, He repeatedly urges His rage.[34] This God declares, "I will cause it to rain a very grievous hail," and subsequently the prophets employ the image to describe His wrath.[35] Because of this hail, "men blasphemed God" exactly as Shelley's Prometheus curses his tormentor, the wrathful god Jupiter. Shelley has chosen his imagery to align Aeschylean myth with biblical prophecy. In both traditions wrath, retribution, and curses form the ethical center of interest; here, Shelley raises that moral problem at the outset of his drama. He implicitly identifies Jupiter with Jehovah *and* with Satan, revealing that both embody ideas of wrath and vengeance. Again, the device and its ethical tenor appear also in Blake, in the 1795 color prints, for example, which compare Jehovah with Satan (figs. 6 and 7). For both poets, the multiple reference serves to universalize the moral theme.

The most frequent image with which Shelley binds his Aeschylean and Hebrew originals is thunder: it was the thunder of the "almighty Tyrant" that chained Prometheus (1.161–62); in Aeschylus, "the Father will shatter this jagged cliff with thunder,"[36] and thunder and lightning are his regular weapons. The image was especially useful for Shelley, however, because the Hebrew God "sent thunder and hail" repeatedly;[37] according to Isaiah, God sends thunder and earthquake with His threats,[38] and the Book of Revelation employs the image ten times.

The problem of retribution, the common theme of Aeschylus, the prophecies, *A Refutation of Deism*, *The Age of Reason*, and *Political Justice*, is introduced so immediately because the play's central action is precisely Prometheus's revocation of that curse. That revocation is his only act, and from it all the play's other developments proceed. He begins that action by saying, "The curse / Once breathed on thee I would recall" (1.58–59), a wish that arises from an emotional change—"I hate no more" (1.57)—and that issues in his retraction.[39] What follows is a complex interweaving of Prometheus and Jupiter: the portrayal of Prometheus uttering his curse identifies him with Jupiter because personal distinction disappears in the face of mental identity.[40] Describing himself rather than Jupiter, he calls on the whirlwinds that accompanied his rage (1.66); *his* curse was "thunder" and earthquake (1.68–69). The memory of the curse is preserved in the language of Genesis: "there stood / Darkness o'er the day like blood" (1.101–2). This line recalls Genesis 1:2—"and darkness was upon the face of the deep"—but ominously. Prometheus's curse is said to have brought thunder, tempest, fire, and earthquake (1.162–67). His wish to recall the curse brings on a character who is neither Prometheus nor Jupiter, but both.

The Zoroastrian machinery that introduces the Phantasm of Jupiter has been explicated by Curran. Other explanations of the system of doubling have also been offered, but the Phantasm is quite consistent with Shelley's own poetic need and philosophical principles.[41] Shelley elsewhere lists the wide variety of "thoughts" that "are also to be included in the catalogue of existence" (*Prose*, 7:59): the phantasms' realm that Earth describes similarly contains "the shadows of all forms that think and live" (1.198), and also "dreams and the light imaginings of men, / And all that faith creates, or love desires" (1.200–201). This intellectual or imaginative space is related to Shelley's tentative speculations on afterlife, as a study of his prose will reveal; within the poem, it provides an image fusing the imaginative forms of Prometheus and Jupiter.

The Phantasm arrives with the sound of whirlwind, "earthquake, and fire, and mountains cloven" (1.232), so we recognize at once the Aeschylean and Hebrew gods. He holds "a sceptre of pale gold, / To stay steps proud" (1.235–36), so that we see Milton's Satan.[42] The golden sceptre Shelley takes from Esther 5:2, where it is held by Ahasuerus. When the Phantasm speaks, he adopts the stance and language of Ezekiel: "A spirit seizes me, and speaks within: / It tears me as fire tears a thunder-cloud" (1.254–55). To underscore the fact that his speech presents the vision of the Old Testament prophets, Shelley makes Panthea inform us that his vision darkens heaven (1.256–57). With the first line of that speech, Shelley identifies that theology with Satan: the "calm, fixed mind" (1.262) of the cursing Prometheus, whose curse the Phantasm repeats, is a detail from Milton's characterization of Satan.[43] The ire of the omnipotent is expressed by lightning and hail, as was the anger of the Hebrews' God. That God moved in darkness, according to Genesis 1:2, and so, according to Prometheus's curse, does Jupiter (1.276–77). Here, however, he is a "malignant spirit," as, for Blake, the God of the Old Testament "is a very Cruel Being" (*V.L.J.*, *E.*, p. 555).

In Shelley's poem, the victim of vengeance becomes its perpetrator:

> I curse thee! let a sufferer's curse
> Clasp thee, his torturer, like remorse,
> Till thine Infinity shall be
> A robe of envenomed agony;
> And thine Omnipotence a crown of pain.
>
> (1.286–90)

This curse casts its object in the role of Christ, the archetypal victim of the "crown of pain." Jupiter and Prometheus, both sharing aspects of Satan and Jehovah, further complicate their identity by sharing this image and role; Prometheus too must suffer the "pillow of thorns" as a victim of vengeance (1.563).

Jupiter is, in fact, an aspect of Prometheus, of the one mind whose operations enclose the lyrical drama. Thus Prometheus says, "I gave all / He has, and in return he chains me here" (1.381–82); and the moment of closest identification between Jupiter and Prometheus contains within itself that same formulation, though in more complex form. In his curse, Prometheus constitutes Jupiter, by his own attribution bringing this god into being. He addresses Jupiter in terms that are not warranted by anything we ever see of Jupiter: "Thou who art the God and Lord—O thou / Who fillest with thy soul this world of woe" (1.282–83). The following line refers to "all things of Earth and Heaven," implying that the world of woe is, at least temporally, the world at large. Shelley had himself defined God as "the Soul of the Universe" (*Letters*, 1:35); in his note to *Queen Mab* 7:13, Shelley repeats that formulation, and quotes Holbach at great length. What Shelley learned from Holbach, and also perhaps from Locke, was that the construction of a personal god from this spirit or force is an attribution. Holbach writes that "it is very difficult, if not impossible to prevent man from making himself the sole model of his divinity. Indeed, man sees in his God nothing but a man," and "his own mind was the standard of the mind that regulated nature."[44] Earlier, Locke had written that "even the most advanced notion we have of GOD is but attributing the same simple ideas which we have got from reflection on what we find in ourselves."[45] Shelley adopts and expresses the same idea: "Mankind . . . have not failed to attribute to the universal cause a character analogous with their own" (*Prose*, 6:238). Jupiter is analogous with Prometheus, and on a precisely ethical scale: what is attributed to god is "the horrible legacy of accumulated vengeances" (*Prose*, 6:238). The theologies of wrath and vengeance, drawn from Aeschylus and the Old Testament, are here placed in a psychological framework. Here and throughout Shelley's poem they represent a mental and therefore human problem, not the transcendental condition that they were for Shelley's poetic precursors. As such, this ethical issue provides structure for the major action of the poem, Prometheus's revocation and repentance of his curse.

Carl Grabo is correct in affirming that Prometheus is subject to Jupiter "in the same way that a man is subject to the thoughts which have been his."[46] It is misleading, however, to ascribe this thought to Shelley's supposed Platonism or Neoplatonism: Milton, too, had placed heaven and hell within the mind, as we have seen, and the usage of the tyrannical beast as a symbol for ideological oppression, to be overthrown from within, is as old as the Bible, as almost every commentator makes plain. Within a philosophical context, Hume had portrayed the mind as subject to its own projected fictions, including time, space, causality, and deity; Godwin's *Political Justice* had mounted a theory of reform on mental renovation: "Make men wise, and by that very operation you make them free."[47] The corollary is obvious throughout Godwin's work and Shelley's: enslaved men are shackled by mind-forged manacles. Foremost among these is the crippling and restrictive deity that men project and to which they submit themselves.[48]

From this perspective, the meaning of Prometheus's revocation unfolds. He hears the Phantasm repeat the curse and immediately revokes it: "It doth repent me: words are quick and vain; / Grief for awhile is blind, and so was mine. / I wish no living thing to suffer pain" (1.303–5). Shelley has carefully chosen those words: *repent* has a biblical rather than classical origin. The Hebrew God repents himself in Genesis 6:6, and thereafter with great frequency. According to classical legend, it was Prometheus who brought fire, the means of sustaining life, to man; in Genesis, that action was God's, and it was this deed that He first repented. In Shelley's account, the bringer of the fire of life repents his destructive act, not his creative act.

The significance of *blind* in this speech is complex. The word refers back to line 9, where Prometheus says that he is "eyeless in hate." That phrase in turn goes back to *Samson Agonistes*, which opens with Milton's parallel hero "eyeless in *Gaza*."[49] Substituting a psychological term for a topographical one (*hate* for *Gaza*), Shelley has already begun to transform his source; Prometheus's acquisition of sight at exactly the instant of his revocation of the curse portrays a vision that Milton's hero never attained. Prometheus has broken the cycle of hate and vengeance in which his prototypes—in Aeschylus, the Bible, and Milton—had remained trapped. As the lyrical drama began in night, while "during the Scene, Morning Slowly Breaks," so too, in a moral frame, Prometheus has undergone an accession of light. His power of vision and his wrath exclude one another.

At the same time, Prometheus is drawn closer to the figure of Christ, disjoining himself from the tyrannical and angry god: "Jesus Christ opposed with earnest eloquence the panic fears and hateful superstitions which have enslaved mankind for ages" (*Prose*, 6:236). Shelley devotes *Prometheus Unbound* to exactly the purpose that he had earlier attributed to Jesus Christ's words: "Having produced this favorable disposition of mind Jesus Christ proceeds to qualify and finally to abrogate the system of the Jewish law" (*Prose*, 6:243). Like Shelley's Prometheus, Jesus Christ "selects the law of retaliation as an instance of the absurdity and immorality" of that system. Shelley had read *The Age of Reason* and admired its author;[50] in that book, Paine had argued that "whenever we read the obscene stories, the voluptuous debaucheries, the cruel and torturous executions, the unrelenting vindictiveness, with which more than half the Bible is filled, it would be more consistent that we called it the word of a Demon, than the word of God."[51] In *A Refutation of Deism* Shelley echoes this argument, in more psychological terms: "Barbarous and uncivilized nations have uniformly adored, under various names a God of which themselves were the model; revengeful, blood-thirsty, grovelling and capricious. The idol of a savage is a demon that delights in carnage. . . . But I appeal to your candour, O Eusebes, if there exist a record of such grovelling absurdities and enormities so atrocious, a picture of the Deity so characteristic of a demon as that which the sacred writings of the Jews contain" (*Prose*, 6:34). Shelley repeats the word *curses* in his prose treatment of theology; the word and the theology are obviously important in *Prometheus Unbound* as well. But just as the vengeful god comes to Shelley's poem from many sources, so also does his contrary, the Christ-like Prometheus: the principles that he embodies "have been the doctrines of every just and compassionate mind that ever speculated on the social nature of man" (*Prose*, 6:247). Again, Shelley's enclosure of his mythic systems within a philosophy of mind makes his vision at once more particularly human and more universal than the myths that he would transform. Like Paine delighting in the sublime poetry of the Bible, and simultaneously abhorring its ethic, Shelley undertakes to transform biblical myth. He achieves this transformation by expanding his vision to include classical, oriental, and Enlightenment materials, as a means of reducing that vision's coordinates to mental terms.

That fusion of religious forms, achieved in part by the association of Prometheus with Jupiter and both figures with God, Christ, and Satan, is only one aspect of the poem's complexity. "The Oppressor of mankind" raises a political theme that is pertinent to the idea of vengeance.[52] Shelley's preface to *The Revolt of Islam* includes an explicit analysis of this idea in terms of the French Revolution: the violence which that revolution elicited and the reprisal and despair which followed it are unnecessary concomitants of the same system of repression and retribution that Shelley delineates in theological terms. Shelley learned from Godwin the close relations that subsist between mental and political form; his symbolic art enables him to unify those levels of reference more compactly and more completely than discursive prose can do.[53]

In one section of the poem the religious and political levels of Shelley's meaning are so clearly presented and so evidently woven together that they do not deserve to be called obscure—certainly not more so than the similar comparisons by Priestley, Faber, and others. Furies torment Prometheus with two visions, closely related; these, in turn, introduce a series of almost perfectly balanced pairs. The first of these visions is of Christ, or rather it is the symbolic and ethical complex that Shelley constructed around Christ; the second is a portrait of the ruined French Revolution, and the violence and misery that followed it. That these visions are presented together serves to highlight their essential unity, suggesting that the two visions embody the same principle. First, "one came forth of gentle worth, / Smiling on the sanguine earth" (1.546–47); his gentle words outlived him, the furies tell Prometheus, and became "like swift poison" (1.548). That "poison" is drawn from Shelley's characterization of Jupiter (1.35); here, the image serves to identify the moral state into which religion fell, "withering up truth, peace, and pity" (1.549). Those are precisely Jupiter's effects. The furies taunt Prometheus:

> Dost thou boast the clear knowledge thou wakendst for man?
> Then was kindled within him a thirst which outran
> Those perishing waters; a thirst of fierce fever,
> Hope, love, doubt, desire—which consume him forever.
>
> (1.542–45)

Immediately, they present a parallel picture of Christ's failure and despair: "Hark that outcry of despair! / 'Tis his mild and gentle ghost / Wailing for the faith he kindled" (1.553–55). Developing what is only a slight hint in Aeschylus,[54] Shelley identifies both Prometheus and Christ with the hope of immortality that his own prose treats so ambivalently.[55] The furies close this vision by implying that Prometheus has become Christ: "And the future is dark, and the present is spread / Like a pillow of thorns for thy slumberless head" (1.562–63).

Immediately the furies present a parallel vision of the French Revolution, arising in hope and failing in despair:

> See! a disenchanted nation
> Springs like day from desolation;
> To Truth its state is dedicate,
> And Freedom leads it forth, her mate;
> A legioned band of linkèd brothers
> Whom Love calls children.
>
> (1.567–72)

A second semichorus of furies completes the vision:

> See how kindred murder kin!
> 'Tis the vintage-time for Death and Sin:
> Blood, like new wine, bubbles within,
> Till Despair smothers
> The struggling world, which slaves and tyrants win.
>
> (1.573–77)

The furies employ language from the Book of Revelation, interpreting
that prophecy in terms of the French Revolution, precisely as Faber had
done, and they echo the disgust and despair with that revolution's
failure which Faber had expressed. Both by means of parallelism with
the vision of Christ and by use of biblical vocabulary, then, the furies'
song combines political and religious reference. The ethical basis of this
identification is clear from the vocabulary: their winepress is drawn
from Revelation 14:19—it is "the winepress of the wrath of God." The
furies' view of the world is transferable, clearly, from religious to
political terms: in each case, love degenerates to wrath. The pattern of
prophecy, and of Shelley's particular prophecy, is of course the reverse;
at this point in the play, morning is slowly breaking from this moral and
ideological darkness.

As the Book of Revelation consists of a single vision variously re-
peated from different perspectives, this recasting of Revelation in
terms of the French Revolution is similarly repeated from different
points of view. Panthea recapitulates the vision: she has seen a youth
"nailed to a crucifix" (1.585) and, next,

> The heaven around, the earth below
> Was peopled with thick shapes of human death,
> All horrible, and wrought by human hands;
> And some appeared the work of human hearts.
>
> (1.586–89)

Her version serves to humanize further the original religious vision.
Prometheus himself repeats the vision of the crucified Christ (1.597–
602), and then brings it to a humanized context:

> I see, I see
> The wise, the mild, the lofty, and the just,
> Whom thy slaves hate for being like to thee:
> Some hunted by foul lies from their heart's home . . .
> Some linked to corpses in unwholesome cells . . .
> . . . sons are kneaded down in common blood
> By the red light of their own burning homes.
>
> (1.604–15)

Next, a fury recapitulates the same vision, but recasts it in psychologi-
cal terms. This version, Shelley has his characters repeat, is worse:

In each human heart terror survives
The ravin it has gorged; the loftiest fear
All that they would disdain to think were true:
Hypocrisy and custom make their minds
The fanes of many a worship, now outworn.
They dare not devise good for man's estate,
And yet they know not that they do not dare.
The good want power, but to weep barren tears;
The powerful goodness want: worse need for them;
The wise want love, and those who love want wisdom;
And all best things are thus confused to ill.
Many are strong and rich, and would be just,
But live among their suffering fellow men
As if none felt: they know not what they do.

(1.618–31)

Here the furies reverse the vision, beginning with the state-of-the-nation question and ending with an allusion to Christ; they continue the process of humanizing the vision, but diabolically: their psychological account is "worse" than the mythic and political formulations. The final inversion embodied in their speech is their perversion of Christ's words of forgiveness, which they use as torment—"they know not what they do." Prometheus then locates these furies and their work within the mind, and he also further defines Jupiter:

Ah woe! Alas! pain, pain ever, forever!
I close my tearless eyes, but see more clear
Thy works within my woe-illumed mind,
Thou subtle Tyrant!

(1.635–38)

It will seem strange, perhaps, to recognize in this scene of torment and despair the beginning of Prometheus's unbinding and resumption of power; the furies' torment is generally recognized as an interruption in the redemption that his pity has begun. In fact, however, this scene itself encloses his redemption, or at least its progress: he has recognized Jupiter as a force within his mind. Shelley's art subtly but firmly reinforces this progress: the furies locate fanes of worship within human minds (1.621–22). Those words artfully recall an earlier line, spoken by Mercury: "Bend thy soul in prayer, / And like a suppliant in some gorgeous fane / Let the will kneel within thy haughty heart" (1.376–78). As Prometheus recognizes the implications of this interiority, he gradually recovers the power he has relinquished. The overthrow of Jupiter, who is a mental projection, is not dramatized until act 3; but its psychological dynamics are under analysis in act 1.

The same twofold vision is repeated still again. Prometheus introduces the next recasting of the vision with words drawn from Shelley's model: "There are two woes" (1.646), he says, repeating Revelation 9:12. There, as here, a vision of woe that nevertheless issues in redemption is symbolically variegated, over and over again. Prometheus says:

> The nations thronged around, and cried aloud,
> As with one voice, "Truth, Liberty, and Love!"
> Suddenly fierce confusion fell from Heaven
> Among them: there was strife, deceit, and fear;
> Tyrants rushed in, and did divide the spoil.
> This was the shadow of the truth I saw.
>
> (1.650–55)

Again, Revelation and the French Revolution are used to interpret one another, but here Shelley includes a new perspective. The last line in that quoted passage suggests, first, that Prometheus's words are a shadow of his vision, a prophetic caveat that is commonplace in Shelley and in the Bible. It also implies that history—the French Revolution—is a shadow of something else. Historical events are the visible shapes taken by visionary ideas. This formulation, made explicit in *A Philosophical View of Reform*, *A Defence of Poetry*, and the preface to *Prometheus Unbound*, is implied by the pattern of the twofold vision: a divine form is presented, and then a worldly event that symbolically recapitulates it. As Time is the shadow of Eternity, so too is political history the shadow of intellectual forms.

What follows in act 1 is one of the most concise interfusions of subject and object, thought and thing, in all of English poetry. The Earth speaks:

> To cheer thy state
> I bid ascend those subtle and fair spirits
> Whose homes are the dim caves of human thought,
> And who inhabit, as birds wing the wind,

Its world-surrounding ether; they behold
Beyond that twilight realm, as in a glass,
The future: may they speak comfort to thee!

(1.657–63)

Shelley's use of *ether* refers to an idea developed by Sir Isaac Newton: in the General Scholium to the *Principia,* Newton assigns a special meaning to this traditional term and concept, though here Newton puts it forward only tentatively. In contrast to the ancient concept of ether (the fifth element), and in contrast to Descartes' concept of a subtle *matter*, Newton writes of a "subtle Spirit which pervades and lies hid in all gross bodies." Newton's theory had fostered a large body of scientific speculation in the eighteenth century, whose product was a vision of an immaterial energy either infusing or constituting both mind and matter.[56] The scientific allusions that Grabo so painstakingly documents enrich the texture of Shelley's symbolic art by employing the theory of science according to which the laws of metaphor apply: things represent immaterial force. The antecedent of "its" (1.661) is, grammatically, "thought"—and thus Shelley identifies ether with thought. Shelley's "spirits" are ideas, "whose homes are the dim caves of human thought," and that metaphor is one of the most recurrent in *Prometheus Unbound*: to recall its meaning here is to unfold acts 2 through 4. The cave is drawn from Plato's *Republic*, but Plato used the metaphor to present a transcendental vision; Shelley rehabilitates the metaphor for his own purposes, restoring the cave to *human* thought. That Plato is not Shelley's only conscious source is evident from the image's previous appearance: "prophetic caves" (1.352) recall the cavern of the Sibyl, from book 6 of the *Aeneid*.[57] It may be that Shelley alludes both to Plato and to the cavern of the Sibyl; it is certain that he restores prophecy and philosophy to specifically "human thought."

Here as elsewhere Shelley's art employs tradition but does not rely upon it: his theory depends, in fact, on the convertibility of that same formulation into his own poetic terms. In that speech by the Earth, Shelley does not rest content with the complex interpenetration of Newton's science, Plato, and Sibylline tradition. The metaphor of the birds, firmly visualized in exterior space, but used for thoughts firmly enclosed within the human mind, is Shelley's demonstration of a fact at once technically poetic and also metaphysical: metaphor recapitulates the ontology of an intellectual philosophy. "It imports little to inquire whether thought be distinct from the objects of thought. The use of the words *external* and *internal*, as applied to the establishment of this distinction, has been the symbol and the source of much dispute. This is merely an affair of words" (*Prose*, 7:65). Shelley states explicitly that language—and especially poetic language— "has relation to thoughts alone" (*Prose*, 7:113). Philosophical history and Shelley's multidimensional art are both attempts to redeem this metaphysical principle from the charge of solipsism. The superiority of the greatest poets "consists in the presence of those thoughts which belong to the inner faculties of our nature, not in the absence of those which are connected with the external, . . . perfection consists in an harmony of the union of all" (*Prose*, 7:123). Thus, Shelley's passage embraces not only metaphysics, which "may be defined as an inquiry concerning those things belonging to, or connected with, the internal nature of man" (*Prose*, 7:342n.), but also natural science. Plato, prophecy, and the other levels of that passage's reference are enclosed within an earthly framework; it is the Earth, after all, who speaks.

Those spirits of human thought identify themselves: they "bear the prophecy / Which begins and ends in thee" (1.690–91). They are the six angels whose trumpets are heard in Revelation, chapter 9; Shelley rewrites that scriptural book to identify its visions "as the thoughts of man's own mind" (1.685). Here, as in Revelation, the sounding of the last spirit or angel is reserved until "the mystery should be finished," i.e., act 3.[58] The first spirit has been conveyed on a trumpet's blast, like his biblical prototype; what he has heard and reports is Shelley's human adaptation of Christian ethics: "'Twas the soul of love; / 'Twas the hope, the prophecy, / Which begins and ends in thee" (1.705–7). The second spirit presents a vision of a rainbow's arch on the sea; he has "heard the thunder hoarsely laugh" (1.715), and he has had a vision of "a hell of death" (1.717), images whose biblical sources are obvious. The speech of the second spirit ends with another biblical reference, expressing both self-sacrifice and the doctrine of loving one's enemies: on a wrecked ship, "one . . . gave an enemy / His plank—then plunged aside to die" (1.721–22). The third spirit has come to Prometheus from "beside a sage's bed" (1.723), and he serves to embody the philosophical dimension of prophecy. He recalls the hopeful vision that had "kindled . . . / Pity, eloquence, and woe" (1.729–30), clearly recapitulating the previously "kindled" visions of Prometheus and Christ. He also recapitulates the metaphysics of the previous "shadow" passage: "The world awhile below / Wore the shade its lustre made" (1.731– 32). The twofold vision is thus again recapitulated from yet another perspective: this spirit and his fellows have come to cheer Prometheus; for this purpose the same vision will suffice, symbolically transformed.

The fourth spirit has come from "a poet's lips" (1.737); as these spirits collectively symbolize prophecy, Shelley thus presents the fusion of poetry and philosophy as constituting prophecy. That this was exactly Shelley's idea of prophecy is made clear in the *Defence* (*Prose*, 7:112). In condensed form, this spirit's lines present Shelley's concept of visionary art: "Nor seeks nor finds he mortal blisses / But feeds on the aerial kisses / Of shapes that haunt thought's wildernesses" (1.740– 42). When we recognize in those "wildernesses" the allusion to Revelation 12:6, we can perceive Shelley's reason for his preferred prophetic form: that form is best susceptible of his constant mental reference. The visionary poet—John of Patmos, Milton, or Shelley— does not heed natural objects in themselves: "But from these create he can / Forms more real than living man" (1.747– 48). Shelley's latent exegesis refers us from the shadow to the intellectual substance of visionary art; to paraphrase, the poets' natural imagery, religious notions, and political forms "are merely the mask and the mantle in which these great poets walk through eternity enveloped and disguised" (*Prose*, 7:129). The fifth and sixth spirits repeat the same twofold vision in different form; they portray a luminous figure of love, tracked by ruin, which is called its "shadow" (1.779). The chorus of spirits cites the Book of Revelation again, affirming that "Death's white and winged steed" (1.780) will be quelled within Shelley's new prophecy,[59] which, as they conclude by reminding Prometheus, "begins and ends in thee" (1.800).

The reference of Shelley's prophecy, therefore, is clearly to the human mind. Still, it is no more solipsistic than Shelley's political writing, which refers reform to intellectual renovation just as firmly as Godwin's had done. Shelley's political prose argues for "the inevitable connection between national prosperity and freedom, and the cultivation of the imagination and the cultivation of scientific truth, and the profound development of moral and metaphysical enquiry" (*Prose*, 7:52). *Political Justice* is a sustained elaboration of that same theory. Thomas Paine also expresses what was to become Shelley's leading principle: "Revolutions . . . have for their object a change in the moral condition of governments" and not merely specific reforms. His concerns are not only with political particulars but rather include matters whose significance expands to "universal extent," and so Paine concerns himself with such subjects as commerce and also with those revolutionary means that flow "from moral principles."[60] "Wisdom, Justice, Love, and Peace" (1.796) are meaningless unless interpreted as mental entities; Shelley's devotion of his art to these mental objects does not limit his reference to the least significant, the merely personal: it enables him to unite all contexts, all major fields of human thought and reform, into one. The only medium susceptible of such intense condensation is visionary art.

The themes, major action, and aesthetic techniques of *Prometheus Unbound* have been presented in act 1; for that reason, it has been necessary to examine the opening act in some detail. What follows in Shelley's lyrical drama is exactly what follows in Revelation: Shelley's Christ-figure, Prometheus, sends a message to Asia, and a series of obscure but gradually brightening panels unfolds, until, at the rhapsodic conclusion, a new heaven and earth have been created. These visionary panels recapitulate one another like those of the biblical prophecy, varying symbols, emphasis, and tone; their veiled but constant interweaving serves gradually to raise their audience's minds to the perception of final unity. Before we examine that process in these later scenes it will be useful to expand upon one more strategy that has already been employed in act 1 and that binds it to subsequent scenes.

This strategy is twofold. First, because all persons are modifications of one mind, as *On Life* argues they are, many *dramatis personae* can symbolize the same mental state. In that way, the poet gathers diversity into unity. Second, each symbolic character simultaneously represents a multitude. Blake also uses such multiple reference, as I have shown above, and perhaps both poets derive the technique from traditional biblical typology. In any case, these principles have already been suggested in the characters of Jupiter and Prometheus, and are also evident in that of Mercury. Mercury says to Prometheus, "Aye from thy sight / Returning, for a season, Heaven seems Hell" (1.358–59). That line recalls Satan's interiorization of hell in *Paradise Lost,* just as Prometheus attributes an interior hell to Jupiter by comparing the tyrant's soul to "a hell within" (1.56); Prometheus himself undergoes a hellish internal torment (1.636–37). All four figures, then—Jupiter, Prometheus, Mercury, and Satan—have been grouped within a single moral state. Simultaneously, Mercury's use of that line invokes other contexts. When Shelley quotes Milton's Satan in the *Defence,* he uses that interiorization of hell to clarify a point in the intellectual philosophy, as we have seen. He goes on in that passage to relate poetic art to both statements: "Poetry defeats the curse which binds us to be subjected to the accident of surrounding impressions" (*Prose,* 7:137). That sentence is the best short gloss on *Prometheus Unbound* that exists. Even the minor character, Mercury, therefore, is woven into the larger unit of the satanic moral state: he is one with Jupiter and also with Prometheus. Simultaneously, he invokes a complex range of associations, mythic and philosophical. These two kinds of multiplicity *complicate* each symbol and part of Shelley's drama, and at the same time *connect* all its parts into a cohesive whole.

Similarly, entire acts of the play are complex within themselves and also largely recapitulatory of one another. Act 2 opens in the morning that has slowly been breaking throughout act 1. Asia's opening speech describes the coming spring in terms that identify the season with the morning, both with Prometheus, and act 1 with act 2:

> As suddenly
> Thou comest as the memory of a dream
> Which now is sad because it hath been sweet;
> Like genius, or like joy which riseth up
> As from the earth, clothing with golden clouds
> The desert of our life.
>
> (2.1.7–12)

These lines recall those of the Earth in act 1: "Joy ran, as blood within a living frame, / When thou didst from her bosom, like a cloud / Of glory, arise—a spirit of keen joy!" (1.156–58). Asia's lines also reproduce the emotional movement from sweetness to sadness, a progression that characterized the repeated visions of act 1. Asia says that Panthea wears "the shadow of that soul by which I live" (2.1.31), recalling 1.832–33, and also the repeated formulations of original brilliance fallen to shadow that characterized the same repeated visions. That repetition is even more obvious when Panthea reports Prometheus's words: "Sister of her whose footsteps pave the world / With loveliness—more fair than aught but her / Whose shadow thou art" (2.1.68–70). These lines recapitulate the prophetic spirits' description of "the form of Love" (1.763).

"His footsteps paved the world with light" (1.767), and this same image assimilates Asia with Love, with Christ, and with Prometheus: the prophetic spirits' line suggests all these figures.

The major action of act 2 is the journey of Asia to the cave of Demogorgon. When we recognize her as a modification of Prometheus, then we can perceive that this entire act is an expanded version of what has already occurred. The cave of Demorgorgon should remind us of the "caves of human thought" into which so much meaning was gathered in act 1. Asia's journey is a symbolic exfoliation of what occurred when the prophetic spirits' song had ended: their sounds "through the deep and labyrinthine soul, / Like echoes through long caverns, wind and roll" (1.805–6). Act 2 is therefore rich with music, and it is "echoes" that conduct Asia to the cavern of Demogorgon. Panthea enters act 2 as "Aeolian music" (2.1.26); she is "made the wind / Which fails beneath the music that I bear" (2.1.50–51). She describes the voice of Prometheus as "footsteps of far melody" (2.1.89), linking the imagery of music and the form of Love, whose "footsteps," like Asia's, "paved the world with light."

Echoes arrive to conduct Asia to the cave of Demogorgon, announcing themselves in terms that identify them with the echoes of act 1: "Our voice recedeth / Through the caverns hollow" (2.1.174–75). These echoes end the scene with a few lines that encapsulate the drama:

> O follow, follow
>   Through the caverns hollow;
> As the song floats thou pursue,
> By the woodland noontide dew,
> By the forests, lakes, and fountains,
> Through the many-folded mountains,
> To the rents, and gulfs, and chasms
> Where the Earth reposed from spasms
> On the day when he and thou
> Parted, to commingle now,
>   Child of Ocean!
>
>   (2.1.196–206)

These lines gather together the earthquake and splitting rocks of act 1 with a brighter prospect: commingling. Asia and Prometheus are to be unified. This sexual union symbolizes cosmic unification, here as in the Book of Revelation and also in Dante's *Divine Comedy*, which Shelley elsewhere calls "the most glorious imagination of modern poetry" (*Prose*, 7:128).[61] Their marriage symbolizes a union of mental faculties, one with another; but it symbolizes also, in the Bible, Dante, and Shelley, the joining together of God and man. This final and cosmic unity is the final cause of Shelley's elaborate poetic unifications: he would blend and unite earth and heaven. The echoes' song contains a hint of this purpose: the "dew" that they mention is recalled from 2.1.130–31, where it is called "stars." This blending of an image of earth with one of sky symbolizes that union of earth and heaven which is more elaborately projected by the twofold vision of act 1; it is repeated in 2.1.168, and carried into the next scene by the image of "clouds of dew" (2.2.7).

Because, according to Shelley's *Defence*, the gaining of heaven is the human mind's release from the "curse which binds us to be subjected to the accident of surrounding impressions," and because it is poetry that defeats that curse, every poetic unification of thought and thing is also a signal of apocalyptic redemption. Shelley's preface alerts his readers to this technique, and acts 1 and 2 are linked to one another by metaphors that make those classes of thought interconvertible. The predominant kind of metaphor in act 1 converts thoughts to things: thus Mercury advises Prometheus to clothe his secret "in words, and bid it clasp his throne" (1.375); the furies are themselves "dread thought beneath" his "brain" (1.488), but they are exteriorized into sensible form; the Earth describes Jupiter's revenge "as rainy wind through the abandoned gate / Of a fallen palace" (1.217–18); omnipotence is seen as a crown (1.290). This technique, a condition of all poetic art, implies a relation between internal and external things, making poetry capable of expressing "beautiful idealisms." But, not content with that much relation, in act 2 Shelley superimposes over these metaphors their exact reverse: a weather comes "as the memory of a dream" (2.1.8); spring is "like a thought" (2.1.2); snow accumulates "as thought by thought is piled" (2.3.40).[62] This technique has two implications: first, the distinction between thoughts and things is nominal; that is, it is a matter of words, as Shelley argues so frequently in his prose. Second, the poet is struggling to embody in his art that which is difficult to "clothe . . . in words." Prometheus declared that his description of his vision was but a shadow of the vision itself; Shelley complained in his own voice of the difficulty of masking and mantling his intellections in words (*Prose*, 6:202n.). His poem strains language past its surface: words cannot transcend the subject-object dichotomy on which language is based. Shelley would suggest, through the orchestration of the verbal forms, "the gathered rays which are reality" (3.3.53). Through harmonious arrangement, poetry can suggest more than words can mean; for this reason, "poetry redeems from decay the visitations of the divinity in Man" (*Prose*, 7:137).

Another verbal technique by which Shelley commingles thought with thing is far more conventional, yet charged with special philosophical significance for him. Referring to his curse, for example, Prometheus calls upon "ye icy Springs, stagnant with wrinkling frost, / Which vibrated to hear me, and then crept / Shuddering through India!" (1.62–64). This humanization of natural objects is conventional in all myth; for Shelley's purposes, the device is especially useful because it unites his landscape with his characters. In act 2 the same device is used, with a difference: Panthea says that "multitudes of dense white fleecy clouds / Were wandering in thick flocks along the mountains, / Shepherded by the slow, unwilling wind" (2.1.145–47). This speech immediately precedes the echoes' musical call to pass through the caverns. Thus, it serves as another signal of the parallelism between the acts, as in act 1 Panthea mentions "flocks of clouds" immediately before the spirits of prophecy arrive to send "echoes through long caverns." The image calls attention to the difference between the two parallel acts, joining imagery of earth and sky, like the dew-stars, as another minute signal of this act's purpose: to enable Prometheus and Asia, like heaven and earth, and man and his own relinquished mental powers, "to commingle now."

That commingling is symbolized so repeatedly, in such poetic detail, that almost any passage will serve to exemplify it. Panthea's description of her first dream is especially useful for this purpose, because it gathers together major imagery from other passages, compresses multiple references, and invokes prophetic tradition. The presentation of dreams had been a prophetic commonplace since the Book of Daniel, and exegesis often involves dream-interpretation, as Isaac Newton, among others, makes abundantly clear. Panthea's dream begins with the language of Christian prophecy:

> . . . the overpowering light
> Of that immortal shape was shadowed o'er
> By love, which, from his soft and flowing limbs,
> And passion-parted lips, and keen, faint eyes,
> Steamed forth like vaporous fire an atmosphere
> Which wrapped me in its all-dissolving power
> As the warm ether of the morning sun
> Wraps ere it drinks some cloud of wandering dew.
> I saw not, heard not, moved not, only felt
> His presence flow and mingle through my blood
> Till it became his life, and his grew mine.
>
> (2.1.71–81)

That "immortal shape" is at once Christ, Prometheus, the "form of Love," and the transfigured Asia who is yet to be. Panthea's dream is another version of the twofold vision from act 1: after this luminous absorption her being is "condensed" (2.1.86), and the joy-bringing sounds cease (2.1.92), leaving her again separate from the form of Love. The inability of the mind to sustain the visionary state is a recurring idea in Shelley:

> As summer clouds dissolve, unburthened of their rain;
>   As a far taper fades with fading night,
>   As a brief insect dies with dying day,
>   My song, its pinions disarrayed of might,
>   Drooped; o'er it closed the echoes far away
> Of the great voice which did its flight sustain,
>   As waves which lately paved his watery way
>   Hiss round a drowner's head in their tempestuous play.
>
> ("Ode to Liberty," 278–85)

Shelley writes explicitly about the difficulty of sustaining vision: "When composition begins, inspiration is already on the decline" (*Prose*, 7:135). The problem arises from the basic formula of all prophecy: inspiration. For Shelley, inspiration is a psychological problem rather than a transcendental one: "This power arises from within." Its accession and disappearance are precise parallels of the love that falls to ruin and the light that turns to shadow. Here, in Panthea's account of her dream, Shelley has further interiorized the terms, but preserved the pattern of the vision. Significantly, however, he has modified the tone in act 2: the passage, like its successors, is radiant with hope. Even as her "being was condensed . . . the rays / Of thought were slowly gathered" (2.1.86– 87). The dew-clouds and the "ether" of the consolation in act 1 are repeated here, and even the "shadow," so ominous in act 1, is redeemed: she sees an "immortal shape" that is "shadowed o'er," not by desolation, as in act 1, but by love.

Asia herself reports the second dream of Panthea, which she sees directly in her sister's eyes. This vision is Prometheus's, because he sends it; it is Panthea's, because it appears in her eyes; and yet it is Asia's, because she reads it and casts it in language. The three figures are, therefore, united by this vision. The same dream also redeems the shadows that darkened the visions of act 1: "I see a shade, a shape, 'tis he, arrayed / In the soft light of his own smiles" (2.1.120– 21). This dream shares the new, bright tone of hope: "Say not those smiles that we shall meet again / Within that bright pavilion which their beams / Shall build o'er the waste world?" (2.1.124– 26). Prometheus is arrayed in the light of his own smiles because the prophecy begins and ends in him; the vision's radiant glory "lives unchanged within" him (2.1.65). This shift of the traditional locus of inspiration redeems the form of prophecy for Shelley's humanistic purposes. He knew that "prophecy in its very nature implies some degree of obscurity, and is always, as the Apostle elegantly expresses it, 'like a light glimmering in a dark place, until the day dawn, and the day-star arise.'"[63] Shelley's contemporary critics, including William Godwin and *The Quarterly Review*, complained of his poem's obscurity; but as Lowth, Shelley, and most other visionary theorists recognized, that obscurity is a condition of prophetic art. It is also a symbol. Obscurity, and the gradual accession of light, are a theme in prophecy as well as a technique. Shelley restores this symbol and this idea to human terms in act 1, revealing that Jupiter is Prometheus's dark attribution; at the outset of act 2 he dramatizes the corollary—that illumination springs from within the mind of man.

The Earth's introduction of prophecy to cheer Prometheus thus defines the scope of that art within the terms of "human thought," as we have seen. Another image in that passage further complicates the lines, but renders them even more consistent with the idea of prophecy revealed in act 2: the prophet beholds, "as in a glass, / The future" (1.662– 63), and is therefore identical with Prometheus, as the meaning of his name reveals. A passage from Lowth so precisely explains Shelley's strategies as to warrant quoting:

The mind of man is that mirror of Plato, which as he turns about at pleasure, and directs to a different point of view, he creates another sun, other stars, planets, animals, and even another self. In this shadow or image of himself, which man beholds when the mirror is turned inward towards himself, he is enabled in some degree to contemplate the souls of other men: for, from what he feels and perceives in himself, he forms conjectures concerning others; and apprehends and describes the manners, affections, conceptions of others from his own. Of this assemblage of images, which the human mind collects from all nature, and even from itself, that is, from its own emotions and operations . . . the more evident and distinct are those which are formed from the impressions made by external objects on the senses; and of these, the clearest and most vivid are those which are perceived by the eye. Hence poetry abounds more in those images which are furnished by the senses, and chiefly those of the sight; in order to depict the obscure by the more manifest, the subtile by the more substantial.[64]

Prometheus gradually discovers that Jupiter is exactly such a "shadow or image of himself," projected outward. The universality of mental forms that Lowth describes is precisely the basis of prophecy in Shelley's understanding, too: "Not that I assert poets to be prophets in the gross sense of the word, or that they can foretell the form as surely as they foreknow the spirit of events: such is the pretence of superstition, which would make poetry an attribute of prophecy, rather than prophecy an attribute of poetry. A poet participates in the eternal, the infinite, and the one" (*Prose*, 7:112). The prophet beholds the future in the sense that he beholds the mental forms that shape it, perceiving the analogy between what passes "when the mirror is turned inward towards himself" and the configurations shaping the universe of human minds. This principle, at once philosophical and visionary, elucidates Shelley's imagistic strategies and his constant, bewildering pilgrimage from inside to outside and back; it also informs the structure of his lyrical drama. "As far as relates to his conceptions, time and place and number are not" (*Prose*, 7:112). Shelley had read that in prophecy "there should be time no longer,"[65] and thus produces in *Prometheus Unbound* a unity of time among his acts that recapitulates the unity of persons among his characters. The philosophical causes of this unity are to be found in Shelley's skeptical idealism, and their poetic form is visionary art.

These principles make intelligible the most enigmatic section of the poem, the journey to the cave of Demogorgon and Asia's interview with him there. This episode must be interpreted, I shall argue, in terms of the visionary principles that Shelley has made so clear, in terms of act 1, with which act 2 is parallel, and in terms of the absolute unity that structures the entire poem. Then this troublesome section of the poem will yield a greater simplicity, or at least less desperate confusion than appears now in studies of the poem.[66]

Act 2, from scene 2 to its finish, is a miniature *Divine Comedy*. Asia—a modification of Prometheus—travels through a dark forest, first downward then up, and arrives finally at beatification. Like scene 1, scene 2 is a recasting of the vision immediately preceding it; spirits sing of "voluptuous nightingales."

> When one with bliss or sadness fails—
> And through the windless ivy-boughs,
> Sick with sweet love, droops dying away
> On its mate's music-panting bosom. . . .
>
> (2.2.26–29)

Then another nightingale lifts the melody "till some new stream of feeling bear / The song, and all the woods are mute" (2.2.34–35). This passage duplicates the earlier picture of Panthea and Ione (2.1.46–49), which in turn recapitulates act 1, 756–60. That passage in act 1 presented the prophetic spirits' song; its recapitulation in act 2, scene 2, presents another chorus of spirits—or the same, symbolically recast. Here, "sounds overflow the listener's brain / So sweet that joy is almost pain" (2.2.39–40), repeating the emotional paradox from act 1: "And hark! their sweet, sad voices! 'tis despair / Mingled with love, and then dissolved in sound" (1.756–57). Here, in act 2, scene 2, "there is heard through the dim air / The rush of wings" (2.2.36–37). This repeats 2.1.25–26: "Hear I not / The Aeolian music of her sea-green plumes." That line is in turn a pointed inversion of the furies' arrival—"I hear the thunder of new wings" (1.521)—counterpointed in act 1 by the music of the airborne prophetic spirits.

The infernal beginning of act 2, scene 2, is indicated by the stage setting, "a Forest, intermingled with Rocks and Caverns." Shelley alludes to the parallel opening of the *Inferno*: there, the speaker finds himself

in a gloomy wood, astray
Gone from the path direct: and e'en to tell,
It were no easy task, how savage wild
That forest, how robust and rough its growth,
Which to remember only, my dismay
Renews, in bitterness not far from death.[67]

Shelley also alludes, by this forest, to his biblical prototype—the wilderness of Revelation 12:6. Here, that wilderness will be transformed into "a paradise of wildernesses" (2.5.81). Both Shelley and Dante clarify their mental reference: Dante writes that, after seeing a "planet's beam," there followed "a little respite to the fear, / That in my heart's recesses deep had lain";[68] Shelley also internalizes his imagery, writing that "like many a lake-surrounded flute, / Sounds overflow the listener's brain / So sweet that joy is almost pain" (2.2.38–40). In both poems, we are in a mental universe, but Shelley more compactly combines his darkness with paradise: "The gloom divine is all around" (2.2.22).

To stress that the journey to Demogorgon is through a mental universe, Shelley invokes other contexts. A faun asks,

. . . have others other lives,
Under pink blossoms or within the bells
Of meadow flowers, or folded violets deep,
Or on their dying colors, when they die,
Or in the sunlight of the spherèd dew?

(2.2.83–87)

The natural science used in this passage is drawn from Shelley's reading in Erasmus Darwin and other scientists who speculated on exactly that kind of universal animation.[69] The incorporation of this knowledge here combines with the mythic animation of natural forms used throughout the drama to annihilate the distinction between thought and its object by firmly enclosing both within Shelley's one-mind philosophy.

The journey through this realm is effected by music: "Echoes, music-tongued . . . draw / . . . All spirits on that secret way" (2.2.42–45). When Asia and Panthea have arrived at their destination, Panthea reports that "hither the sound has borne us—to the realm / of Demogorgon" (2.3.1–2). Music transports one through mental space. Further, we have already made this journey: in the shape of Panthea and Ione, this feminine modification of Prometheus has already, in act 1, journeyed "through the deep and labyrinthine soul, / Like echoes through long caverns" (1.805–6). That music and journey, of which act 2 is a repetition from a different perspective, was the prophetic song that has already begun and ended within Prometheus. The journey to Demogorgon's realm does not follow Prometheus's revocation of the curse, chronologically; it is rather a retelling of that action in a new symbolic framework.

Another signal of that symbolic identity is Asia's metaphor for the realm of Demogorgon: "Fit throne for such a Power!" (2.3.11). The singing spirits inform her that the journey to this throne must proceed downward and inward, "through the shade of sleep" (2.3.56). Asia hints that she is aware that the scene she beholds is a projection—"And if thou be / The shadow of some spirit lovelier still" (2.3.12–13)—but it is Shelley's prose that interprets this "throne" most clearly, both as it functions here and in act 1. This poetical landscape has been "created by that imperial faculty, whose throne is curtained within the invisible nature of man" (*Prose*, 7:113). Asia engages in the same error of attribution that Mercury prescribes for Prometheus: "I could fall down and worship that and thee" (2.3.16), she says, unwittingly following the advice of Jupiter's minister: "Bend thy soul in prayer" (1.376). The change in the object of worship is less significant than the common pattern: Shelley's subject is the exteriorization, attribution, and worship of that which arose from within. Thus, in *The Revolt of Islam*,

> Some moon-struck sophist stood
> Watching the shade from his own soul upthrown
> Fill Heaven and darken Earth, and in such mood
> The Form he saw and worshipped was his own,
> His likeness in the world's vast mirror shown.
>
> (8.6)

Asia here represents that condition of mind in which Prometheus believed Jupiter "the God and Lord . . . / Who fillest with thy soul this world" (1.282–83), but from a milder ethical perspective. Prometheus's statement was part of his curse; Asia in this mental state says of the tyrant that "curses shall drag him down" (2.4.30). I do not argue that Asia is locked in the same intensity of hatred that bound Prometheus; her ethos is less satanic than Prometheus's precisely to the extent that act 2 is more luminous and hopeful than act 1. But her attribution and her willingness to curse Jupiter parallel, with diminished severity, those of Prometheus prior to the sounding of the prophetic song in act 1.

This strategy of patterning, whereby multiple structures are assembled in order to reveal the unity that they share, enters the details of Shelley's poetry, just as his ontological theme of mental philosophy enters his particular metaphors. Just as act 2 is superimposed over act 1, to reveal differently the same vision, so too the function of the echoing spirits' song—which is symbolically identical with the prophetic spirits' song—assembles multiple images as analogies for a single idea. The sensible diversity of these images is designed to dissolve into the intellectual unity of their common tenor, exactly as the diverse symbols and tones of acts 1 and 2 are designed to reveal the "beautiful idealisms" masked and mantled by each:

> While the sound whirls around,
>   Down, down!
> As the fawn draws the hound,
> As the lightning the vapour,
> As a weak moth the taper;
> Death, despair; love, sorrow;
> Time both; to-day, to-morrow;
> As steel obeys the spirit of the stone,
>   Down, down!
>
>   (2.2.63–71)

Such a technique, like biblical synchronism, embodies intellectual philosophy. If thoughts are identical with things, as in Shelley's philosophy they are, and "all things exist as they are perceived; at least in relation to the percipient" (*Prose*, 7:137), then the use of metaphor, multiple symbolism, and thematically parallel acts reproduces Shelley's philosophy in poetic form, by converting sensibles to intelligibles.

Shelley's biblical context, too, is as apparent here as it was in act 1; the "throne" to which Asia and the song of the spirits refer is mentioned thirty-eight times in the Book of Revelation. To reach it, Asia must pass "through the veil" (2.3.59), and she sees it only when "the veil has

fallen" (2.4.2). *Apokalypsis* means "unveil"; the song of the six pro-
phetic spirits in act 1, and what follows here in act 2, are both rewritings
of John's Apocalypse. What Asia and Panthea see has "neither limb, /
Nor form, nor outline; yet we feel it is / A living spirit" (2.4.5–7). Well
might they feel that it is: prodigious power has been attributed to
whatever they think is here. He has been said to wield a "mighty law"
(2.2.43); when Panthea sees nothing but darkness, she accordingly
engages in attribution: "I see a mighty darkness" (2.4.3). She per-
ceives "rays of gloom" (2.4.4), which lodge us in Milton's hell, where
Shelley read of "darkness visible."[70] This allusion reinforces the mental
landscape of their journey, because Milton makes clear, as Shelley
points out, that "the mind is its own place, and of itself can make a
Heaven of Hell, a Hell of Heaven." This allusion also binds acts 1 and 2
together. At the falling of the veil, it is this "mighty darkness" that is
revealed, "filling the seat of power" (2.4.3).

What follows is one of the most annoying sort of interviews: one
consults a self-proclaimed authority who is in fact utterly uninforma-
tive. Demogorgon says that he can tell "all things thou darest demand"
(2.4.8), but all of his answers are meaningless: he tells Asia nothing that
she does not already know. Asia asks, "Who made the living world?"
and Demogorgon begs the question, saying only "God" (2.4.9). As
Shelley had understood since at least 1811, that bare word is merely a
device by which ignorance disguises itself as piety: "Before we doubt or
believe the existence of any thing it is necessary that we should have a
tolerably clear idea of what it is—The word 'God' has been [and] will
continue to be the source of numberless errors until it is erased from
the nomenclature of Philosophy" (*Letters*, 1:35). When Asia presses the
question by rephrasing it, Demogorgon can only repeat himself
(2.4.11). Her own language, however, is more informative: she lists "all
/ That it [the world] contains—thought, passion, reason, will, / Imag-
ination" (2.4.9–11), defining a mental universe. As her questions grow
gradually more complex and specific, Demogorgon repeats "Merciful
God" (2.4.18), changing his response only by substituting the phrase,
"He reigns" (2.4. 38, 31), a phrase that he mechanically repeats three
times without assigning its words any meaning. Asia, meanwhile, grows
more and more helpful herself, eventually supplying a seventy-eight-
line philosophical history of the universe (2.4.32–109).[71] Time is a
fallen "shadow," she says; thought "pierces this dim universe like light";
Prometheus himself embodied power in the form of Jupiter when he

"clothed him with the dominion of wide Heaven." Asia reports the gifts that Prometheus gave mankind, deviating from Aeschylus's similar list primarily by heightening the intellectual nature of the gifts and by more fully identifying man with God:

> He gave man speech, and speech created thought,
> Which is the measure of the universe;
> And Science struck the thrones of earth and Heaven,
> Which shook but fell not; and the harmonious mind
> Poured itself forth in all-prophetic song,
> And music lifted up the listening spirit
> Until it walked, exempt from mortal care,
> God-like, o'er the clear billows of sweet sound.
>
> (2.4.72–79)

This passage casts its gathered rays backward over earlier parts of the poem and forward over what is yet to be revealed. The fact that political and religious tyrannies are under simultaneous attack is made as clear here as in Shelley's prose; so too is the vision of prophecy as mental projection. To walk on billows of sound is quite as godlike, perhaps, as to walk on water: the bringing together of God and man, heaven and earth, is very nearly approached at this point in Asia's history.[72] When she winds her stirring address to its peroration, in which "man looks on his creation like a God / And sees that it is glorious" (2.4.102–3)—an obvious recasting of Genesis 1:4 in purely humanistic terms—she asks who "drives him on, / The wreck of his own will" (2.4.103–4), not perceiving that she has answered her own question. Demogorgon's answer is as meaningless and uninformative as his earlier ones: "All spirits are enslaved who serve things evil: / Thou knowest if Jupiter be such or no" (2.4.110–11). She is thrown, again, on her own wits.

When Asia then asks Demogorgon for a definition of God, he admits that "I spoke but as ye speak" (2.4.112); that is, he has told her nothing that she did not already know. His famous declaration that "the deep truth is imageless" (2.4.116) is merely a means of avoiding the necessity of answering the question. This evasion follows his confession that "a voice / Is wanting" (2.4.115–16), a confession that well might annoy Asia, who has come to him on the assurance that "in the world unknown / Sleeps a voice unspoken" (2.1.191–92), specifically to pose her questions to "such a Power" (2.3.11) as is here enthroned. She finds an essentially speechless darkness. She does not, however, express disappointment, but rather discovery: "So much I asked before, and my heart gave / The response thou hast given; and of such truths / Each to itself must be the oracle" (2.4.121–23). She asks one more question, to which, she now knows, an answer will come "as my own soul would answer" (2.4.125): "When will the destined hour arrive?" (2.4.128). In response Demogorgon does nothing, saying only, "Behold!" (2.4.128). For this remark he is sometimes credited with engineering and enacting the entire transformation of the world. What follows is Asia's vision, of charioteers drawn by rainbow-winged steeds who trample the wind; it is Asia's transformation that follows in turn, as she bursts into radiance (not, like Demogorgon, darkness) when her presence is "unveiled" (2.5.20).

In the cave of Demogorgon, then, Asia has been talking to herself. This "great confrontation scene is essentially one of self-communion," as Curran observes.[73] Demogorgon has been difficult or impossible to define to anyone's satisfaction precisely because he does not exist, considered apart from the fruitful solitude in which Asia's mind unfolds itself. He has been invisible, he has supplied no information, he has done nothing: he has been attributed into existence.

But that is not to say that he does not exist at all: symbols are objectifications, as the imagination renders its idealisms in visible forms. But it is Shelley's project, as it was Blake's, to reclaim this process of symbolism, of creation, for the mind. The nexus of thought and thing, of thought and action, is humanly real, and Demogorgon's scene in act 2 launches the transfigured Asia and the liberated Prometheus into realization—in the sense of *discovery* and in the sense of *actualization*. But the process that he represents is a mental one: Blake's Albion reified and distanced his own faculties at the expense of torment and enslavement, and so did Shelley's Prometheus; Asia's transfiguration and Prometheus's liberation result not from the cooperation of an external agent whose help might be implored—they result from the unveiling of a mental power, and that power is found within.

Thus Demogorgon has been clearly located within the human mind. His cave is one of "the dim caves of human thought" (1.659); it is the human soul that Panthea describes as caverns (1.805–6), and for that reason Asia has traveled downward and inward to reach it. He fills the throne of power, a seat that Asia had projected outside herself; but this throne is precisely that which "is curtained within the invisible nature of man." When the throne is unveiled, as it is in the Book of Revelation, this "imperial faculty" is revealed. What Asia discovers is no transcending deity of the sort that she thought she should worship; she discovers the power of her mind. Like the prophetic song of act 1, Asia's journey to Demogorgon transforms the vision of John by rendering its humanism more clear and more complete.

It is misleading, however, to identify Demogorgon with the imagination, poetic or otherwise: he is not portrayed imagining anything, nor does he originate new forms. It is also misleading to identify him, as Wasserman has done, as "the repealing powers that are outside the One Mind, outside Existence."[74] Wasserman notes, in support of this bewildering claim, that Shelley contemplated locating Demogorgon's realm "beyond the world of being";[75] but Shelley certainly would have understood that that which is distinct from all that is, is not. Wasserman affirms that Demogorgon is "Primal Power," as Mary Shelley had written in her note to *Prometheus Unbound*, but he confuses the issue by insisting that "we must also recognize his isolation and absolute difference from the world."[76] Shelley does refer, in 1811, to an "existing power of existence" (*Letters*, 1:101), but he predicates *existence* of it, not remoteness from existence; and in any case, Shelley came to recognize, later if not in 1811, that such a formulation is, like the answers of Demogorgon, double talk.[77] "For when we use the words *principle, power, cause,* &c., we mean to express no real being" (*Prose*, 6:208). Wasserman's study includes all those terms in its analysis of Demogorgon, but in such a way as both to predicate a thing and simultaneously to claim that it is remote from existence. It is more likely, perhaps, that it is unnecessary to reify Demogorgon into a transcendental absolute of any sort, including Necessity, just as it was unnecessary for Prometheus to reify Jupiter. If we do not so reify him, we avoid contradictions. "Asia awakens the slumbering Demogorgon to action in accordance with his inviolable law of process,"[78] but it is contradictory to imagine a primal power, an ultimate force, asleep; and his "inviolable law" will be violable indeed if he sleeps through so much. If he is distinct from that law, he remains to be defined; if he is identical with it, his power, his law, and its inviolability sleep with him.

Still, Wasserman's account of Demogorgon is one of the better interpretations to date.[79] The more common interpretation, which reifies Necessity into an agent, ignores the careful interiorization of Demogorgon and his realm. In the creation of religious forms, "the harmonious mind / Poured itself forth in all-prophetic song" (2.4.75–76). Such a formulation stops short of transcendental realities, but credits Shelley with what, by the evidence of his philosophical prose, he deserves: an unwillingness to claim knowledge of that which his own definitions do not render knowable.[80]

In a similar scene in Shelley's later lyrical drama, *Hellas*, Mahmud *mistakenly* assumes that he has a supernatural vision, of the Phantom of Mahomet the Second: the phantom "seems—he is, Mahomet!" (l. 841). In *Hellas*, however, Ahasuerus contradicts this superstition, immediately and explicitly: "What thou see'st / Is but the ghost of thy forgotten dream" (ll. 841–42). The apparently supernatural figure is a "portion of thyself"; and the scene in *Hellas* dramatizes Mahmud's recognition of that fact: he learns to address the phantom as, "Imperial shadow of the thing I am" (l. 900). Here, as in *Prometheus Unbound*, Shelley dramatizes one mind's discovery that its superstitions are its own work and that its ghosts and gods are projections of itself.

Asia's transformation completes act 2 of *Prometheus Unbound*, and it completes the plot of the drama by resolving its central problem. Demogorgon had said that "a voice / Is wanting," and now that voice arrives and sounds:

> . . . thy lips enkindle
> With their love the breath between them;
> And thy smiles before they dwindle
> Make the cold air fire.
>
> (2.5.48–51)

This diction reminds us that Prometheus had "kindled" in man a "thirst which outran" mortal limits. Her smiles are Prometheus's: "Say not those smiles that we shall meet again / Within that bright pavilion which their beams / Shall build o'er the waste world" (2.1.124–26). Those lines were initially spoken of Prometheus's illuminated form, after he had undergone the passage from moral darkness to light in act 1; Asia has made that same passage in act 2.

The end of the Divine Comedy that is act 2 presents the attainment of paradise, but it is the fallen world redeemed, not replaced. The end returns us to the opening of the act, but with the new perception that its scene is "a paradise of wildernesses." Like the end of Dante's poem, act 2 contains poetic embodiments of its mental heaven: these are what John Freccero has called "anti-images" when they occur in the *Paradiso*:

> One of the most memorable occurs in the first heaven (III, 15), where spirits appear within the Moon and are described as "a pearl upon a milk white brow." The comparison is obviously self-defeating as far as its function to convey information is concerned: we are told simply that the poet saw white upon white. The point is of course the *difference*, which we are unable to see, yet within which all of the reality of the *Paradiso* is contained.[81]

The achievement of such a metaphor is to transcend sense-experience, even while employing the language of sense. Shelley's anti-images at the end of act 2 thus employ synesthesia; the Voice sings to Asia:

> . . . none beholds thee—
> But thy voice sounds low and tender
> Like the fairest—for it folds thee
> From the sight, that liquid splendour,
> And all feel, yet see thee never.
>
> (2.5.60–64)

Her invisibility, presented in sensory language, is as insusceptible of concrete perception as the folding of Asia from sight by sound; the effect is to expand the mind's faculties beyond the limits of exterior sense. To do this is to tear the veil: Asia's "limbs are burning / Through the vest which seems to hide them" (2.5.54–55). The poem, as Shelley elsewhere writes of poetry itself, has lifted the veil from the hidden beauty of the world.

Acts 3 and 4 are progressively brightening versions of that which has already occurred twice: the renovation of vision.[82] This kind of structure, in which the sequence of time is displaced by a sequence of perspectives, is implied by the poem's subtitle, "A Lyrical Drama in Four Acts." (That phrase names a form that Shelley will use again, for *Hellas*.) He describes the form in his preface: a lyrical drama is "a series of lyric pictures"; the poet has "wrought upon the curtain of futurity . . . figures of indistinct and visionary delineation." This last phrase suggests that Shelley invokes the form's religious derivations, and especially that earlier form of lyric, "the vision or apocalyptic prophecy, which employs the indirection of the trope to imply its perceptions."[83] These poems are dramas, not only because they are composed in dialogue, but also because their structure is precisely an interaction of perspectives; they are lyrics not only because of their obvious musical elements, but also because of their subjectivity—but this subjectivity follows from their focus on perspectives, *not* from the poet's self-expression. They are dramatic in that their principles are conflict and action—interaction—but they are lyrical in that their personal tone, which arises from the individualized perspectives that they embody, is essential, just as "the personal tone remains and is essential to the lyricism of such passages as those in Isaiah 5:1 . . . Psalm 137 . . . and II Samuel 1:19."[84]

Acts 3 and 4 also display another structural characteristic: symbolism is progressively exteriorized, to expand as well as to vary the point of view. In act 1, the action and imagery are often internal: the furies come "from the all-miscreative brain of Jove" (1.448); they say to Prometheus that they "will be dread thought beneath thy brain" (1.488), and so Prometheus says, "I close my tearless eyes, but see more clear / Thy works within my woe-illumed mind" (1.636–37). The ethical issue, in act 1, is also internal, focused on the movement from disdain to pity (1.53): Prometheus says, "I hate no more, / As then, ere misery made me wise" (1.57–58). In act 2, imagery moves outward from Prometheus, as Panthea goes from him to Asia, and as echoes lead Panthea and Asia from visions of dreams onto *their* journey: "Come, sweet Panthea, link thy hand in mine, / And follow, ere the voices fade away" (2.1.207–8). The ethical issue in act 2 also moves outward; Asia asks Demogorgon, "Who made the living world?" (2.4.9), and "Who reigns?" (2.4.32). She also narrates the history of the relationship of Prometheus and Jupiter, and so it is clear that the ethical focus of this act is on relationships (of god and man, or Titan and Olympian). Aptly, the salient vehicle in act 2 is dialogue, not (as in act 1) monologue.

In act 3, much imagery is of travel again, but the terrestrial coverage is more obvious, as the Spirit of the Earth and then the Spirit of the Hour report the social effects, across the earth, of Prometheus's regeneration. The ethical unity displayed here is a global and millenarian harmony among people, expressed in social and political terms: "Thrones were kingless, and men walked / One with the other" (3.4.131–32). This movement of the symbolism—from pure mind to political and social organization—is typical of radical thought in the period; it is evident, for example, in the title of one of Robert Owen's late works, *Revolution in Mind and Practice* (1849). That a mental renovation precedes, empowers, and prophesies universal change is, again, a leitmotif in Godwin's *Political Justice*. Owen's early work, *A New View of Society* (1813), expresses the correlative concern with perspective—a new *view* precedes and precipitates a new social order, according to the millenarian political tradition in which Shelley's radical drama takes a place. But this political theme does not circumscribe the drama's ends; a visionary poem sharing both aims and strategies with Blake's *Jerusalem* (though that poem was, of course, unknown to Shelley), Shelley's drama does what neither the philosophy of Godwin nor the political program of Owen can do: it unifies a psychological center with a cosmic circumference, and act 4 thus transposes the ethical norm of harmony, peace, and love into cosmic terms. The ecstatic song-and-dance of the Earth-sphere and Moon-chariot repeat on a planetary level the theme of marriage-union, which is embodied more centrally in the union of Prometheus and Asia, ironically in the union of Jupiter and Thetis,[85] and metaphysically in the creation of a new heaven and earth (see 4.164–65).

Certainly each level of reference is present in each act, but emphases and perspectives shift among the scenes. Thus in act 3 Jupiter places himself in the ethical center of the poem, as Prometheus had defined it in act 1: Jupiter refers to "my curses" and "my wrath's night" (3.1.11, 13). He also attributes power to the same locus to which almost everyone else has attributed it— "Demogorgon's vacant throne" (3.1.21). He employs the image of dew rising, and he invokes the harmonies that have already unified earth with heaven (at 2.5.97) though he knows it not. He assembles his Old Testament complex of "thunder," "fiery wheels," and "earthquake" (3.1.47, 50), all of these images linking this scene to act 1. Demogorgon arrives, again refuses to identify himself (3.1.52), and the two disappear, like one of Jupiter's prototypes, "into the bottomless void" (3.1.76).[86]

As Wasserman has shown, "there is, then, no 'fatal child' at all. The myth of Jupiter, Thetis, and their offspring is present only to be parodied, not to be understood as the content of Prometheus' secret."[87] In fact, Demogorgon is Jupiter's progeny insofar as all the modifications of Prometheus's mind, including Jupiter, have attributed him into being. Similarly, Prometheus had attributed Jupiter into being: both tumble into the void outside existence, at least until the mind recalls them. Oliver Elton has complained that making Prometheus "both the installer of Jupiter and his victim" is "very well in the interpretation, which is that man has invented the gods of false theology, who become his tyrants; but in the myth it is confusing."[88] Elton is right, and that same point is equally valid with regard to Jupiter and Demogorgon: the two pairs are symbolically the same. This confusion is not a flaw, however, but an achievement of Shelley's visionary art: he *is* writing an interpretation of Aeschylus's play and of the myth, not a continuation of them. Further, his twisting of the myth into a shape that is susceptible only of intellectual interpretation is identical with his twisting of images into anti-images: time, space, and exteriority itself are obliterated in a poem whose scene, like that of sacred prophecy, is the theater of the mind.

Scene 2 recapitulates scene 1 from a different perspective: Apollo's. Apollo narrates the overthrow of Jupiter, repeating the imagery of "thunder," "whirlwind," "lightning," and "hail" (3.2.11–15). He ends his speech by returning us to the simultaneous acts 1 and 2: "But list, I hear / The small, clear, silver lute of the young spirit / That sits in the morning star" (3.2.37–39). The same sunrise has been illuminating the poem from its beginning. In act 1 this same "eastern star looks white" (1.825). In act 2 "the point of one white star is quivering still" (2.1.17). In the structure of *Prometheus Unbound*, like the structure of the Book of Revelation, there is no time; instead, each scene depicts a state of vison: Prometheus's, Asia's, Jupiter's, Apollo's.

Prometheus's unbinding is reported in a stage direction to act 3, scene 3. Imagery from preceding acts is then repeated to be redeemed: the "shadow" that darkened earlier pages merges with the anti-images of act 2 to become the "shadow of beauty unbeheld" (3.3.7). The prophetic caves that were at first presented in act 1 (ll. 805–6) served there to internalize an image from Earth (see 1.252). Act 2 repeats this movement, Asia progressing from worship of externals to a radiant image of light that emanates from within; again, the image of the cave is used, Demogorgon's cave being the locus of her discovery of her own mental power. In act 3 the vision of the cave appears again: Prometheus announces that he and Asia will dwell there, in apparently ceaseless mental activity.[89] They will "make / Strange combinations out of common things, / Like human babes in their brief innocence" (3.3.31–33). A gloss on this passage appears in the essay *On Life:*

Let us recollect our sensations as children. . . . We less habitually
distinguished all that we saw and felt, from ourselves. They seemed as
it were to constitute one mass. There are some persons who, in this
respect, are always children. Those who are subject to the state called
reverie, feel as if their nature were dissolved into the surrounding
universe, or as if the surrounding universe were absorbed into their
being. They are conscious of no distinction. And these are states which
precede, or accompany, or follow an unusually intense and vivid ap-
prehension of life. (*Prose*, 6:195–96)

Prometheus's speech comes immediately after his union with what he
calls "thou light of life" (3.3.6). Unification of subject and object is thus
one level of meaning in the scene. From Shelley's preface onward, it has
been a pervasive theme and technique of his poetic art. The passage
on undifferentiated unity introduces a passage on art:

And lovely apparitions, dim at first,
Then radiant—as the mind, arising bright
From the embrace of beauty (whence the forms
Of which these are the phantoms) casts on them
The gathered rays which are reality—
Shall visit us, the progeny immortal
Of Painting, Sculpture, and rapt Poesy,
And arts, though unimagined, yet to be.

(3.3.49–56)

The mind's projection of light constitutes reality: the attribution of
beauty is a specifically aesthetic act, but as acts 1 and 2 have drama-
tized, it manifests the same intellectual activity that generates re-
ligious, political, and philosophical forms. The theory elaborated in the
Defence is embodied in *Prometheus Unbound*.

Prometheus's description of the cave contains lines that apparently
contradict any identification of Prometheus with mankind: "We will sit
and talk of time and change / As the world ebbs and flows, ourselves
unchanged— / What can hide man from mutability?" (3.3.23–25).
Hearing "echoes of the human world" (3.3.44), Prometheus seems to
detach his identity from it.[90] To recall that spirits from the human mind
came to console Prometheus with a prophecy that was actually con-
tained within him, and that echoes were the symbolic stand-ins for
these spirits in act 2, is to recognize that Prometheus in the cave is

hearing or will hear the prophecy that he has heard elsewhere and
before: "The grammatical forms which express the moods of time, and
the difference of persons, and the distinction of place, are convertible
with respect to the highest poetry." In illustration Shelley cites three of
his models for *Prometheus Unbound*: "Aeschylus, and the book of Job,
and Dante's *Paradise*" (*Prose*, 7:112). Shelley is not insisting on a
distinction, he is annihilating distinction. The form of intellection that
is symbolized by Prometheus is timeless. It is precisely Shelley's pur-
pose to wed earth and heaven in the figure of the prophet—not to
separate them.

This pattern is common in Shelley's poetry: what appears to separate
time and eternity in fact identifies them. This view of prophecy—as an
operational form, not an introversional escape—Shelley voices in 1820:
"If faith is a virtue in any case it is so in politics rather than religion; as
having a power of producing that a belief in which is at once a prophecy
& a cause" (*Letters*, 2:191). Thus while it has seemed to some readers
that in *Hellas* Shelley has split time from eternity,[91] the poet's own note
better explains his poem's strategy: "It is the province of the poet to
attach himself to those ideas which exalt and ennoble humanity." Words
that require stress are *poet* and *humanity*. Shelley writes that

> Greece and her foundations are
> Built below the tide of war,
> Based on the crystalline sea
> Of thought and its eternity.
>
> > (*Hellas*, ll. 696–99)

But in that poem as in *Prometheus Unbound* the implications are no more
transcendental than this: "We are all Greeks. Our laws, our literature,
our religion, our arts have their root in Greece" (*Hellas*, preface). The
eternity is of *thought*, and thought is human and natural, not transcen-
dental at all.

Another device of Shelley's lyrical dramas makes interpretation com-
plex. Each poem calls itself a "prophecy," and "prophecy is dramat-
ically structured"; but as the poem's conflicts are "among its various
perspectives,"[92] then the prophecy is lyrical. In *Hellas* Shelley splits his
perspectives dramatically—juxtaposing the Indian slave and the Greek
captive women, for example—and he separates his own voice from
both perspectives in his note: "Let it not be supposed that *I* mean to

dogmatise" (my stress). In *Prometheus Unbound* a different symbolism splits perspectives, linguistically: a form of thought (Prometheus) seems to view mankind as distinct from itself. The metaphorical formulation is thus potentially misleading. "Most words are so—No help" (*Prose*, 6:202n.). When a mind employs symbols for its own components, it seems to refer to external objects, but the "instruments of our knowledge form part of our organism, which forms part of the external world."[93] Prophecy concerns itself with "the struggle of all men as they travel toward a Jerusalem that must be discovered within before it can be established without."[94] Shelley's poetic *form* and his philosophical *problem* (the dichotomy of subject and object) are thus adapted to one another, but it is no part of his symbolic design to divide man from the world, or his poem's ethos from either man *or* the world.

The seventh trumpet sounds at Prometheus's command:

Go, borne over the cities of mankind
On whirlwind-footed coursers: once again
Outspeed the sun around the orbèd world;
And as thy chariot cleaves the kindling air,
Thou breathe into the many-folded shell,
Loosening its mighty music; it shall be
As thunder mingled with clear echoes.

(3.3.76–82)

The usage of whirlwind and thunder links this passage to the biblical prophecies and to act 1, but only to transform them into a new and human vision. No longer is Prometheus bound by his own projections onto an altar of a rock; no longer does he receive a prophecy as if it were from without. He has recognized what the spirits of human thought had told him from the beginning: the prophecy is his.

Furthermore, it is naturalized: the vision of the prophetic cavern is repeated yet again, this time in the voice and viewpoint of Earth. As this act embodies a millenarian and political point of view, so this particular version of the prophetic cavern includes both political history and a secular source of inspiration.[95] Earth reports that

There is a Cavern where my spirit
Was panted forth in anguish whilst thy pain
Made my heart mad, and those who did inhale it

Became mad too, and built a Temple there
And spoke and were oracular, and lured
The erring nations round to mutual war.

(3.3.124–29)

At the general transformation, the regeneration of Prometheus, this same breath of earth no longer inspires madness and war, but "circles round / Like the soft waving wings of noonday dreams, / Inspiring calm and happy thoughts" (3.3.144–46).

Earth's speech continues the secularization of scripture—it is a torch-bearer of Earth who walks on water (3.3.156), and with his image the Earth assimilates Prometheus to a human pattern. At the now-deserted temple of Prometheus, youths once bore a lamp "through the divine gloom" (3.3.169); an analogy is life of mortal men, "who bear the untransmitted torch of hope / Into the grave across the night of life" (3.3.171–72); this natural and human viewpoint is (in Earth's perspective) identified with the triumph of Prometheus, "as thou hast borne it most triumphantly / To this far goal of Time" (3.3.173–74). In this act, therefore, through the earthly viewpoint, Prometheus's triumph, and his cave of prophecy, and his accomplished millennial goal, are all assimilated to the mortal and human level of reference; divinity and humanity unite, in the figures of Earth's metaphors and in the millennial teleology.

The following scene again shifts and multiplies viewpoints, opening with a vision of the Spirit of the Earth—and this time "it is not Earthly" (3.3.1). As "it moves / The splendour drops in flakes upon the grass" (3.3.4–5) and Shelley then transforms this image from Wordsworth's "Ode: Intimations of Immortality." First he establishes a naturalistic reference (to electricity, as both Grabo and Curran illustrate),[96] and then he humanizes this force mythologically.[97] Shelley predicates (in the voice of Panthea) seven actions of this planetary force— "It loved," "it came to drink . . . it thirsted," "it made its childish confidence," it "told her / All it had known or seen," it "reasoned," and it "called her" (3.4.16–22). These are predicable of humans only: linguistically, human and natural forces are identified.

Metaphorically, in the speech of the Spirit of the Earth, nature and man, thing and thought, are again interfused— "toads and snakes and loathly worms" *and* "ill thoughts" are at once redeemed, suggesting a metaphorical or literal identity (3.4.35, 44, 74–75, 77).

Within this scene, perspective is multiplied once more: the global effects of regeneration are narrated by the Spirit of the Hour. He begins with thunder and the abysses of the sky (3.4.98–99), and proceeds with a vision that could "see / Into the mysteries of the Universe" (ll. 104–5). He repeats the emotional oxymorons of act 2 (here, at l. 125), the imagery of the vacant throne from act 2, scene 1 (here, at l. 131), and the Miltonic identification of hell with the human mind (ll. 134–36). The Spirit of the Hour tells that men and women have "made Earth like Heaven" (l. 160), but this visionary goal and language is (consistently with the tenor of act 3) human and millennial: renovation includes "thrones, altars, judgement-seats and prisons" (l. 164), effecting the overthrow of "the tyrant of the world" in political and institutionally religious forms. These tyrannies gone, "the man remains" (l. 193). Ominously, perhaps, but consistently with a natural and human level of reference, the Spirit of the Hour reports that man is not exempt "from chance and death and mutability" (l. 201).[98] The millennium reported by the Spirit of the Hour ends, thus, with a humane vision, not of a transcendental or Platonic absolute, "but man: / Equal, unclassed, tribeless and nationless, / Exempt from awe, worship, degree,—the King / Over himself; just, gentle, wise—but man" (3.4.194–97).

In the final act, perspective is expanded once more, from the social and political realities to a cosmic level of reference, already anticipated by the electrical Spirit of the Earth. This final version of the prophecy whose varied repetitions have structured the lyrical drama opens, in act 4, in "a Part of the Forest near the Cave of Prometheus." The preceding scene, containing the report of the seventh trumpeter, the Spirit of the Hour, is set in "a Forest. In the Background a Cave." The identity of place is obvious, and so is the compression of forest and cave, the settings which, in act 2, were still separated. In act 4 a train of dark forms and shadows sings: "We bear Time to his tomb in eternity" (4.14). Here, as in the Book of Revelation and its other great Romantic successor, Blake's *Jerusalem*, we hear at last what has been true of the poetic universe from the beginning: time is an accident of appearance, a form that is penetrated and replaced by the form and themes of visionary art. We hear again that the spirits of prophecy "come from the mind / Of humankind" (4.93–94), and in Shelley's prophecy it is precisely these human thoughts "which build a new earth and sea / And a heaven where yet heaven could never be" (4.164–65). The transformation of Revelation is complete, its ethos purged of wrath and vengeance and its coordinates fully humanized. The poem began as an elaboration of Shelley's prophetic context, subsuming Greek, Italian, and British poetic originals into his own structure, and adapting poetic form to his philosophical insights. Now it has arrived at an explicit statement of the unity that has been latent all along in the poem's metaphors, scenes, acts, *dramatis personae*, and time structure. The mind's power, implicit in all previous scenes, is here celebrated explicitly in lines that openly transform biblical prophecy by enclosing its terms in a human framework: spirits of thought sing that "beyond our eyes / The human love lies / Which makes all it gazes on, paradise" (4.126–28).

In precisely this way—by enclosing its terms in a human framework—Shelley had been transforming biblical episodes for years, and he was to continue to do so throughout his career. Thus he transforms the Sermon on the Mount—"That those who are pure in heart shall see God, and that virtue is its own reward, may be considered as equivalent assertions" (*Prose*, 6:232). Thus in his later lyrical drama he transforms Genesis: "Let there be light! said Liberty, / And like sunrise from the sea, / Athens arose!" (ll. 682–84); the resurrection of Christ is identified with the resurrection of Freedom in Greece (ll. 100–103); and in the vision of Mahmud, Shelley transforms the seven woes of Revelation (ll. 894–97). Sometimes, as in these examples, Shelley's transformations are topical: he applies biblical language to current events. At other times he transcends even his biblical source in his explicit focus on eternity: thus, he parodies Ezekiel—to transcend Ezekiel—in the prologue to *Hellas* (ll. 56–70). But in Shelley's poems both of these techniques focus on humanity; he draws language and incidents from the Bible, but precisely to bring them to a humane application.

In act 4 of *Prometheus Unbound*, imagery from previous visions—Shelley's *and* the Bible's—is swiftly and openly transformed: "whirlwind" is now "of gladness" (4.85); "veils" are "bright" (4.82); "wings" are "soft and swift as thought" (4.91). The abyss to which both Demogorgon and Jupiter have been returned is the human mind (4.99–104), and outward temples disappear, as at the end of the Book of Revelation. In scripture, those temples are replaced by "the Lord God Almighty and the Lamb" who "are the temple" of the holy city; in Shelley's prophecy, they are replaced by "the temples high / Of man's ear and eye" (4.111–12).[99] The last speech of the lyrical drama serves to recapitulate the prophecy that the poem has contained:

This is the day, which down the void abysm
At the Earth-born's spell yawns for Heaven's despotism,
And Conquest is dragged captive through the deep:
Love, from its awful throne of patient power
In the wise heart, from the last giddy hour
Of dread endurance, from the slippery, steep,
And narrow verge of crag-like agony, springs
And folds over the world its healing wings.

                                          (4.554–61)

Demogorgon's lines repeat the internal locus of the throne of power; this recognition was Asia's discovery in act 2, here made plain. But the unification dramatized in each of the acts of the play is here rendered even more complex.

Again, much of the complexity is imagistic: the Voice of Unseen Spirits begins with an image of pale stars fleeing beyond the blue dwelling of the sun; then dark Forms and Shadows "bear Time to his tomb in Eternity" (4.14); then the first image reappears, changed: in their voice, it is "shades" that are chased "from Heaven's blue waste" (4.22–23). These dark Forms have asked for hair and tears to mark "the spoil, which their toil / Raked together" (ll. 32–33), and so their vision is a darkened one; but the brighter Voice of the Unseen Spirits returns, singing that "bright clouds float in Heaven, / Dew-stars gleam on Earth" (ll. 40–41). The Unseen Echoes of act 2 also sing of dew-stars, and here Shelley again binds his acts imagistically, but to reveal both a progressive brightening and expansion of vision.

This act is given chiefly to two duets that are cosmic in scale. Hours sing that "the voice of the Spirits of Air and of Earth / Has drawn back the figured curtain of sleep / Which covered our being" (4.57–59), assigning apocalypse (unveiling) to the elements; but then Shelley, again in the voice of Panthea, reveals that it is "spirits of the human mind" that are "wrapt in sweet sounds as in bright veils" (4.81), and Panthea's imagery recalls act 2:

Child of Light! thy limbs are burning
    Through the vest which seems to hide them. . . .
    But thy voice sounds low and tender
Like the fairest—for it folds thee
    From the sight.

                                          (2.5.54–63)

As acts of the play are woven together, so are voices for the first duet of act 4: the Hours sing, then the Spirits of the human mind sing, and then a combined Chorus of Spirits and Hours sings: "Weave the web of the mystic measure; / From the depths of the sky and the ends of the Earth" (4.129–30). Sky and earth are indeed united: "Spirits . . . build a new earth and sea / And a Heaven where yet Heaven could never be" (4.164–65). Thus the Chorus announces a new revelation, a new heaven and earth that previous prophecies have not accomplished.

A second duet is the erotic song-and-dance of the moon and the earth. Shelley again employs the art of multiple perspectives. Ione says,

> I see a chariot like that thinnest boat
> In which the Mother of the Months is borne
> By ebbing light into her western cave.
>
> (4.206–8)

These lines recall the imagery of Asia's soul as "an enchanted Boat" (2.5.72), and in both passages the familiar cave appears. Ione's speech is further connected to Asia's transfiguration in act 2 by its use of similar anti-imagery, whereby what is invisible is presented in sensory language; Ione's anti-image is in fact almost identical in strategy with Dante's "pearl upon a milk white brow." Ione says of the spirit in the moon, "Its limbs gleam white, through the wind-flowing folds / Of its white robe, woof of aetherial pearl" (4.222–23). She speaks of "the Deity within" (4.226–27), and uses synesthesia, also used in the scene of Asia's transformation—the chariot's wheels "wake sounds / Sweet as a singing rain of silver dew" (4.234–35).

Panthea's rejoinder, a description of the earth-sphere, contains wheel imagery that is even more obviously a transformation of Ezekiel's vision of the wheels: "Ten thousand orbs involving and involved . . . Sphere within sphere" (4.241–43). In Shelley as in Ezekiel, "The spirit of the living creature was in the wheels" (Ezek. 1:20); "within the Orb . . . the Spirit of the Earth is laid asleep" (4.261–65). One transformation of Ezekiel is imagistic—Shelley's three-dimensional spheres replace the wheels of Ezekiel, for example—but another transformation is ethical. In Ezekiel the vision of the wheels is followed by the voice of the Lord complaining that the children of Israel are "impudent" and "rebellious" (2:3–4). The Lord subsequently says to the children of

Israel, "I will send mine anger upon thee" (7:3). Shelley's passage, in
open contrast, introduces a vision and song of love, "embleming
Heaven and Earth united now" (4.273).

The Earth in fact addresses directly the tyrannical and punitive god,
whose representative in this drama is Jupiter:

"Sceptred Curse,
   Who all our green and azure Universe
Threatenedst to muffle round with black destruction, sending
   A solid cloud to rain hot thunderstones
   And splinter and knead down my children's bones,
All I bring forth, to one void mass battering and blending,

"Until each craglike tower and storied column,
   Palace and Obelisk and Temple solemn,
My imperial mountains crowned with cloud and snow and fire,
   My sea-like forests, every blade and blossom
   Which finds a grave or cradle in my bosom,
Were stamped by thy strong hate into a lifeless mire,

"How art thou sunk . . .
   And from beneath, around, within, above,
   Filling thy void annihilation, Love
Bursts in like light on caves cloven by the thunderball."

                                              (4.338–55)

Ecstatically, the love song proceeds: the moon blossoms into green-
ery and flowers (as the desert does in Isaiah 35), and she sings: "'Tis
Love, all Love" (4.369). Earth reports that the dead are reawakened,
as in Revelation 20, and offers a psychological rendering of Isaiah 11:6–
7: "The wolf also shall dwell with the lamb, and the leopard shall lie
down with the kid; and the calf and the young lion and the fatling
together; and a little child shall lead them. . . . And the lion shall eat
straw like the ox." In Shelley's vision, "Labour and Pain and Grief in
life's green grove / Sport like tame beasts—none knew how gentle they
could be!" (4.404–5).

Man unveils the abyss (4.423), and the "shadow of white Death has
past" from the path of the moon (4.424), and, as this line clearly recalls
Revelation 6:8, it is obvious that Shelley's poem rewrites the scriptural
prophecy. To say this is not to deny the scientific level of reference

explicated by Grabo and others; the love, imaged as a magnet (4.465–66) and as a beam that "passes with the warmth of flame" (4.329), obviously does assimilate gravity, electricity, and electromagnetic radiation. But this multidimensional meaning of Shelley's poem is its theme—biblical and scientific levels of meaning portray the bringing together of heaven and earth, effected here by and in the mind of man, through love. The poem's imagery, allusions, and ethos are united in this vision of a unification of man and the universe. The marriage symbolism from Revelation, applied to the gravitational orbits of earth and moon, contributes to this vision of cosmic unification.

The action of the poem is thus nearly identical with its theme, the multiplicity of perspectives enabling the poet to present his multiple levels of meaning in a vision whose time is simultaneous. The psychological level of reference is made explicit in the drama's closing speech: "Hope creates / From its own wreck the thing it contemplates" (4.573–74). The religious, political, and psychological levels of meaning coincide here, as they did, less obviously, at the drama's beginning; that is the form of prophecy, which proceeds always from darkness to light. On a psychological level, the regeneration of Prometheus is the recovery of his imaginative and cognitive power, bringing him freedom from the fears that had disguised themselves in external form. In religious terms, paradise has been restored to earth, man's gods and his heaven standing revealed as forms that his mind has projected. Politically, man has collectively achieved liberty, recovering the knowledge that commonwealth and king are clothed with power by himself. The angel who has bound the dragon in the bottomless pit is no civil, ecclesiastical, or military authority: that action is effected by powers of the individual human mind: "Gentleness, Virtue, Wisdom, and Endurance" (4.562).[100]

That closing speech is spoken by Demogorgon, but his having the last word does not establish him as a reified deity, any more than he was in act 2—he is still a fiction, "a sense of words" (4.517) of which, universally, minds are capable. No objective deity has overthrown Jupiter, even according to the speech of Demogorgon: "Love from its awful throne of patient power / In the wise heart" (4.557–58) is the agent of redemption, and it is fitting that Demogorgon himself should finally supply the explicitly psychological locus of this "throne" that has appeared in so many visions throughout the drama.

As Revelation begins with Christ's messages to the seven churches in

Asia, and as Prometheus's prophecy has been borne by seven spirits (the first six appearing in act 1, and the seventh delayed until act 3), so Demogorgon's final speech begins with a sevenfold invocation: he addresses, in sequence, Earth, Moon, ethereal powers ("Kings of suns and stars, Daemons and Gods, / Aetherial Dominations"), the "happy dead," the "elemental Genii," the spirits "whose homes are flesh," and, finally, Man.

That Demogorgon's speech is cheerfully accepted by all those he addresses might suggest that he does exist independently, even regally, in the universe of the drama; but the symbolic exteriorization of inner forces is a dominant technique of the play, and Demogorgon's words make the play's humane and psychological focus more obvious than ever. It is love, from within the heart, that overthrows Jupiter. "Gentleness, Virtue, Wisdom, and Endurance" are the seals that bar the pit over Destruction, whereas in Revelation 20:3 it is an angel who casts the dragon into the pit, "and set a seal upon him." In Revelation, the dragon (serpent, devil, or Satan) can "deceive the nations no more, till the thousand years should be fulfilled: and after that he must be loosed a little season"; this is the millennium, a thousand blessed years on earth. When, in the biblical account, Satan is then loosed again, "fire came down from God out of heaven" and devoured Satan's minions, and Satan is then "tormented day and night for ever and ever."

In Shelley's prophecy, to rain fire and to torment rebels for ever and ever are the ways of Jupiter, not the ways of the redeemer of mankind. Instead, Love, Gentleness, Virtue, Wisdom, and Endurance "are the spells by which to reassume / An empire o'er the disentangled Doom" (4.568–69), *if* the serpent is freed after the peaceful millennium. (As in act 2, Demogorgon is no source of knowledge on this point.)

"Life, Joy, Empire" (4.578) are not Demogorgon's, and Victory is not of Necessity, Primal Power, God, or any other tyrant over humanity; it belongs *alone* to human powers, and specifically to these powers: "To suffer woes . . . To forgive wrongs . . . To defy Power which seems Omnipotent [as Demogorgon has seemed to some critics] / To love, and bear; to hope" (4.570–73). Demogorgon thus ends the drama, precisely by restoring liberty and power to the human mind and heart.

Shelley assigns no person, not even Jesus Christ, and no power, not even imagination, the status of creative deity. To shape and to illuminate is less, perhaps, than to create *ex nihilo*; but Shelley's skeptical idealism never violates itself by predicating a deity that its principles render unintelligible. Man is "Godlike" but not God. The consummation of prophecy is an increase in human power that Shelley embodies in metaphor; poetry itself "is as it were the interpenetration of a diviner nature through our own" (*Prose*, 7:136). Arrayed in the light of his own energies, man can, in the terms of Prometheus's vision, transform the earth on which he gazes; he casts on the earth the mind-made rays of reality, just as he shackled himself with mind-forged manacles in act 1. It is both an imaginative act and its political concomitant that can render "the gloom divine"; imagination redeems the human mind, and it thereby redeems religion, political life, and even the earth.

In the preface to his next lyrical drama, Shelley says explicitly that the external political changes to which he looks arise from a spirit before which tyrants tremble. In both poems the spirit is an inner and outer force, belonging to mind and to its objects. Psychological renovation enables this outer revolution, whereby "Love . . . folds over the world its healing wings."

This unification is the achievement of *Prometheus Unbound*.

EPILOGUE

"The Sublime System"

Jerusalem and *Prometheus Unbound* are comparable examples of Romantic prophecy: they share traditions, most obviously the traditions of visionary aesthetics and Enlightenment philosophy; each embodies an apocalypse that is humanistic rather than transcendental; each employs a structure that annihilates time, renovating the form of consciousness; each displaces materialism with an intellectual philosophy embodied in the intellectual semantics of symbols; each portrays the overthrow of a covenant of law by a covenant of mercy; and each ends with a marriage that is based at once on the biblical symbol from Revelation and the philosophical union of subject and object. Further, each uses the central myth of overthrow to express a radical political interpretation that is exactly simultaneous with psychological and philosophical levels of meaning.

Despite these complex similarities, these poems were not written in reaction to one another: there is little or no question of influence.[1] Instead, there is a common cultural matrix that includes literary and philosophical tools and traditions. The poets used these to solve shared problems, independently producing outstanding examples of one poetic form. I have called this form Romantic prophecy, but I must stress again that this term does not imply an appeal from the poets to any exterior agency or authority; it implies the rebirth of a biblical form in a secular universe, newly shaped to embody the philosophical visions of not one or two but a generation of major poets. All the major Romantic poets and many of the minor ones either wrote Romantic prophecies or wrote poems incorporating elements of the form.

This fact is not surprising, given an age whose art is so dominated by the idea of imagination that it becomes a common theme in its poems. As Shelley writes, translating Spinoza's tract "On Prophecy," "With the exception of Christ, none ever apprehended the revelations of God

without the assistance of imagination, that is of words or forms imaged
forth in the mind, and . . . therefore . . . the qualification to prophecy
is rather a more vivid imagination than a profounder understanding than
other men" (*Prose*, 7:274). Surely Shelley would have heard the tone of
deprecation in that remark; but surely, too, Shelley's use of the word
imagination in this passage is less simply deprecatory. Shelley writes
elsewhere that "the great instrument of moral good is the imagination"
(*Prose*, 7:118), and that "the office and character of a poet participates
in the divine nature as regards providence, no less than as regards
creation" (*Prose*, 7:123), clearly expressing a commitment to a positive
value of imagination beyond what Spinoza implies. Its usage in this
passage, therefore, enriches Shelley's conception of prophecy: this
theme of imagination was an ethical and ontological problem, and not
merely a poetic one. Blake's entire poetic canon is devised to embody
and engender a philosophical vision: imagination is the principle that
binds his art in union with other forms of thought and perception.

   That principle also connects major poets of the period: Coleridge,
for example, developed a theory of imagination that accounts equally
for the productions of art and also "all human Perception."[2] E. S.
Shaffer has correctly observed that Coleridge formed a "secular theory
of inspiration,"[3] and the remark is pertinent to other poems besides
"Kubla Khan." In "Religious Musings" the poet is summoned by a
cherub's trump and lifted to a height of vision; in this same poem
Coleridge indicates explicitly his simultaneous usage of contrary con-
texts, affirming in a note that the poem's penultimate paragraph "is
intelligible to those, who, like the Author, believe and feel the sublime
system of Berkley [*sic*]."

   Other Romantic prophecies assimilate other contexts, as we have
seen, founding this assimilation on philosophical principle. Henry More
had done the same, aligning biblical and Platonic literature, precisely
because each employs intellectual symbolism.[4] After him, Joseph
Priestley and others supply still more precedent for Shelley, whose
major poems assume pagan and Christian contexts to lay bare their
common mental origin. His art asks to be approached from several
perspectives at once, and so does that of Blake and other romantics.
Thus many commentators approached the Bible, producing a body of
criticism that "is an intermediary between philosophy and literary
criticism," as Shaffer writes of German authors in the eighteenth and
nineteenth centuries.[5] This approach, though Shaffer does not de-

velop the point, also had a lengthy English tradition, and it is here that foundations were laid for the Romantic transformation of visionary form.

Ronald L. Grimes has argued that for Blake, "visionary time is not so much a segment of a uniformly divided line as it is a quality of perception,"[6] and in that sentence Grimes touches on the philosophical cause of all the Romantics' interest in antichronological structure. The poets are engaged in renovating the forms of thought through the transformation of perception. The denial of externally imposed authority, including the conventional concept of time, is based on the cognitive activity of the human mind: "As the Eye—such the Object" (*E.*, p. 634). For Shelley too the mind bestows reality on what it beholds; for both writers the *form* of visionary art effects the *purpose* of a modern philosophy.

Vocabulary has also been adapted, by the time of the Romantic period, for secular purposes: Henry More, Berkeley, and Swedenborg agree in defining *spiritual* as "mental." Blake's doctrine that "Mental Things are alone Real" has its precedent in visionary theory as well as Enlightenment philosophy: in the terms of that theory, the conversion of sensible thing to intelligible thought and the reference of knowledge to mental activity both make of imagination a literary and epistemological principle. Further, most commentators and all Romantic poets are seldom far from political issues. Thus *Milton, Jerusalem*, and *Prometheus Unbound* present the parallel pairs of Milton/Satan, Los/Spectre, and Prometheus/Jupiter. Each of these pairs enacts a display of internal reform, dramatizing a refusal to engage in violent opposition. This refusal overturns orthodox theologies of vengeance. Each symbolic pair also supplies a psychological paradigm, in which the mind is released from the tyrannies of guilt and projected authority. These same ethical coordinates easily take on political significance, as they do in Shelley's "Address to the Irish People" and "Proposals for an Association of Philanthropists." John Taylor Coleridge was correct on this point in his review of the *Revolt of Islam*: Shelley "would erase the Decalogue, and every other code of laws."[7] The religious and political implications of Shelley's visionary art, which the reviewer found so disturbing, form part of Shelley's multidimensional purpose.

Abrams has written of the traditional Christian tendency "to internalize apocalypse by transferring the theater of events from the outer earth and heaven to the spirit of the single believer."[8] Abrams has also

brought this tradition forward to the Romantic period, and thus sum-
marizes the "high Romantic argument": "Faith in an apocalypse by
revelation had been replaced by faith in an apocalypse by revolution,
and this now gave way to faith in an apocalypse by imagination or
cognition. In the ruling two-term frame of Romantic thought, the mind
of man confronts the old heaven and earth and possesses within itself
the power . . . to transform them into a new heaven and new earth, by
means of a total revolution of consciousness."[9] Abrams admits that this
formulation is a "drastic simplification," and it *is* that, in part because
the poets never abandoned prophecy's simultaneous multiplicity of
meaning. A wish to settle on a single or final meaning will be constantly
frustrated by Romantic prophecies, poems that, one comes to fear,
cannot be discussed at all without drastic simplification. Their meaning
consists in large part of the revolution that they enact in the reader's
mind, but goes past this limited reference to dramatize and to antici-
pate interpersonal, political, religious, and cosmic change. Thus Baker,
author of a Platonic interpretation of *Prometheus Unbound*, complains
that Cameron's political interpretation widens to become, "in effect,
the traditional moral interpretation with some political ornamenta-
tion."[10] As Baker's statement implies, and as Cameron's method sug-
gests, the major limitation of any approach to this poem or to other
Romantic prophecies must be the difficulty or impossibility of ade-
quately treating all levels of reference at once. Criticism cannot match
the poems' peerless complexity.

   As is so often the case, Coleridge expresses the philosophical basis of
that complexity: "The ground of existence, and the ground of the
knowledge of existence, are absolutely identical."[11] Both enjoy their
birth into being within, and in terms of, consciousness. Art repeats the
process in miniature: "Poetry . . . is purely human; for all its materials
are from the mind, and all its products are for the mind."[12] Coleridge's
formulation applies to the symbolism of other Romantic idealists: "Art
itself might be defined as of a middle quality between a thought and a
thing."[13] Art recapitulates creation: "Now what the Globe is in Geogra-
phy, *miniaturing* in order to *manifest* the Truth, such is a Poem to that
Image of God."[14] In a godless universe enclosed within human terms,
such as Shelley's, the poem repeats no external deity's pattern; rather
the poet generates the birth of perceptions identical in kind with those
that form all reality. In a world such as Blake's, where Jesus Christ is
precisely the human imagination, the formation of symbols both re-

peats and changes the formation of human experience. Similarly, it has justly been said of Jeremiah that "the historical events of his day merely supplied him with imagery."[15] As all the Romantic writers are likely to have remembered, Ezekiel describes the state of inspiration in the following terms: "I know the things that come into your mind."[16] Employing more modern philosophies, they also knew that "we receive but what we give,"[17] and that the prophet, whose qualification is imagination, must know the things that come *from* the human mind. Shelley's spirit of prophecy is also the spirit of the age in whose poetry it is no object, nor institution, nor God, but rather the human faculty, love, "which makes all it gazes on, Paradise."

Notes

Prologue: "The Eternal, the Infinite, and the One"

1. M. H. Abrams, *Natural Supernaturalism: Tradition and Revolution in Romantic Literature* (1971; rpt. New York: Norton, 1973), p. 11.

2. See Earl R. Wasserman, *Shelley: A Critical Reading* (Baltimore: Johns Hopkins University Press, 1971), especially pp. 131–53. Metaphysical criticism—even of literary prose of the period—is still so uncommon that in 1981 Wendell V. Harris argues afresh for the relevance of this approach, which is to study "assumptions about the nature of what we know and how we know it, the root problems of metaphysics," from which "all the rest of a person's thought grows." See Harris, *The Omnipresent Debate: Empiricism and Transcendentalism in Nineteenth-Century English Prose* (DeKalb: Northern Illinois University Press, 1981), pp. 3–20, esp. p. 6.

3. Leslie Stephen, *History of English Thought in the Eighteenth Century*, 3d ed. (1902; rpt. New York: Harcourt, Brace and World, 1962), 1:11.

4. I refer to chapters 1 and 11 of Northrop Frye's *Fearful Symmetry: A Study of William Blake* (1947; rpt. Princeton: Princeton University Press, 1969).

5. I quote from E. B. Murray, "*Jerusalem* Reversed," *Blake Studies* 7, no. 1 (1974): 11.

6. Frye, *Fearful Symmetry*, p. 11.

7. See David V. Erdman, *Blake: Prophet against Empire: A Poet's Interpretation of the History of His Own Times*, 3d ed. (Princeton: Princeton University Press, 1977); Kenneth Neill Cameron, *The Young Shelley: Genesis of a Radical* (New York: Macmillan, 1950); and idem, *Shelley: The Golden Years* (Cambridge: Harvard University Press, 1974).

8. Peter F. Fisher's suggestive study of Blake's intellectual context takes a more generalized point for its thesis: "Both the spirit of enlightenment and revolution burned in him as intensely as in any of his contemporaries, but they were content with a relatively superficial kind of revolution—the kind that altered external conditions and man's apparent relationship to them. Blake was more ambitious, and he sought to redeem the entire perspective of history by an apocalyptic revolt in the ground of the human mind." See *The Valley of Vision: Blake as Prophet and Revolutionary*, ed. Northrop Frye (Toronto: University of Toronto Press, 1961), p. 142. I shall be demonstrating that a more precise analysis of two traditions—biblical prophecy and Enlightenment philosophies of mind—will show with greater clarity what this vision of redemption was, both historically and specifically for Blake and Shelley.

9. Jean H. Hagstrum, *William Blake: Poet and Painter. An Introduction to the Illuminated Verse* (1964; rpt. Chicago: University of Chicago Press, 1969), p. 98.

10. Frye, *Fearful Symmetry*, pp. 356–403.

11. "The dominant structural control over *Hellas*, then, is a complex of the various temporal modes and historical designs of freedom and oppression, elaborated in such a fashion as to assimilate the present to all of time"; since "tyranny is for Shelley a spirit, a disposition of the soul, not external events," it follows that "theistic religion and political tyranny" share a common basis, and they are therefore (according to Wasserman) simultaneous dimensions of Shelley's reference. See *Shelley: A Critical Reading*, pp. 385–86 and, generally, 374–413.

12. Leslie Tannenbaum has also called attention to this biblical technique, and pointed out its relevance to Blake: Tannenbaum cites Mede as the authority for the perception "that Revelation abandons chronological in favor of synchronic order that permits the prophet to expand upon and clarify particular issues." See *Biblical Tradition in Blake's Early Prophecies: The Great Code of Art* (Princeton: Princeton University Press, 1982), p. 38. Earlier, Joseph Anthony Wittreich, Jr., had applied Mede's principle of synchronism to the poetry of Milton and Blake: see Wittreich, "Opening the Seals: Blake's Epics and the Milton Tradition," in *Blake's Sublime Allegory: Essays on "The Four Zoas," "Milton," "Jerusalem,"* ed. Stuart Curran and Wittreich (Madison: University of Wisconsin Press, 1973), p. 43; and Wittreich, *Visionary Poetics: Milton's Tradition and His Legacy* (San Marino, Calif.: Huntington Library, 1979), pp. 38–39.

13. Erdman, *Blake: Prophet against Empire*, pp. 189–92.

14. Joseph Anthony Wittreich, Jr., *Angel of Apocalypse: Blake's Idea of Milton* (Madison: University of Wisconsin Press, 1975), pp. 189–219.

15. Emanuel Swedenborg, *True Christian Religion*, trans. anon. (London: J. Phillips and J. Denis and Son, 1781), par. 156.

16. Paul Henri Thiry, Baron de Holbach, *The System of Nature; or, Laws of the Moral and Physical World*, trans. H. D. Robinson (1889; rpt. Ann Arbor, Mich.: University Microfilms, 1963), p. 52.

17. Ibid., pp. 174–77.

18. Ibid., p. 180.

Chapter 1: Prophecy and the Philosophy of Mind

1. Prophecy had always been a philosophical form: "If we wish to reconstruct the world of ideas and aspirations which filled the heart of an earnest Jew at the beginning of the Christian era, it is to this literature [i.e., apocalyptic literature] that we must have recourse for materials." See R. H.

Charles, "Apocalyptic Literature," *A Dictionary of the Bible Dealing with Its Language, Literature, and Contents*, ed. James Hastings et al. (New York: Charles Scribner's Sons, 1898), 1:109a. Likewise, "The prophetic writings embodied great principles both of belief and practice," to quote W. Sanday, "Bible," *Encyclopaedia of Religion and Ethics*, ed. James Hastings et al. (New York: Charles Scribner's Sons, 1910), 2:566b. In the Book of Revelation John endeavors "to set forth the divine philosophy (or theology) of history," J. W. Bowman observes in "Revelation," *The Interpreter's Dictionary of the Bible: An Illustrated Encyclopedia*, ed. George Arthur Buttrick et al. (New York: Abingdon, 1962), 4:68.

2. See, for example, Thomas Goodwin, *An Exposition upon the Revelation* (1639), in *The Works of Thomas Goodwin* (London: Printed by J. Darby and S. Roycroft, 1681–1704), 2:2. Citing other authorities, Christopher Hill, in *Antichrist in Seventeenth-Century England* (London: Oxford University Press, 1971), has shown that seventeenth-century biblical criticism "moved from Antichrist in Rome, through Antichrist in the bishops or the whole state church, to Antichrist in every man" (p. 130) and that "the Holy War is conducted inside each believer" (p. 171). In *Milton and the English Revolution* (New York: Viking Press, 1977), Hill explicates "the radical doctrine which saw heaven and hell *merely* as internal states" (p. 311), pointing out that for many interpreters, "the Fall, the Second Coming, the Last Judgment and the end of the world were all events which take place on earth within the individual conscience" (p. 309).

3. Thus Martin Rist writes that "Revelation is by any criterion the finest example of an apocalypse in existence," and he defines *apocalypse* as "a specific type of literature . . . which conforms to a distinctive and readily recognizable pattern of thought." See his introduction to the Book of Revelation in *The Interpreter's Bible* (New York: Abingdon, 1957), 12:347. I shall be arguing that Revelation was understood by many of its English interpreters, through the Romantic period, not only to "conform" with a pattern of thought, but to condition and to promote such patterns of thought, thus addressing itself specifically to issues of intellectual philosophy.

I should mention here that, throughout my argument, I shall not be observing the specifically modern tendency "to differentiate apocalypticism from Old Testament prophecy, which is primarily if not exclusively concerned with this life and this age of human history, rather than with the next life and the age to come" (ibid.). The distinction will not prove helpful when the literary *form* of prophecy is the subject of study, and the historical fact is that, during the periods that I study, John's prophecy was not widely believed to deviate thus from Old Testament prophecy: its literary continuity with Old Testament prophecy is a commonplace among commentators, and the ideological focus of Revelation commentary *is* on "this life and this age of human history," as I shall be showing at some length.

4. I prefer Shelley's phrase, *intellectual philosophy*, to the conventional term *empiricism* because I would include Descartes, whose philosophy is rational rather than empirical, and Newton, whose system is mathematical. The line of Descartes, Locke, Newton, Berkeley, and Hume comprises a shifting but coherent body of thought whose major emphasis is mind: so the poets perceived them, and so I treat them here. For different treatments of empiricism in nineteenth-century literature, see Harris, *The Omnipresent Debate*, especially pp. 3–41. In *Energy and the Imagination: A Study of the Development of Blake's Thought* (Oxford: Oxford University Press, 1970), Morton D. Paley also surveys Enlightenment philosophers, including Descartes, Locke, Berkeley, and Hume, to show their relevance to Blake, though Paley is not concerned with other Romantic poets, and though he focuses more simply and narrowly on the philosophers' concepts of imagination—see especially pp. 214–30.

5. See Stephen, *History of English Thought in the Eighteenth Century*, 1:21.

6. To identify this contradiction, compare Locke, 4.17.23, with the title, *The Reasonableness of Christianity*.

7. See especially George Berkeley, *A Treatise Concerning the Principles of Human Knowledge*, pars. 29–33 and 146ff.

8. For a different perspective on this point, see Carl L. Becker, *The Heavenly City of the Eighteenth-Century Philosophers* (1932; rpt. New Haven: Yale University Press, 1969), pp. 128–29 et passim.

Useful books on British thought in the eighteenth century, as that body of thought is relevant to the Romantic poets, include the following: Basil Willey, *The Eighteenth-Century Background: Studies in the Idea of Nature in the Thought of the Period* (1940; rpt. Boston: Beacon Press, 1961); A. A. Luce, *Berkeley's Immaterialism: A Commentary on His "A Treatise Concerning the Principles of Human Knowledge"* (1945; rpt. New York: Russell and Russell, 1948); C. E. Pulos, *The Deep Truth: A Study of Shelley's Scepticism* (1954; rpt. Lincoln: University of Nebraska Press, 1962); Ernest Lee Tuveson, *The Imagination as a Means of Grace: Locke and the Aesthetics of Romanticism* (Berkeley and Los Angeles: University of California Press, 1960); and Wasserman, *Shelley: A Critical Reading*. My conclusions differ from the conclusions of each of these writers, but I am indebted to them all. Specifically, I shall be arguing that these studies do not profit from their exclusion of the openly visionary philosophies that were contemporary with the major texts of British empiricism.

9. See Karl Mannheim, *Ideology and Utopia: An Introduction to the Sociology of Knowledge*, trans. Louis Wirth and Edward Shils (1936; rpt. New York: Harcourt, Brace and World, n.d.), p. 6.

10. See René Descartes, *Discourse on Method*, trans. Laurence J. Lafleur, 2d ed. (Indianapolis: Bobbs-Merrill, 1956), p. 7. Subsequent citations will be found in the text.

11. An extreme form of this procedure appears among modern phenomenologists, in the technique (of Husserl and others) called "bracketing existence": here, the issue is so utterly one of mental forms that "it is quite irrelevant whether the object described exists or not." See Richard Schmitt, "Phenomenology," *The Encyclopedia of Philosophy*, ed. Paul Edwards (1967; rpt. New York: Macmillan and The Free Press, 1972), 6:140–41.

12. For Fraser's remarks, see his edition of Locke's *An Essay Concerning Human Understanding* (1894; rpt. New York: Dover Publications, 1959), p. lxxii.

13. Henry More, *Antidote against Atheism*, 1.5.2; I quote from *The Philosophical Writings of Henry More*, ed. Flora Isabel MacKinnon (New York: Oxford University Press, 1925), p. 259.

14. See Frye, *Fearful Symmetry*, p. 23. In his response to Locke's argument, "Blake is protesting against the implication that man is material to be formed by an external world and not the former or imaginer of the material world." Regrettably, Frye is not concerned to analyze Locke's doctrine, however, or its history. See also Fisher, *The Valley of Vision*, p. 108.

15. See, for example, Tuveson, *The Imagination as a Means of Grace*, pp. 5–7.

16. Luce, *The Dialectic of Immaterialism: An Account of the Making of Berkeley's "Principles"* (London: Hodder and Stoughton, 1963), p. 61.

17. Tuveson, *The Imagination as a Means of Grace*, p. 2.

18. For a discussion of attribution theory, see Albert H. Hastorf, David J. Schneider, and Judith Polefka, *Person Perception* (Reading, Mass.: Addison-Wesley, 1970).

19. Tuveson, *The Imagination as a Means of Grace*, pp. 19–21.

20. Sir Isaac Newton, *Opticks; or, A Treatise of the Reflections, Refractions, Inflections and Colours of Light*, based on the 4th ed. (1730; rpt. New York: Dover, 1952), p. 405. Subsequent citations will be found in the text.

21. For a summary and a critique of this interpretation, see Carl Grabo, *A Newton among Poets: Shelley's Use of Science in "Prometheus Unbound"* (1930; rpt. New York: Gordian Press, 1968), pp. 100–102; and Donald Ault, *Visionary Physics: Blake's Response to Newton* (1974; rpt. Chicago: University of Chicago Press, 1975), pp. 9–11.

22. Isaac Newton, *The Mathematical Principles of Natural Philosophy*, trans. Andrew Motte (1729; rpt. London: Dawsons, 1968), 2:393.

23. The most famous and typical misunderstanding of Berkeley's philosophy was that of Samuel Johnson, who inadvertently demonstrated the validity of Berkeley's system by kicking a rock; see James Boswell, *The Life of Samuel*

Johnson Together with Boswell's Journal of a Tour to the Hebrides and Johnson's Diary of a Journey into North Wales, ed. G. B. Hill, rev. G. F. Powell (1934– 50; rpt. Oxford: Oxford University Press, 1971), 1:471.

24. Frye has called attention to this argument of abstract ideas (see "The Case Against Locke," in *Fearful Symmetry*, especially pp. 14–17); but Frye's famous chapter is not a philosophical analysis of the problem such as (I am claiming) is warranted for the study of Blake and Shelley. Frye confuses or identifies, for example, *reflection, generalization,* and *abstract ideas*, but Locke and Berkeley do not confuse or identify them in the same way. In a general sense, it is both useful and correct to observe that the "acceptance of the *esse-est-percipi* principle unites the subject and the object" (p. 17), but it is a confusion of philosophical history to say that "by introducing the idea of 'reflection' we separate them again" (p. 17). The relation of Locke to Berkeley (and of both to Blake and Shelley) warrants more precisely philosophical analysis because more than a general outlook is involved.

25. Luce, *Berkeley's Immaterialism*, pp. 38–67.

26. Here again, Luce, in *Berkeley's Immaterialism*, covers this material at length; some of Luce's conclusions differ from my own.

27. Jean Piaget, *Psychology and Epistemology: Towards a Theory of Knowledge*, trans. Arnold Rosin (1971; rpt. New York: Viking Press, 1972), pp. 1–2; Ulric Neisser, *Cognition and Reality: Principles and Implications of Cognitive Psychology* (San Francisco: W. H. Freeman, 1976), p. 52.

28. Neisser, *Cognition and Reality*, p. 57.

29. William Jones, *A Course of Lectures on the Figurative Language of Scripture* (1786), in his *Theological and Miscellaneous Works*, 6 vols. (London, 1826), 3:6, quoted in Tannenbaum, *Biblical Tradition in Blake's Early Prophecies*, p. 59.

30. Tannenbaum, *Biblical Tradition in Blake's Early Prophecies*, p. 77.

31. John Wesley, *Explanatory Notes upon the New Testament* (1764; New York: Lane & Tippett, 1847), p. 6. Peter F. Fisher had stated generally this characteristic of prophetic language, more than a decade before Tannenbaum explained it with such scholarly detail, and (of course) before my own explication of its philosophical basis. See *The Valley of Vision*, p. 83.

32. Henry More, *An Explanation of the Grand Mystery of Godliness* (1660), in *The Theological Works of the Most Pious and Learned Henry More* (London: Joseph Downing, 1708), p. i.

33. Stephen, *History of English Thought in the Eighteenth Century*, 1:1.

34. Becker, *The Heavenly City of the Eighteenth-Century Philosophers*, pp. 33–118, is especially useful on Hume and his context.

35. Stephen, *History of English Thought in the Eighteenth Century*, 1:267.

36. Morton D. Paley relates Hume's concept of imagination to Blake, where, it seems to me, the relation is much more problematic; Paley, of

course, does not analyze Hume's issues and methods, instead explicating Blake's thought and its antecedents more generally. See *Energy and the Imagination*, pp. 25–27.

37. David Hume, *A Treatise of Human Nature*, ed. L. A. Selby-Bigge (1739; rpt. Oxford: Oxford University Press, 1973), p. 67. Subsequent citations will be found in the text.

38. Becker, *The Heavenly City of the Eighteenth-Century Philosophers*, pp. 71–129.

39. Holbach, *The System of Nature*, p. 48.

40. Joseph Priestley, *Disquisitions Relating to Matter and Spirit. To Which is Added the History of the Philosophical Doctrine Concerning the Origin of the Soul*, 2d ed. (London: Printed by Pearson and Rollason for J. Johnson, 1782), 1:iii. This passage appears in Priestley's Introduction, which is paginated separately from the preceding front matter.

41. Ibid., p. iv.

42. Holbach, *The System of Nature*, p. 50.

43. Ibid., p. 33.

44. For a discussion of Holbach in this connection, see W. H. Wickwar, *Baron d'Holbach: A Prelude to the French Revolution* (London: George Allen & Unwin, 1935), pp. 123, 218 et passim.

45. Stephen J. Stein, introduction to Jonathan Edwards, *Apocalyptic Writings*, vol. 5 of *The Works of Jonathan Edwards*, ed. John E. Smith (New Haven: Yale University Press, 1977), p. 1. Thus Murray Roston is misleading, in my view, when he remarks that "In biblical prophecy, which constitutes the main body of biblical poetry, there was little room for such philosophical speculations as are to be found, for example, in the book of Job"; see *Prophet and Poet: The Bible and the Growth of Romanticism* (Evanston: Northwestern University Press, 1965), pp. 68–69. Such a statement, intended to explicate the Bible as a background to Romanticism, obscures the intensely philosophical interest in biblical prophecy that such poets as Blake and Shelley expressed; further, it simply contradicts the openly philosophical exegesis that flourished in England for centuries, which derived an aesthetic from prophecy for philosophical poetry, and which, in consequence, I shall be explicating.

Quite apart from English Romanticism, H. Gunkel has observed that already, in much older tradition, "the prophets became poets and thinkers." He is quoted in Claus Westermann, *Basic Forms of Prophetic Speech*, trans. Hugh Clayton White (Philadelphia: Westminster Press, 1967), p. 28. It is this conception of the prophet, a conception common to the Romantic writers and traditional before them, that I explicate here.

46. Christopher Hill, *The World Turned Upside Down: Radical Ideas During the English Revolution* (1972; rpt. Harmondsworth: Penguin, 1980), p. 92.

47. Stein, introduction to Edwards, *Apocalyptic Writings*, p. 6.

48. Ernest Lee Tuveson, *Millennium and Utopia: A Study in the Background of the Idea of Progress* (Berkeley and Los Angeles: University of California Press, 1949), pp. viii–ix.

49. Ibid., pp. 3–4. In this connection, Tuveson cites Hajo Holborn, "History and the Humanities," *Journal of the History of Ideas* 9 (1948): 65.

50. Grabo, *A Newton among Poets*, pp. 100–103; Ault, *Visionary Physics*, pp. 8–14.

51. See M. H. Abrams, "English Romanticism: The Spirit of the Age," in *Romanticism Reconsidered*, ed. Northrop Frye (New York: Columbia University Press, 1963), pp. 26–72; Abrams, *Natural Supernaturalism*, pp. 37–44 and 327–56; F. B. Curtis, "Blake and the Booksellers," *Blake Studies* 6, no. 2 (1976): 171; Roston, *Poet and Prophet*, p. 141 et passim; E. S. Shaffer, *"Kubla Khan" and "The Fall of Jerusalem": The Mythological School in Biblical Criticism and Secular Literature 1770–1880* (Cambridge: Cambridge University Press, 1975), pp. 17, 20, 23, et passim; Wittreich, "'Sublime Allegory': Blake's Epic Manifesto and the Milton Tradition," *Blake Studies* 4, no. 2 (1972): 15–44; Joseph Anthony Wittreich, Jr., "Opening the Seals: Blake's Epics and the Milton Tradition," in *Blake's Sublime Allegory*, ed. Curran and Wittreich, pp. 23–58; Wittreich, *Angel of Apocalypse*, pp. 188–219; and Wittreich, *Visionary Poetics*, pp. xiv, 4, et passim.

52. More, *An Explanation of the Grand Mystery of Godliness*, in *Theological Works*, p. 124. Also see Wittreich, *Visionary Poetics*, p. 7 and note.

53. Signor Pastorini [Charles Walmesley], *The General History of the Christian Church*, 2d ed. (London: J. P. Coghlan, 1798), p. iv. This phrase appears in the anonymous editor's preface.

54. J. Bicheno, *The Signs of the Times* (Providence, R.I.: Carter and Wilkinson, 1794), p. 10.

55. Joseph Mede, *The Key of the Revelation*, trans. Richard More, 2d ed. (London: Printed for Philip Stephens, 1650), p. 72.

56. Cf. J. W. Bowman's statements: "All apocalyptic literature is dramatic in character, its varied scenes being reported as 'visions' by the seer"; "John's book is highly dramatic in style. . . . The book readily divides itself into seven Acts, each Act having in turn seven Scenes." See *The Interpreter's Dictionary of the Bible*, 4: 58, 61.

57. Richard More, unpaginated translator's note in his translation of Mede's *The Key of the Revelation*. Cf. Westermann's observation: "In the prophetic books . . . there is not one single vision account in which the prophet *only* sees. *Always*, without exception, hearing is associated with the experience of seeing." See *Basic Forms of Prophetic Speech*, p. 25.

58. Robert Lowth, *Lectures on the Sacred Poetry of the Hebrews*, trans. G. Gregory (1787; rpt. New York: Garland, 1971), 2:18. E. F. Siegman has

observed that the specifically poetic component of prophecy is itself a composite form, "using symbols and imagery of every kind"; see "Apocalypse," *New Catholic Encyclopedia*, ed. William J. McDonald et al. (New York: McGraw-Hill, 1967–74), 1:658. H. Gunkel also observes that "within . . . prophetic speeches an almost boundless diversity prevails: promise and threat, a recounting of sins, admonitions, Priestly Torah, historical retrospection, disputations, songs of all kinds, short lyrical passages, liturgies, parables, allegories, etc." Thus, "genres . . . have been extensively appropriated by the prophets." Gunkel is quoted in Westermann, *Basic Forms of Prophetic Speech*, pp. 25–26.

59. Lowth, *Lectures on the Sacred Poetry of the Hebrews*, 2: 68, 69.

60. Goodwin, *An Exposition upon the Revelation*, 2: 2, 5.

61. Ibid., pp. 29, 32, 39. Thus, much later, C. Steuernagel writes that "the individual character of the prophet" results in part from his "religious and moral understanding," and in part from abilities that are "inward and personal." He is quoted in Westermann, *Basic Forms of Prophetic Speech*, p. 16. It may be, as Westermann comments, that "this is quite unmistakably the language of an idealistically colored religious individualism" (p. 17), but I am arguing precisely that such an idealism colored the Romantics' understanding of prophecy, and that *their* idealistic reading of biblical prophecy arose from English exegetical tradition.

62. A. C. Charity, *Events and Their Afterlife: The Dialectics of Christian Typology in the Bible and Dante* (Cambridge: Cambridge University Press, 1966), p. 160.

63. Emanuel Swedenborg, *The Apocalypse Revealed*, trans. the Rev. T. B. Hayward and the Rev. John Worcester (Philadelphia: J. B. Lippincott & Co., 1881), par. 7; idem, *True Christian Religion*, pars. 12, 156.

64. More, *Apocalypsis Apocalypseos; or, The Revelation of St. John the Divine Unveiled* (London: Printed by J. M. for J. Martyn and W. Kettilby, 1680), p. 5. This point will seem to manifest More's Platonic idealism, a doctrine which, as J. H. Muirhead argues in *The Platonic Tradition in Anglo-Saxon Philosophy* (London: George Allen and Unwin, 1931), p. 26, sometimes shows a unity of principle with Christianity; to demonstrate this unity was part of More's project. William Warburton, however, is *not* interested in Platonism, but in "the high Antiquity of *Egypt*" when he also argues that "where God teaches the Prophet . . . the [external] *significative Action* is generally changed into a *Vision*." See *The Divine Legation of Moses Demonstrated* (2d ed. 1741; rpt. New York: Garland, 1978), 2: 66, 83.

65. More, *Apocalypsis Apocalypseos*, p. 197.

66. Thus Wittreich writes that "often in prophetic literature the devaluation of reason is accompanied by the exaltation of the imagination" (*Visionary Poetics*, p. 29); and Morton W. Bloomfield observes that "all writers on

prophecy had to give the imagination a place of some importance." See *"Piers Plowman" as a Fourteenth-Century Apocalypse* (New Brunswick, N.J.: Rutgers University Press, 1961), p. 174.

Morton D. Paley also explicates concepts of visionary or prophetic imagination, citing John Smith, a Cambridge Platonist: "The Prophetical scene or Stage upon which all apparitions were made to the Prophet, was his Imagination" (quoted in *Energy and the Imagination*, p. 236). Paley comments: "This conception . . . was not meant to apply to anything outside the Bible. Neither was Spinoza's assertion that the prophets perceived God through the imagination, but by insisting on the imaginative nature of prophecy, such views prepared the way for literary criticism of the Bible as sublime poetry." He continues, most relevantly for my purposes, "It then remained for William Blake to argue that all scriptures were sublime poems, including Milton's and his own."

67. Lowth, *Lectures on the Sacred Poetry of the Hebrews*, 2:15.

68. Austin Farrer, *A Rebirth of Images: The Making of John's Apocalypse* (1949; rpt. Boston: Beacon Press, 1963), p. 17.

69. Wittreich cites Tasso in this connection: "The art of composing a poem resembles the plan of the universe." See Torquato Tasso, *Discourse on the Heroic Poem*, trans. Mariella Cavalchina and Irene Samuel (Oxford: Clarendon Press, 1973), pp. 77–78; quoted in Wittreich, *Visionary Poetics*, p. 12. On p. 18, citing George Puttenham, Wittreich again raises the analogy, but he leaves the issue in strictly aesthetic terms, not considering—as both commentators and poets certainly *did* consider—the ontological and epistemological implications of this analogy. Thus poets, like God, "contrive a universe out of their own brain." See George Puttenham, *The Arte of English Poesie*, ed. Edward Arber (1589; rpt. London: English Reprints, 1869), p. 20; quoted in Wittreich, *Visionary Poetics*, p. 18. The relevance of that claim to the theories of knowledge that I have outlined above should be obvious—as it was to the major Romantic poets.

70. See Mede, *The Key of the Revelation,* p. 64, where Mede cites the *Onirocriticis* of Nicolaus Rigaltius. See also Warburton, *The Divine Legation of Moses*, 2:159. Warburton cites the *Onirocriticis* in Artemidorus's version, and relates to biblical symbolism the "allegorical" or "tropical" imagery interpreted by the *Onirocriticis*.

71. Such an inference is not unwarranted: "It has been computed that in the 404 verses of Apocalypse, 518 OT citations and allusions are found . . . 278 of the 404 verses are made up of reminiscences of Scripture." See Siegman, "Apocalypse," *New Catholic Encyclopedia*, 1:658. The recognition of this shared symbolic vocabulary is almost universal—see, for example, Wesley, *Explanatory Notes upon the New Testament*, p. 652.

72. The distinction between kinds of language is discussed by Roland

Barthes in *Elements of Semiology*, trans. Annette Lavers and Colin Smith (1967; rpt. New York: Hill and Wang, 1977), pp. 9–12. On the figurative and visual component of prophecy, see Warburton, *The Divine Legation of Moses*, 2:66–206 passim.

73. Piaget, *Psychology and Epistemology*, p. 2. Historically, this visionary emphasis on flux, on perpetually ongoing action, actually bridges the conventionally observed categories of transcendentalism (like More's) and empiricism (like Hume's)—see, e.g., Harris, *The Omnipresent Debate*, pp. 22, 25.

74. Many modern commentators agree; thus J. A. MacCulloch writes that the earlier chapters of the Apocalypse present "a series of visions, which are concurrent rather than successive." See "Eschatology," *Encyclopaedia of Religion and Ethics*, 5:387. I shall argue that this principle from biblical aesthetics informs major Romantic poems; here, I argue that the device reorders the perceptions of a prophecy's audience, displacing the order of time by an order of perspective.

This principle, as R. H. Charles has pointed out, is Mede's version of an ancient method of reading the Apocalypse—the method of recapitulation, traceable to Victorinus of Pettau, who was martyred under Diocletian. Charles summarizes the interpretive theory: "The Apocalypse does not represent a strict succession of events following chronologically upon one another, but under each successive series of seven seals, seven trumpets, seven bowls the same events are dealt with." See *Studies in the Apocalypse: Being Lectures Delivered before the University of London*, 2d ed. (Edinburgh: T. & T. Clark, 1915), p. 11; for Charles's discussion of Mede, see pp. 38–39.

75. Mede, *The Key of the Revelation*, pp. 1–9.

76. Swedenborg, *The Apocalypse Revealed*, par. 4.

77. That the *effect* of recapitulation—of synchronism—is to expand perspective is attested by the language of E. F. Siegman, when he summarizes modern developments of this technique: "The septenaries of the seals (6.1–8.1) and the trumpets (8.2–9.21) describe the future of the world from the glorification of Christ to the Last Judgment, mentioned as early as 11.15–18, with emphasis upon world events. The section 12.1–21.8 covers the same period, but centering on the role of the Church. The millennium describes the same period from another viewpoint." ("Apocalypse," *New Catholic Encyclopedia*, 1:658). This coupling of structure (recapitulation) with epistemology (the multiplying of viewpoints) binds visionary art to the philosophy of mind.

In the context of Protestant commentary, which chiefly influenced Blake and Shelley, however, Siegman's conservative approach needs to be qualified: common among Protestants since the Reformation was a historical interpretation that was simultaneous with this synchronic vision: thus, for example, Moses Lowman and Jonathan Edwards agree, in their commentaries on

Revelation, that the Protestant Reformation was an event predicted in the prophecy of the vials; Edwards also maintains that synchronism is a valid method—see Edwards, *Apocalyptic Writings*, ed. Stein, pp. 56–57, 251 and note.

78. More, *An Explanation of the Grand Mystery of Godliness*, in *Theological Works*, pp. 11, ii. See also Warburton, *The Divine Legation of Moses*, 2:94–95.

79. See Stein's introduction to Edwards, *Apocalyptic Writings*, pp. 1–2.

80. See, e.g., Joseph Anthony Mazzeo, "New Wine in Old Bottles: Reflections on Historicity and the Problem of Allegory," in his *Varieties of Interpretation* (Notre Dame, Indiana: University of Notre Dame Press, 1978), pp. 50–51; and Tannenbaum, *Biblical Tradition in Blake's Early Prophecies*, p. 93.

81. More, *Apocalypsis Apocalypseos*, p. 197.

82. Swedenborg, *The Apocalypse Revealed*, 1:3; *True Christian Religion*, par. 156.

83. Swedenborg, *The Apocalypse Revealed*, par. 1; *True Christian Religion*, par. 33.

84. More, *Apocalypsis Apocalypseos*, pp. 127, 52, xxvi, 199, 163, 69. Thus, even among reformers, a conservative and Augustinian interpretation persists: John Calvin, for example, rejects literal millenarianism—see Stein, introduction to Jonathan Edwards, *Apocalyptic Writings*, p. 3.

85. More, *Apocalypsis Apocalypseos*, p. 30. Cf. Charity: "He who follows Christ . . . is already sharing in the eschatological kingdom of God" (*Events and Their Afterlife*, p. 160).

86. More, *An Explanation of the Grand Mystery of Godliness*, in *Theological Works*, pp. 45, 43, 46.

87. Joseph Priestley, *The Doctrines of Heathen Philosophy, Compared with Those of Revelation* (Northumberland: John Binns, 1804). See also David Shelley Berkeley, *Inwrought with Figures Dim: A Reading of Milton's "Lycidas"* (The Hague: Mouton, 1974), pp. 28–32; Paul J. Korshin, "The Development of Abstracted Typology in England, 1650–1820," in *Literary Uses of Typology*, ed. Earl Miner (Princeton: Princeton University Press, 1977), p. 155; Barbara Kiefer Lewalski, "Typological Symbolism and the 'Progress of the Soul' in Seventeenth-Century Literature," in *Literary Uses of Typology*, ed. Miner, p. 103; and Tannenbaum, *Biblical Tradition in Blake's Early Prophecies*, pp. 92, 314n.

88. Isaac Newton, *Observations upon the Prophecies of Daniel and the Apocalypse of St. John* (London: Printed by J. Darby and T. Browne, 1733), pp. 18–19, 254, 14. Of course Newton was not alone in his terrestrial emphasis: cf. Arthur Bedford's *The Scripture Chronology Demonstrated by Astronomical Calculations* (1730), which refutes Newton, but with maps and chronological

tables; and Nathaniel Lardner, *The Credibility of the Gospel History* (17 vols., 1727–57), "a historical apology for the data of Christian revelation." On both Bedford and Lardner, see Stein, introduction to Jonathan Edwards, *Apocalyptic Writings*, p. 67.

89. More, *An Explanation of the Grand Mystery of Godliness*, in *Theological Works*, pp. 4, 328.

90. The quoted phrase appears in the subtitle of More's *Conjectura Cabbalistica* (1653), reprinted in *A Collection of Several Philosophical Writings of Dr. Henry More*, 4th ed. (London: Printed by Joseph Downing, 1712), with separate pagination.

91. Hill, *The World Turned Upside Down*, p. 91.

92. See Hill, *Antichrist in Seventeenth Century England*, pp. 90–91, 130 et passim.

93. I cannot agree with Marjorie Reeves's *The Influence of Prophecy in the Later Middle Ages: A Study in Joachimism* (Oxford: Oxford University Press, 1969), p. viii, that, in the seventeenth century, "prophecy as an attitude towards the future" became "outmoded." In fact, Reeves's valuable study supplies descriptions of Joachim's prophetic literature that illuminate with almost equal aptness the later literature that forms my subject; what she says of Joachim is true of many eighteenth-century commentators, and is also characteristic of the form that I shall be calling Romantic prophecy: "Contemporary happenings form part of the material on which Joachim's mind fed. His meditations . . . were not concerned with a dead history but with a continuing drama. . . . Contemporary events illumined the concords of Scripture; the study of the Testaments gave the clue to the vast events on the threshhold of which Joachim believed he stood" (p. 10). To recognize that this mode of thought did *not* cease with the seventeenth century, we need only to cite Priestley's statement that political revolutions of the eighteenth century were "distinctly and repeatedly foretold in many prophecies, delivered more than two thousand years ago." See *Letters to the Right Honourable Edmund Burke, Occasioned by His Reflections on the Revolution in France, &c.*, 3d ed. (London: Printed by Thomas Pearson, and sold by J. Johnson, 1791), p. 150. Cf. also Bicheno's statement that the French Revolution "is undoubtedly the theme of prophecy" (*The Signs of the Times*, advertisement, p. ix).

Because Thomas Newton and others do concern themselves with practical matters, it is misleading to assert, as Sacvan Bercovitch does, that "the American Puritans changed metaphor to fact. . . . The New World and the remnant now arrived to redeem it were sacred as well as worldly facts. They represented the fulfillment of scriptural promises. . . . History for them was prophecy postdated, and prophecy, history antedated. . . . On these grounds, in defiance of exegetical convention, they recast the modern world as a setting for Armageddon." See "Emerson the Prophet: Romanticism,

Puritanism, and Auto-American-Biography," in *Emerson: Prophecy, Metamorphosis, and Influence*, ed. David Levin (New York: Columbia University Press, 1975), p. 2. The fact is that "exegetical convention" is not *defied* but rather *continued* by such temporal focus: see Reeves, *The Influence of Prophecy in the Later Middle Ages*, p. 10; Hill, *The World Turned Upside Down*, p. 91; George Stanley Faber, *A Dissertation on the Prophecies*, 5th ed. (London: Printed for F. C. and J. Rivington, 1814), 1:xx; and Norman Cohn, *The Pursuit of the Millennium* (London: Secker & Warburg, 1957), pp. 9, 10, 20.

Bercovitch goes on to apply his interpretation to the English Romantic poets, writing that "as a prophetic company, these poets had no country" but were instead guilty of "retreat to the kingdom within" (p.14). This denial of the political pertinence of Romantic prophecy rests on such simplifications as the following: "Blake's Albion symbolizes spiritual wholeness" (p. 14). This is not my view, as will become apparent.

94. Thomas Newton, *Dissertations on the Prophecies*, 3d ed. (London: J. and R. Tonson, 1766), 3: 334, 352. Roston misunderstands the temporal focus of such commentary when he writes that "by the end of the eighteenth century the literalist (and hence literary) approach had won the day" (p. 59). Conservative commentators continued to argue for a "spiritual sense" of prophetic literature, not a literal one, and radical commentators read so figuratively as to discern the French Revolution beneath the Bible's symbols. Though Roston does not mention that political event, it came in fact to dominate English commentary on biblical prophecy in the late eighteenth century.

95. In this connection, compare Hill's statements of the relation of prophecy to politics with this generalization, by William Haller: audiences of English preachers, 1570–1643, took interest specifically "in the psychology of spiritual struggle" and thus English preachers "set out to describe the warfare of the spirit, to portray the drama of the inner life." See *The Rise of Puritanism; or, The Way to the New Jerusalem Set Forth in Pulpit and Press from Thomas Cartwright to John Lilburne and John Milton, 1570–1643* (New York: Columbia University Press, 1938), pp. 32, 33. It is my contention that neither Hill nor Haller is incorrect in his emphasis, except by exclusion: biblical literature, and especially literature of prophecy, is characterized precisely by this multiple reference to the worlds within and without.

For a different formulation of these two kinds of reference, see Wittreich, *Visionary Poetics*, p. 26. More simply, Wittreich subordinates the one level of reference to the other: "The prophet's objective is to re-form history—an objective dependent upon the renovation of individual men." I argue that the relation is more complex: if inner renovation facilitates the reformation of history, it is also true that history—a sustained symbol-system—derives its importance from the *mental* truths that it embodies. Thus, I cannot agree that "prophecy . . . reminds us that vision, unless it inspires action, is nothing, the mental activity involved in its interpretation being a correlative of the later activity that will effect its implementation" (p. 34); instead, history is often perceived as a correlative of prior and universal mental forms. It is in this way that, as More says, a prophecy "may be applicable . . . in any particular Place or Age of the World" (*Apocalypsis Apocalypseos*, p. 12). As Wittreich himself argues elsewhere, prophecy is "not concerned with outward action," but "instead expresses and reveals the mind" (p. 34).

96. Earl R. Wasserman, *The Subtler Language: Critical Readings of Neo-classic and Romantic Poems* (Baltimore: Johns Hopkins University Press, 1959), pp. 101–68.

97. J. F. C. Harrison, *The Second Coming: Popular Millenarianism 1780–1850* (New Brunswick, N.J.: Rutgers University Press, 1979), p. 12.

98. Two studies of Spenser in this connection are Angus Fletcher, *The Prophetic Moment: An Essay on Spenser* (Chicago: University of Chicago Press, 1971); and Kathleen Williams, "Milton: Greatest Spenserian," in *Milton and the Line of Vision*, ed. Joseph Anthony Wittreich, Jr. (Madison: University of Wisconsin Press, 1975), pp. 25–55. On Milton as an exemplar of visionary poetics, see Leland Ryken, *The Apocalyptic Vision in "Paradise Lost"* (Ithaca: Cornell University Press, 1970); Austin C. Dobbins, *Milton and the Book of Revelation: The Heavenly Cycle* (University: University of Alabama Press, 1975); Wittreich, "'A Poet Amongst Poets': Milton and the Tradition of Prophecy," in *Milton and the Line of Vision*, ed. Wittreich, pp. 97–142; and Wittreich, *Visionary Poetics*.

99. Cohn, *The Pursuit of the Millennium*, pp. 7, xiv, 20, 100.

100. Tuveson, *Millennium and Utopia*, p. 30.

101. Significantly, this philosophical complexity distinguishes Christian prophecy, which culminates in the Book of Revelation, from the secular prophecies studied by Rupert Taylor in *The Political Prophecy in England* (New York: Columbia University Press, 1911). Taylor writes of secular prophecies in which "an attempt is made to foretell coming events of a political nature" (p. 2). I write, rather, of the prophetic art for which Shelley, among others, claims multiple meanings: the prophetic poet "beholds the future in the present" and "participates in the eternal, the infinite"; according to this point of view, and with regard to this prophetic art, it is "superstition which would make poetry an attribute of prophecy rather than prophecy an attribute of poetry" (*Prose*, 7:112).

102. Karl Kroeber, *Romantic Narrative Art* (1960; rpt. Madison: University of Wisconsin Press, 1966), pp. 56, 64.

103. Dr. Twisse, unpaginated preface to Mede, *The Key of the Revelation*. So too C. Stuhlmueller observes that, in apocalyptic literature, "almost every earthly element acquired symbolic value." See "Apocalyptic," *New Catholic*

Encyclopedia, ed. William J. McDonald et al. (New York: McGraw-Hill, 1967), 1:663.

104. More, *An Explanation of the Grand Mystery of Godliness*, in *Theological Works*, pp. 117–18.

105. Emanuel Swedenborg, *The Apocalypse Explained*, trans. L. H. Tafel and John Whitehead (New York: The American Swedenborg Printing and Publishing Society, 1911–12), par. 597.

106. I quote from the anonymous *Prophetic Conjectures on the French Revolution* (Philadelphia: William Young, 1794), p. 4, and from Faber, *A Dissertation on the Prophecies*, 1:87.

107. Swedenborg, *The Apocalypse Explained*, pars. 41, 419e.

108. Henry More, *Synopsis Prophetica; or, The Second Part of the Enquiry into the Mystery of Iniquity* (1664), reprinted in *The Theological Works of the Most Pious and Learned Henry More*, p. 532.

109. Faber, *A Dissertation on the Prophecies*, 1:90.

110. Ibid., pp. 89, 137.

111. *Prophetic Conjectures*, p. 4.

112. More, *An Explanation of the Grand Mystery of Godliness*, in *Theological Works*, pp. 122, 1.

113. Lowth, *Lectures on the Sacred Poetry of the Hebrews*, 2:65.

114. See More, *An Explanation of the Grand Mystery of Godliness*, in *Theological Works*, pp. 170, 278, et passim; idem, *Synopsis Prophetica*, in *Theological Works*, p. 532 et passim; and idem, *Apocalypsis Apocalypseos*, pp. xxvi–xxvii, 12, et passim.

115. See Swedenborg, *The Apocalypse Revealed*, par. 1 et passim; Faber, *A Dissertation on the Prophecies*, 1:89.

116. The quoted phrases are from Mede, *The Key of the Revelation*, pp. 40–41 in the separately paginated essay on "The Interpretation of the Little Book"; for his explanation of the six seals, see pp. 40–67 in the main body of the *Key of the Revelation*.

117. More, *An Explanation of the Grand Mystery of Godliness*, in *Theological Works*, pp. 115, 123, 126, 228.

118. Thomas Newton, *Dissertations on the Prophecies*, 3:213.

119. Swedenborg, *The Apocalypse Explained*, pars. 624d and 388c.

120. More, *A Prophetical Exposition of the Seven Epistles Sent to the Seven Churches in Asia* (1669), reprinted in *The Theological Works of the Most Pious and Learned Henry More*, p. 719; Newton, *Observations upon the Prophecies*, p. 304.

121. More, *Synopsis Prophetica*, in *Theological Works*, running head to chapter five, pp. 557, 538.

122. Newton, *Observations upon the Prophecies*, p. 16; Frank E. Manuel,

The Religion of Isaac Newton (Oxford: Oxford University Press, 1974), pp. 19, 95.

123. Manuel, *The Religion of Isaac Newton*, pp. 95–96.

124. Newton, *Observations upon the Prophecies*, pp. 10, 276.

125. More, *Synopsis Prophetica*, in *Theological Works*, pp. 526, 528, 525, 529.

126. D. H. Lawrence, *Apocalypse* (1931; rpt. New York: Viking Press, 1971), p. 87.

127. More, *Synopsis Prophetica*, in *Theological Works*, pp. 530, 531.

128. Milton, *Areopagitica*, ed. Ernest Sirluck, in *Complete Prose Works of John Milton*, ed. Don M. Wolfe et al. (New Haven: Yale University Press, 1959), 2:552–58. Tannenbaum points out Milton's use of typology here; see *Biblical Tradition in Blake's Early Prophecies*, p. 88.

129. See Charity, *Events and Their Afterlife*, pp. 157–58.

130. Tannenbaum, *Biblical Tradition in Blake's Early Prophecies*, p. 88.

131. Wesley, *Explanatory Notes upon the New Testament*, p. 694.

132. See Tannenbaum, *Biblical Tradition in Blake's Early Prophecies*, p. 91 and chapter 4, passim.

133. Mazzeo, "New Wine in Old Bottles," pp. 64–65. On biblical typology as a figural technique, see, besides Mazzeo and Tannenbaum, Erich Auerbach, *Mimesis: The Representation of Reality in Western Literature*, trans. Willard R. Trask (1953; rpt. Princeton: Princeton University Press, 1968), especially pp. 16–17, 73, and 555; and Hans W. Frei, *The Eclipse of Biblical Narrative: A Study in Eighteenth and Nineteenth Century Hermeneutics* (New Haven: Yale University Press, 1974), especially pp. 25–31.

134. More, *Synopsis Prophetica*, in *Theological Works*, pp. 535–36; idem, *Apocalypsis Apocalypseos*, p. 46.

135. A. B. Peganius, *A Genuine Explication of the Visions of the Book of Revelation*, trans. "H. O." (London: Printed by W. G. and sold by Moses Pitt, n.d.), pp. 48, 35–36.

136. More, *Apocalypsis Apocalypseos*, p. 9.

137. Swedenborg, *The Apocalypse Explained*, par. 21.

138. More, *Apocalypsis Apocalypseos*, p. 12.

139. Samuel Taylor Coleridge, "France: An Ode," ll. 40–41, in *Coleridge: Poetical Works*, ed. Ernest Hartley Coleridge (1912; rpt. Oxford: Oxford University Press, 1969).

140. Harrison, *The Second Coming*, p. 5.

141. Thompson, *The Making of the English Working Class* (1963; rpt. New York: Vintage, 1966), p. 50. See also Clarke Garrett, *Respectable Folly: Millenarians and the French Revolution in France and England* (Baltimore: Johns Hopkins University Press, 1975). Garrett identifies Mede as a founder of an English tradition of "scholarly millenarianism" (p. 123), and then cites

Priestley and others in that tradition who perceived "the French Revolution as herald of the millennium" (p. 137).

142. Curtis, "Blake and the Booksellers," p. 171.

143. See Alexander Gilchrist, *The Life of William Blake*, ed. W. Graham Robertson, 2d ed. (London: John Lane, 1907), p. 94; and G. E. Bentley, Jr., *Blake Records* (Oxford: Oxford University Press, 1969), pp. 39–44.

144. William F. Halloran, "*The French Revolution*: Revelation's New Form," in *Blake's Visionary Forms Dramatic*, ed. David V. Erdman and John E. Grant (Princeton: Princeton University Press, 1970), pp. 30–56.

145. Mannheim, *Ideology and Utopia*, p. 38.

146. Faber, *A Dissertation on the Prophecies*, 1: 87, xx, 132; 2:114. Also see, in that work, 1, sig. A2r, and 1:135.

147. Priestley, *Letters to the Right Honourable Edmund Burke*, pp. 150, 143–44.

148. Bicheno, *The Signs of the Times*, Advertisement, p. i; and p. 9.

149. Walmesley, *The General History of the Christian Church*, p. v. The passage appears in the anonymous editor's preface.

150. *Prophetic Conjectures*, pp. 70, 5, 70. So too, the sermons of John Willison (d. 1750) were published after his death with the title, *A Prophecy of the French Revolution . . .* (1793); see Stein, introduction to Jonathan Edwards, *Apocalyptic Writings*, p. 69.

The eclectic procedure of compiling commentaries was also not uncommon; Matthew Poole and John Collinges, for example, collected and summarized prior commentaries, and these writers were especially favorable toward Mede's commentary. See Stein, introduction, pp. 59–60.

151. See Lawrence, *Apocalypse*, pp. 3–13.

152. Abrams, *Natural Supernaturalism*, p. 334.

153. Newton, *Observations upon the Prophecies*, p. 254.

154. Bicheno, *The Signs of the Times*, p. 10; see also *Prophetic Conjectures*, p. 4. Referring to other commentators, Wittreich writes that "the various visions of any given prophecy act as interpreters for all that goes before them," so that each vision is a commentary on a preceding vision (*Visionary Poetics*, p. 32). As I shall argue below in my chapters on Blake and Shelley, this principle of order informs Romantic prophecies as well as the Book of Revelation.

155. Mannheim, *Ideology and Utopia*, p. 3.

156. Lowth, *Lectures on the Sacred Poetry of the Hebrews*, 1:16.

Chapter 2: "Humanity Divine": Blake's *Jerusalem*

1. More, *A Prophetical Exposition of the Seven Epistles Sent to the Seven Churches in Asia*, in *Theological Works*, p. 752.

2. E. B. Murray, "*Jerusalem* Reversed," *Blake Studies* 7, no. 1 (1974): 11.

3. For a discussion of the complex relations between Blake's texts and designs, see W. J. T. Mitchell, *Blake's Composite Art: A Study of the Illuminated Poetry* (Princeton: Princeton University Press, 1978).

4. *Jerusalem* exists in significantly different versions, varying in the order of its plates and also in symbolic detail. These differences occur largely between the colored and uncolored copies of the poem, Blake completing only one colored copy, so far as is known, before his death (copy E). I quote from the Erdman edition—therefore using the plate-order of the Erdman edition—and I note significant differences between the colored and uncolored copies when necessary. My authorities are copy A (British Museum Department of Prints and Drawings), copy E, in facsimile (London: Trianon Press for The William Blake Trust, 1951), and the posthumous copy I (Lessing J. Rosenwald collection, Library of Congress).

5. Irene H. Chayes, "The Marginal Design of *Jerusalem* 12," *Blake Studies* 7, no. 1 (1974): 51–76.

6. See Wittreich, *Angel of Apocalypse*, p. 316n.

7. Swedenborg, *The Apocalypse Explained*, pars. 517, 1188.

8. Wittreich, *Angel of Apocalypse*, p. 316n.

9. See John 10: 1, 2, 7, 9; Rev. 4:1; Swedenborg, *The Apocalypse Explained*, pars. 259, 260½.

10. This translation appears in *The Apocalypse Explained*, where Hebrew *tohu* is literally rendered "void" (Swedenborg, *The Apocalypse Explained*, par. 419e). Blake's knowledge of Hebrew is problematic but likely: the *Night Thoughts* illustrations and *Milton* contain Hebrew, and in 1803—that is, before writing *Jerusalem*—Blake reported his good progress with the language. Two discussions of Blake's knowledge of Hebrew are Harold Fisch, "William Blake," *The Encyclopedia Judaica* (Jerusalem: Keter Publishing House, 1971), 4:1071–72; and Arnold Cheskin, "The Echoing Greenhorn: Blake as Hebraist," *Blake: An Illustrated Quarterly* 12 (1978–79): 178–83.

11. David Bindman reads this watercolor more cheerfully: it depicts "the mercy of Christ" and "Christ's creative role"; see *Blake as an Artist* (Oxford: Phaidon, 1977), p. 188. Bindman also perceives its dire implications, though—the picture implies "man's fall into division" (p. 191).

12. Locke, *Essay Concerning Human Understanding*, 2.11.17.

13. Newton, *Opticks*, p. 77.

14. Swedenborg, *The Apocalypse Explained*, par. 595.

15. Blake shows his knowledge of Newton amply in *Jerusalem*, and elsewhere too. In "To Venetian Artists," for example, he simultaneously discusses Newton's theories of light and God (l. 1).

16. Newton, *Opticks*, p. 168.

17. William Blake, *The Illuminated Blake*, annotated by David V. Erdman (Garden City, N.Y.: Doubleday, 1974), p. 282.

18. Terence Allan Hoagwood, "*The Four Zoas* and 'The Philosophick Cabbala,'" *Blake: An Illustrated Quarterly* 12 (1978): 87–90.

19. See Martin Butlin, "A Newly Discovered Watermark and a Visionary's Way with His Dates," *Blake: An Illustrated Quarterly* 15 (1981): 101–3.

20. This interpretation goes back to Philo's reading, whereby, as J. M. Evans says, "Sense-perception was born when the mind relaxed its attention, when, as Genesis had it, Adam fell asleep." See Evans, *"Paradise Lost" and the Genesis Tradition* (Oxford: Oxford University Press, 1968), p. 72.

21. Gershom G. Scholem, *On the Kabbalah and Its Symbolism*, trans. Ralph Manheim (New York: Schocken Books, 1965), p. 68.

22. William Warburton also discusses the traditional belief that God first taught writing to man with the Ten Commandments, but Warburton refutes this view. See *The Divine Legation of Moses Demonstrated*, 2:139ff.

23. Scholem, *On the Kabbalah and Its Symbolism*, p. 69.

24. Cf. Westermann, *Basic Forms of Prophetic Speech*, p. 15.

25. Quoted in ibid., p. 15.

26. For Henry More, this line from Paul connected cabbalistic theory with Revelation. See *An Explanation of the Grand Mystery of Godliness*, in *Theological Works*, p. 228.

27. On this theory, see Wittreich, "'Sublime Allegory'" and also his "Opening the Seals."

28. For a useful index of More's statements on this point, see *Philosophical Writings of Henry More*, ed. MacKinnon, p. 264.

29. Newton, *The Mathematical Principles of Natural Philosophy*, 2:393.

30. Swedenborg, *The Apocalypse Revealed*, par. 24.

31. Swedenborg, *The Apocalypse Explained*, par. 36; *The Apocalypse Revealed*, par. 24.

32. Blake, *The Illuminated Blake*, p. 284.

33. See More, "The Philosophick Cabbala," in *Conjectura Cabbalistica*.

34. Sir Geoffrey Keynes, *Drawings of William Blake: Ninety-Two Pencil Studies* (New York: Dover, 1970), entry 83.

35. Florence Sandler, "The Iconoclastic Enterprise: Blake's Critique of 'Milton's Religion,'" *Blake Studies* 5, no. 1 (1972): 20.

36. Locke, *Essay Concerning Human Understanding*, 4.29.3.

37. Faber, *A Dissertation on the Prophecies*, 1:132.

38. See Frye, *Fearful Symmetry*, pp. 356–403.

39. John Howard, *Blake's "Milton": A Study in the Selfhood* (Cranbury, N.J.: Fairleigh Dickinson University Press, 1976), p. 15. Within Revelation commentary, *Israelismus* is defined by More; see *Synopsis Prophetica*, in *Theological Works*, p. 530.

40. "Like Milton, Blake inverts whatever patterns he inherits from tradition—his art is continually engaged in inversional transformations," according to Wittreich, "Opening the Seals," p. 55.

41. Harold Bloom, "The Bard of Sensibility and the Form of Prophecy," *Eighteenth-Century Studies* 4 (1970): 6–20, reprinted in idem, *The Ringers in the Tower: Studies in Romantic Tradition* (Chicago: University of Chicago Press, 1971), pp. 65–80; Joanne Witke, *"Jerusalem*: A Synoptic Poem," *Comparative Literature* 22 (1970): 265–78; Stuart Curran, "The Mental Pinnacle: *Paradise Regained* and the Romantic Four-Book Epic," in *Calm of Mind: Tercentenary Essays on "Paradise Regained" and "Samson Agonistes" in Honor of John S. Diekhoff*, ed. Joseph A. Wittreich, Jr., (Cleveland: Case Western Reserve University Press, 1971), pp. 133–62; Frye, *Fearful Symmetry*, pp. 356–403; Karl Kiralis, "The Theme and Structure of William Blake's *Jerusalem*," in *The Divine Vision: Studies in the Poetry and Art of William Blake*, ed. Vivian de Sola Pinto (London: Victor Gollancz, 1957), pp. 141–62; Edward J. Rose, "The Structure of Blake's *Jerusalem*," *Bucknell Review* 11 (1963): 35–54.

42. Roger R. Easson, "William Blake and His Reader in *Jerusalem*," in *Blake's Sublime Allegory*, ed. Curran and Wittreich, pp. 309–28.

43. Curran, "The Structures of *Jerusalem*," in ibid., pp. 329–46.

44. In *Blake's Composite Art*, Mitchell recognizes that "the poem is some species of 'antiform,' that its structure is a denial of our usual ideas of structure" (p. 165). Mitchell however deduces not the traditional form that Blake knew thoroughly and embraced explicitly—the form of prophecy—but rather "encyclopedic anatomy" (p. 175), a compound of form-titles that Mitchell draws from Frye. All the characteristics that Mitchell adduces in support of this generic classification— "the intellectual, philosophical emphasis, the deliberate disregard for mimetic form, the exhaustive scope, the dialectical procedure, and the insistence on an insomniac for its ideal reader" (p. 176)—are more usefully seen as acknowledged elements of traditional prophecy. An awareness of these elements aids understanding of *Jerusalem*, and Mitchell usefully insists on their importance; but to ascribe them to an artificial genre that Blake never even mentioned, instead of the genre that he declared his own, is distracting. The subjects as well as the methods of *Jerusalem* arise directly from its formal context—biblical prophecy.

45. Susan Fox, in *Poetic Form in Blake's "Milton"* (Princeton: Princeton University Press, 1976), p. 6, calls this technique "simultaneity" and she identifies it in *Milton*. Discussing that poem's "presentation of its focal event as it occurs in all its minute particulars on all levels of reality" (p. 19), Fox perceives the immense "range of its applicability" (p. 32), and she explicates *Milton* accordingly. She refers in a vague and general way to the biblical prophecies as somehow pertinent, but does not mention that this particular

strategy—synchronism—was a long-recognized signal of Blake's traditional form. Of *Jerusalem* Fox writes, "It may be . . . that what is now considered progressive may ultimately prove circular, that the events of *Jerusalem*, like those of *Milton*, are all the same event witnessed through various perspectives" (p. 14). Finally, though, Fox retreats into what she admits is a "shaky consensus," and concludes that *Jerusalem*'s structure is linear (p. 14). To believe that it is linear is to believe that Blake wrote clumsily, and that his poem is troubled with artless redundancy; to consult the tradition that Blake embraces is to perceive in *Jerusalem* what Mede, More, Newton, and others perceived in Revelation—synchronism, or what Fox calls "simultaneity."

46. Studying a display of Blake's color prints at the Tate Gallery, I noticed a striking example of this kind of ordering: there, the physical juxtaposition of "Elohim Creating Adam" (Fig. 6) and "Satan Exulting Over Eve" (Fig. 7)— which was then lent from the Bateson collection—makes similar motives obvious: the analogy of Elohim and Satan is inescapable. To pass to the "House of Death" (Fig. 1), a little further down the wall, is to find the motif again—and to discover further implications. This pattern is discernible in Martin Butlin, *William Blake*, a catalogue of an exhibition organized in association with the William Blake Trust (London: Tate Gallery, 1978), pp. 59, 64; and in idem, *The Paintings and Drawings of William Blake: Plates* (New Haven: Yale University Press, 1981), nos. 388, 389, 397.

For discussion of the series of large color prints (1795), see Butlin, "The Evolution of Blake's Large Color Prints of 1795," in *William Blake: Essays for S. Foster Damon*, ed. Alvin H. Rosenfeld (Providence, R.I.: Brown University Press, 1969), pp. 109–16; Anne T. Kostelanetz, "Blake's 1795 Color Prints: An Interpretation," in ibid., pp. 117–30; and Butlin, *The Paintings and Drawings of William Blake: Text* (New Haven: Yale University Press, 1981), pp. 156–77.

On *Jerusalem*, Frye makes a brief but useful observation about the poem's structure: "*Jerusalem* is conceived like a painting of the Last Judgement, stretching from heaven to hell and crowded with figures and allusions. . . . Everything said in the text is intended to fit somewhere into this simultaneous conceptual pattern, not to form a linear narrative." See "The Road of Excess" (1963), reprinted in *Romanticism and Consciousness: Essays in Criticism*, ed. Harold Bloom (New York: Norton, 1970), p. 122.

47. Blake, *The Illuminated Blake*, p. 293.

48. Harrison, *The Second Coming*, p. 12. For related statements by Blake, see *M.H.H.*, plates 9 and 12, and the *Book of Urizen*, plate 2.

49. Randel Helms, "Ezekiel and Blake's *Jerusalem*," *Studies in Romanticism* 13 (1974): 131, 133.

50. Ibid., pp. 134, 136.

51. According to Peter F. Fisher: "The Jews took over the outer expression

of prophetic vision as a national heritage and as a divine promise of future political supremacy. In Christianity there is an inner vision which never completely gives way to the outer allegory of the church. It is to this visionary Christianity which survives the religious and political struggles that Blake gives his allegiance." See *The Valley of Vision*, pp. 54–55. Fisher did not live to apply this insight to *Jerusalem*.

52. Curran, "The Structures of *Jerusalem*," p. 333.

53. Wittreich, "Opening the Seals," p. 43. Mitchell makes a similar point about the structure of the *Book of Urizen*, whose first eight chapters contain "alternative performances of the same event"; see "Poetic and Pictorial Imagination in *The Book of Urizen*," in *The Visionary Hand: Essays for the Study of William Blake's Art and Aesthetics*, ed. Robert N. Essick (Los Angeles: Hennessey and Ingalls, 1973), p. 353.

54. I have found no evidence whatever to indicate that Blake ever knew that Hume also treated time as a mental projection rather than a perceived object.

55. So too, Thomas Paine, whose critique of the Bible Blake defended, uses Anglo-Israelite typology in *Common Sense*, where he compares King George with Pharaoh. See *The Selected Works of Tom Paine and Citizen Tom Paine*, ed. Howard Fast (New York: Modern Library—Random House, 1943), p. 25; for this reference I am indebted to Leslie Tannenbaum's *Biblical Tradition in Blake's Early Prophecies*, p. 95.

56. Erdman, *Blake: Prophet against Empire*, pp. 462–87.

57. Paley argues that, by the time of Night IX of *Vala*, "Blake, having abandoned his revolutionary hopes, no longer employs the eschatological conception of the Hebrew prophets, who had looked for a fulfilment of God's design *in* history. He has turned instead to Revelation for a vision of history." According to this new vision, "As apocalypse breaks into history . . . history is itself destroyed." See *Energy and the Imagination*, pp. 163 and 169.

58. More, "The Philosophick Cabbala," in *Collection of Philosophical Writings*, 2: 18, 20. Citations from this work refer to chapter and paragraph numbers.

59. Frye, *Fearful Symmetry*, pp. 356–57.

60. See Milton, *Paradise Regained*, 4:201–84. All quotations in my text from Milton's poems are from *The Works of John Milton*, ed. Frank Allen Patterson et al., 18 vols. (New York: Columbia University Press, 1931–38).

61. See More, *An Explanation of the Grand Mystery of Godliness*, in *Theological Works*, p. 47; Priestley, *The Doctrines of Heathen Philosophy, Compared with Those of Revelation*, p. 64.

62. Cf. Isa. 63:10 and Ezek. 1:3 on the wrathful God; cf. Matthew 4:3, Luke 4:3, and *Paradise Regained* 1:342–56 for Satan's speech on turning stones to bread.

63. See, e.g., Swedenborg, *The Apocalypse Explained*, pars. 388c and 714a; Mary Baker Eddy, *Key to the Scriptures* (1875; rpt. Boston: Christian Science Publishing Society, n.d.), p. 563.

64. Blake recognized his agreement with Berkeley on this principle, if not with Hume; when Berkeley includes pure space among "the children of imagination," Blake underscores the phrase with approval (*E.*, p. 652).

65. Erdman, *The Illuminated Blake*, p. 342.

66. Newton, *Opticks*, pp. 158, 165, 15, xxxi.

67. Ibid., pp. 14–15.

68. Hoagwood, *"The Four Zoas* and 'The Philosophick Cabbala,'"* pp. 88–89.

69. Holbach, *The System of Nature*, pp. 32–33, 41. For further discussion of the relation between Holbach's thought and Blake's, see Howard, *Blake's "Milton"*, pp. 57, 59–60, 264, and my essay, "Holbach and Blake's Philosophical Statement in 'The voice of the Devil,'" *English Language Notes* 15 (1978): 181–86.

70. Holbach, *The System of Nature*, pp. 53, 28, 11.

71. For some circumstantial evidence that also supports this conclusion, see G. E. Bentley, Jr., "Blake and Swedenborg," *Notes and Queries* 199, n.s. 1 (1954): 264–65. See *The Apocalypse Explained*, pars. 1 and 53 for the quoted phrases.

Chapter 3: "The Prophecy Which Begins and Ends in Thee": Shelley's *Prometheus Unbound*

1. As I shall subsequently show, this statement helps to interpret the overthrow of Jupiter. The description of the overthrow of tyrannical religion recalls traditional interpretations of Antichrist. These interpretations are documented by Christopher Hill, in *Antichrist in Seventeenth Century England*, pp. 90–91 et passim. Hill's argument goes on to suggest that, raised to an intellectual level, Antichrist was susceptible of multiple interpretations: "Experience of the religious changes of the revolution taught Milton that new presbyter was but old priest writ large: it convinced Nathaneal Homes and many others that Antichrist could be incarnated in many more forms than the Pope or the bishops" (p. 90). Multiple incarnation, a characteristic of intellectual rather than topical reference, is also a matter of exegetical and philosophical history, as I have argued above.

On Antichrist as oppressive religious form, see Faber: "The life or vital principle of a beast" is "the principle which causes him to be a beast" (*A Dissertation on the Prophecies*, 1:108). Faber specifies this principle: "a superstition affecting universal dominion" (1:110). Thus, the symbol has multiple reference, "including all persons who answer to the several parts of the ample description which is given of the character of that monster" (1:132). Faber, with whom Shelley engaged in philosophical correspondence, differs from Shelley primarily on other matters, most obviously his atheism and radicalism.

2. This list is not exhaustive, but indicative; Grabo has also explicated numerous optical, biological, and astronomical levels of reference, in *A Newton among Poets*, pp. 118–70 et passim. See also Desmond King-Hele, *Shelley: His Thought and Work*, 2d ed. (Teaneck: Fairleigh Dickinson University Press, 1971), pp. 172, 186–97.

3. Cameron has noted the related contexts of Shelley's art, but tends to subordinate mental to political reference: "It is apparent . . . that although Shelley intended Prometheus to stand primarily for the intellectual rebels of his own age, he also represented all those creative intellectuals, from Homer to Hazlitt, who had advanced culture and the cause of humanity." This quotation is from *Shelley: The Golden Years*, p. 496.

4. For such an interpretation—needlessly narrow, in my view— see Charles E. Robinson, *Shelley and Byron: The Snake and Eagle Wreathed in Fight* (Baltimore: The Johns Hopkins University Press, 1976), pp. 1–2, 4.

5. See Wasserman, *Shelley: A Critical Reading*, p. 283. Wasserman notes that the epigraph is given its title in Shelley's notebook. For another comparison of Shelley's lyrical drama with Aeschylus's play, see Bennett Weaver, "*Prometheus Bound* and *Prometheus Unbound*," *PMLA* 64 (1949): 115–33. Weaver argues that Shelley distinguished his protagonist from Aeschylus's: "Together with the Titan of Aeschylus, with Job and Satan and Tasso, his Prometheus should suffer the oppression of tyranny. But there should be in him no important sense of outrage . . . no boasting followed by compromise" (p. 122).

6. Lowth, *Lectures on the Sacred Poetry of the Hebrews*, 1:14.

7. Shelley's *Essay on Christianity* (*Prose*, 6:227–52) is a sustained discussion of Jesus Christ's doctrines from a philosophical, and especially ethical, perspective.

8. Goodwin, *An Exposition upon the Revelation*, 2:2.

9. Letter from Peacock to P. B. Shelley, January 13, 1819, in *The Works of Thomas Love Peacock*, ed. H. F. B. Brett-Smith and C. E. Jones (n.d.; rpt. New York: AMS Press, 1967), 8:215.

10. Peacock, *The Four Ages of Poetry*, in ibid., p. 24.

11. Stuart Curran, *Shelley's Annus Mirabilis: The Maturing of an Epic Vision* (San Marino, Calif.: Huntington Library, 1975), p. 38.

12. Ibid., p. 95.

13. See Willey, *The Eighteenth-Century Background*, p. 213; William Godwin, *Enquiry Concerning Political Justice and Its Influence on Morals and Happiness*, ed. F. E. L. Priestley (Toronto: University of Toronto Press, 1946),

1:25–26n. In this note Godwin concisely summarizes the history of British idealism, naming Locke, Berkeley, and Hume.

14. Francis Bacon, *The Great Instauration*, in *The New Organon and Related Writings*, ed. Fulton H. Anderson (New York: Liberal Arts Press, 1960), p. 29.

15. See Mary Shelley's note to *Prometheus Unbound*, in *The Complete Works of Percy Bysshe Shelley*, ed. Roger Ingpen and Walter E. Peck (New York: Charles Scribner's Sons, 1926–30), 2:268.

16. Curran, *Shelley's Annus Mirabilis*, pp. 45, 214n.

17. For a useful discussion of Shelley's use of myth, see Wasserman, *Shelley: A Critical Reading*, pp. 272–73. For an earlier account, see Douglas Bush, *Mythology and the Romantic Tradition in English Poetry* (1937; rpt. New York: Norton, 1969), pp. 143–62.

18. Mitchell, *Blake's Composite Art*, p. 127.

19. Tannenbaum, *Biblical Tradition in Blake's Early Prophecies*, p. 118.

20. See Mary Shelley's note to *The Revolt of Islam*, in *Complete Works of Shelley*, 1:409.

21. See Faber, *A Dissertation on the Prophecies*, 1:91; 2:105; 1:87; 1:132–33; 1:135.

22. See, for example, Swedenborg, *The Apocalypse Explained*, pars. 110, 175a.

23. Holbach, *The System of Nature*, p. 50.

24. See Godwin, *Enquiry Concerning Political Justice*, 1:26, 37. For evidence of Shelley's reading and rereading of Godwin, see *The Letters of Percy Bysshe Shelley*, ed. Frederick L. Jones (Oxford: Clarendon Press, 1964), 1: 21, 28; *Mary Shelley's Journal*, ed. Frederick L. Jones (Norman: University of Oklahoma Press, 1947), pp. 18, 69–70, 86, 130–31. Mary Shelley indicates that on the same day in 1820 Shelley read Ezekiel and *Political Justice*.

H. N. Brailsford has written a book entitled *Shelley, Godwin and Their Circle* (1913; rpt. Hamden, Conn.: Archon Books, 1969), and Cameron provides a useful discussion of the relation between Godwin's and Shelley's thought in *The Young Shelley: Genesis of a Radical*, pp. 61–70.

25. For a discussion of Shelley's skeptical idealism and its debt to Sir William Drummond, see Pulos, *The Deep Truth*, pp. 24–25 et passim. Pulos correctly observes that "Shelley's acceptance of immaterialism . . . functioned . . . not in conflict but in harmony with" his political radicalism (p. 54).

26. See Hume, *A Treatise of Human Nature*, pp. 371, 385–86.

27. Godwin writes that "the doctrine of necessity will teach us to look upon punishment with no complacence, and at all times to prefer the most direct means of encountering error, the development of truth." See the

218

NOTES TO PAGES 139–142

Enquiry Concerning Political Justice, 1:393. From this position he opposes tyrannicide (1:300–304) and violent revolutions (1:271–72). Book 7 is devoted entirely to the subject of crimes and punishments.

28. John W. Wright places that development even later, pointing to the *Defence of Poetry*. See *Shelley's Myth of Metaphor* (Athens: University of Georgia Press, 1970), p. 8.

29. See Wasserman, *Shelley: A Critical Reading*, pp. 255–57.

30. Robinson argues thus: "Shelley uses the phrase 'one mind' to designate not the ontological unity into which all human minds are subsumed, but rather the epistemological unity of thoughts in an individual human mind." See *Shelley and Byron*, p. 246.

31. Cf. *Paradise Lost*, 4:20–23.

32. Isa. 29:6.

33. Rev. 6:12–16.

34. See Isa. 66:15; Jer. 23:19; Ezek. 1:4.

35. Ex. 9:18; see Isa. 28:2, 28:17; Rev. 8:7, 11:19, 16:21.

36. Aeschylus, *Prometheus Bound*, trans. Herbert Weir Smyth, in *Aeschylus* (1922; rpt. Cambridge, Mass.: Harvard University Press; London: William Heinemann, 1963), 1:309. This is the Loeb Classical Library edition.

37. Ex. 9:23.

38. Isa. 29:6.

39. Milton Wilson argues that "Prometheus is regenerated when he abjures hate for pity, and revenge for forgiveness." See *Shelley's Later Poetry: A Study of the Prophetic Imagination* (New York: Columbia University Press, 1959), p. 71. Ross Greig Woodman disputes that interpretation, arguing that Prometheus "has not yet found the way to release himself from the vicious circle in which good and evil merge in a legalistic morality"; see *The Apocalyptic Vision in the Poetry of Shelley* (Toronto: University of Toronto Press, 1964), p. 111.

40. For different descriptions of this identification, see Wilson, *Shelley's Later Poetry*, p. 64; Woodman, *Apocalyptic Vision*, p. 116; and Wasserman, *Shelley: A Critical Reading*, p. 259.

41. Curran writes that "the Phantasm of Jupiter is a Fravashi . . . a daemonic force resembling that which Socrates claimed to possess and, in the aggregate, bearing affinities with the pantheon of Christian saints. The Fravashis are active, guardian spirits." See *Shelley's Annus Mirabilis*, p. 73. The Phantasm little resembles "Christian saints," perhaps, and may differ significantly from "guardian spirits," but Curran does cite what he calls "an exact source for the double" of Zoroaster, mentioned in 1:191–93—his Fravashi; see *Shelley's Annus Mirabilis*, pp. 73–74, 223n.

Grabo had earlier provided a Neoplatonic interpretation, citing a doctrine of Porphyry; see *"Prometheus Unbound": An Interpretation* (1935; rpt. New York: Gordian Press, 1968), pp. 25–27. Grabo summarizes: "The soul presides over its earthly 'vehicle' which awaits the spirit in the lower world until the decease of the earthly body. The 'shadows of all forms that think and live' are the vehicles prepared for them, having no life of their own until inhabited by the spirits of the dead" (p. 27). Grabo observes, too, that "if the image which resides in Hades is the creation of intellection, as in Platonic theology all worldly existences and the unrealities of matter are, it follows intelligibly enough that all the thoughts, imaginings, and desires of men have likewise their images" (p. 27).

Also prior to Curran's discovery, Cameron had written that "the general concept is ultimately Platonic or Indian, yet in the specific form given by Shelley it is neither, for Shelley's other-world is an inferior image ('shadow') of actuality, whereas in Plato or the *Upanishads* actuality is an inferior image of the One." See *Shelley: The Golden Years*, p. 503.

42. Cf. *Paradise Lost*, 1:294–95.

43. Cf. ibid., 1:97.

44. Holbach, *The System of Nature*, p. 181.

45. Locke, *An Essay Concerning Human Understanding*, 3.6.11.

46. Grabo, *"Prometheus Unbound": An Interpretation*, p. 30.

47. Godwin, *Enquiry Concerning Political Justice*, 1:259.

48. In 1810 Shelley had complained that "religion fetters a reasoning mind" (*Letters*, 1:51).

49. John Milton, *Samson Agonistes*, 1.41.

50. Shelley writes that *The Age of Reason* "was written by that great & good man under circumstances in which only great & good men are ever found; at the bottom of a dungeon under momentary expectation of death for having opposed a tyrant" (*Letters*, 2:143).

51. Thomas Paine, *The Age of Reason, Part the First*, in *The Theological Works of Thomas Paine* (London: R. Carlile, 1819), p. 13.

52. For a discussion of the poem's political reference, see Kenneth Neill Cameron: "The Social Philosophy of Shelley," *The Sewanee Review* 50 (1942): 457–66; "The Political Symbolism of Prometheus Unbound," *PMLA* 58 (1943): 728–53; *Shelley: The Golden Years*, pp. 475–564.

Gerald MacNiece, in *Shelley and the Revolutionary Idea* (Cambridge, Mass.: Harvard University Press, 1969), argues that Shelley "remained the ardent disciple of revolutionary idealism throughout his life" (p. 1), and finds that "Shelley defined the idea of revolution in *Prometheus Unbound*. It must occur within the mind of man, perhaps within the mind of every man before the true change can be expressed in nature and society" (p. 221). MacNiece's use of the word *true* displays his bias, which, it seems to me, slights Shelley's complexity: Shelley's achievement was to refer to *both* levels of reality. Elsewhere, however, MacNiece's study keeps several levels of reference in view: see pp. 7, 239. Carl Woodring, in *Politics in English Romantic Poetry*

(Cambridge, Mass.: Harvard University Press, 1970), observes that Shelley's early poems address a "political idea rather than a political situation" (p. 238) and that in *Prometheus Unbound* events such as the French Revolution provide examples only: "The torturing of Prometheus reveals certain laws that underlay the revolution" (p. 280). Cameron's study also unfolds more than political reference, explicating "the multiplicity of meaning in which Shelley delighted" (see *Shelley: The Golden Years*, p. 523), but ending with emphasis on the poem's reference to "those intellectuals who are interested in 'reform'" and the "radical movement" (p. 564).

53. Maria Gisborne recorded in her journal for August 22, 1820, that Godwin "has not seen the Prometheus, and does not think he shall read it through"; she adds his reason for not reading the poem, a reason which ironically aligns Godwin's judgment with that of *The Quarterly Review*: "He hates to read books that are full of obscurities and puzzles." That Godwin did not in fact read the poem through is also evident from his remark, paraphrased by Gisborne, that Shelley "never writes with a calm, proper tone, but rather with anger, and bitterness, and violence." See *Maria Gisborne & Edward E. Williams: Shelley's Friends, Their Journals and Letters*, ed. Frederick L. Jones (Norman: University of Oklahoma Press, 1951), p. 45. For *The Quarterly Review*'s complaints about the poem's obscurity, see *The Quarterly Review* of October, 1821, reprinted in Newman Ivey White, *The Unextinguished Hearth: Shelley and His Contemporary Critics* (1938; rpt. New York: Octagon Books, 1972), pp. 240–50.

54. See *Prometheus Bound*, pp. 237–39.

55. For Shelley's conflicting attitudes, see *Prose*, 6: 194, 208.

56. See Grabo, *A Newton among Poets*, pp. 89–158. On the history of the concept of ether, see also Mary Hesse, "Ether," *The Encyclopedia of Philosophy*, 3:66–69.

57. Also see Curran, *Shelley's Annus Mirabilis*, p. 77, on Zoroastrian cave-symbolism.

58. Rev. 10:7.

59. Cf. Rev. 6:2.

60. Thomas Paine, *Rights of Man*, in *The Life and Works of Thomas Paine*, ed. William M. Van der Weyde (New Rochelle, N.Y.: Thomas Paine National Historical Association, 1925), 7:5–6.

61. Abrams also compares the union in *Prometheus Unbound* with the bridal union in the Book of Revelation, as one example of the apocalyptic marriage that appears so often in Romantic literature. See *Natural Supernaturalism*, pp. 303–4.

62. For a list of earlier discussions of this technique, see Lawrence John Zillman, ed., *Shelley's "Prometheus Unbound": A Variorum Edition* (Seattle: University of Washington Press, 1959), p. 305.

63. Lowth, *Lectures on the Sacred Poetry of the Hebrews*, 2:65.

64. Ibid., 1:117–18.

65. Rev. 10:6.

66. The most common interpretation of Demogorgon is Necessity: thus Grabo, *"Prometheus Unbound": An Interpretation*, p. 73; Carlos Baker, *Shelley's Major Poetry: The Fabric of a Vision* (1948; rpt. New York: Russell and Russell, 1961), p. 116; and Cameron, *Shelley: The Golden Years*, pp. 512–15. James Rieger has suggestively remarked that "Demogorgon is the Imagination, and his work is the poetry of Creation itself"; see *The Mutiny Within: The Heresies of Percy Bysshe Shelley* (New York: George Braziller, 1967), p. 143. According to Wasserman, in *Shelley: A Critical Reading*, p. 319, Demogorgon is "infinite potentiality." Curran calls Demogorgon "a subsuming power" in *Shelley's Annus Mirabilis*, p. 84. Mary Shelley's statement has perhaps been the guide for these commentators: she calls Demogorgon "the Primal Power of the world"; see note to *Prometheus Unbound*, in *Complete Works of Shelley*, 2:269. Thus Robinson affirms that "Demogorgon . . . is the same figure Shelley in the *Essay on Christianity* called 'God'" (*Shelley and Byron*, p. 119), but he does not mention the fact that in that essay Shelley is summarizing Jesus Christ's apparent doctrines, *not* Shelley's own. Elsewhere Robinson writes that Prometheus and Demogorgon are "two modal representations of the perfection to which human nature might aspire by means of the imagination" (p. 118). I am suggesting that Demogorgon can be more usefully interpreted by reference both to Shelley's principles and to his poem's structure. To do so will obviate inconsistency and confusion.

67. *Inferno*, in *The Divine Comedy of Dante Alighieri*, trans. Henry F. Cary (1805; rpt. New York: P. F. Collier & Son, 1909), p. 5.

68. Ibid., p. 5.

69. Cf. *Queen Mab:*

> I tell thee that those living things,
> To whom the fragile blade of grass,
>   That springeth in the morn
>   And perisheth ere noon,
>   Is an unbounded world;
> I tell thee that those viewless beings,
> Whose mansion is the smallest particle
> Of the impassive atmosphere,
>   Think, feel and live like man.
>
> (2:226–34)

For Grabo's comment on the passage and Erasmus Darwin's theory, see *A Newton among Poets*, pp. 23–24.

70. *Paradise Lost*, 1:63.

71. Milton Wilson observes that positive conclusions emerge from Asia's dialogue with Demogorgon and that "Asia contributes them, not Demogorgon." See *Shelley's Later Poetry,* p. 144.

72. These lines and the whole of Asia's speech reward close study. Curran has shown, for instance, that its similarities with, and differences from, the Earth's comparable speech in act 1 reflect a dramatic interplay of perspectives; see *Shelley's Annus Mirabilis*, p. 42. On the simultaneity of acts 1 and 2, see Bennett Weaver, *Prometheus Unbound* (1957; rpt. Hamden, Conn.: Archon Books, 1969), p. 13.

73. Curran, *Shelley's Annus Mirabilis*, p. 100.

74. Wasserman, *Shelley: A Critical Reading*, pp. 307–8.

75. Ibid., p. 319. Wasserman transcribes the quoted phrase from Shelley's manuscript.

76. Ibid.

77. For another example of just this kind of double talk, see Wilson: "Demogorgon . . . exists at the point where nothing becomes something"; see *Shelley's Later Poetry*, p. 135. Of course Demogorgon *does* dramatize a nexus of intellect and action—and the location in act 2 of this dialogue emphasizes this fact, but Wilson's more useful statements are these: Demogorgon, like the Necessity he is taken to represent, is a fiction (see p. 139), and Demogorgon "is eternal only by courtesy and default" (p. 208).

78. Wasserman, *Shelley: A Critical Reading*, p. 315.

79. Curran provides a useful survey of Shelley's mythological sources and an undogmatic description of Asia's descent to Demogorgon as "a syncretic ritual designed to draw together its many allusions into a conceptualized human framework"; see *Shelley's Annus Mirabilis*, p. 53; also see pp. 38, 51–52, and 85.

80. Pulos, in *The Deep Truth*, p. 77 et passim, explicates the skeptical idealism to which I refer here.

81. I quote the passage from John Freccero's introduction to *The Paradiso*, trans. John Ciardi (New York: New American Library, 1970), p. xii.

82. In *A Study of English Romanticism* (1968; rpt. New York: Random House, n.d., p. 111), Northrop Frye makes a claim that, in his general essay, is not pursued in the minute particulars of the poem: "The unity of *Prometheus Unbound* is the unity of a theme which exists all at once in various aspects, and where the narrative can therefore only move from the periphery into the center and out again." Of course this insight *can* be pursued in the poem's details, and—though Frye's book does not make the point—it can be pursued also in Blake's poetry and in the visionary aesthetic tradition in which both poets' works belong.

83. James William Johnson, "Lyric," *Princeton Encyclopedia of Poetry and*

Poetics, ed. Alex Preminger (1965; rpt. Princeton: Princeton University Press, 1972), p. 463.

84. Ibid., p. 463.

85. Woodman observes that "Shelley, then, by sustaining the parallelism between Prometheus and Jupiter, is simultaneously presenting two approaches to the apocalypse"; Woodman identifies these as "the secular apocalypse of the *philosophes*" and "the pagan apocalypse of the Orphic poets which, with his growing faith in the creative imagination, came to replace his earlier mechanistic philosophy"; see *The Apocalyptic Vision in the Poetry of Shelley*, p. 113. Woodman is correct about the simultaneous structures, but his contextual coordinates may be misleading. Shelley does reject large parts of the French philosophy of material mechanism prior to 1819, but he retains its humanistic emphasis and he makes use of its unification of mind and matter. His "apocalyptic vision," moreover, is not primarily Platonic, Orphic, or pagan at all: he draws on the Bible and the visionary philosophies that incorporate elements of Platonism, and the poem's ethical coordinates arise from biblical tradition.

86. Cf. Rev. 20:1–3.

87. Wasserman, *Shelley: A Critical Reading*, p. 289.

88. Oliver Elton, *A Survey of English Literature: 1780–1830* (New York: Macmillan, 1924), 2:195.

89. Curran observes that "Zoroaster's religious grotto, from which subsequent eastern, Mithraic, and Greek cave worship emanates, becomes itself a symbol—of the creative mind, of the gestating womb of art"; see *Shelley's Annus Mirabilis*, p. 77. More important than the conjectured source is the insight yielded by this speculation: "In exchanging mountain for cave, an external and unresponsive nature for a world of intellectual symbols, Prometheus commits himself to the destiny of man, to a human fellowship and the love that renders it possible" (p. 77).

90. Wasserman, in *Shelley: A Critical Reading*, pp. 255–57, provides a complex explanation of the same problem, citing different passages from the poem and reaching a different conclusion from mine; nevertheless, I am indebted to his analysis.

91. One such reader is Milton Wilson, who finds in *Hellas* a statement of Shelley's "obsessive sense of the insubstantiality and impermanence of this universe in Time and of his reliance on a world of eternal thought, which alone has being, and of which this world of becoming can only provide 'idle shadows.'" See *Shelley's Later Poetry*, p. 182.

92. Wittreich, "'A Poet amongst Poets': Milton and the Tradition of Prophecy," in *Milton and the Line of Vision*, p. 106.

93. Piaget, quoted in Hans G. Furth, *Piaget and Knowledge: Theoretical Foundations* (Englewood Cliffs, N.J.: Prentice-Hall, 1969), p. 24.

94. Wittreich, "'A Poet amongst Poets': Milton and the Tradition of Prophecy," in *Milton and the Line of Vision*, p. 107.

95. A very general hint from Frye accords with this analysis: "A hope based on human love becomes a future-directed hope for the earthly and social regeneration of all mankind"; see *A Study of English Romanticism*, p. 105.

96. See Grabo, *A Newton among Poets*, pp. 140–45, and Curran, *Shelley's Annus Mirabilis*, pp. 106–10.

97. Without reference to the form and ideology of prophecy, Frye briefly observes something similar here: "For Shelley the liberation of man and the liberation of nature are different aspects of the same thing"; see *A Study of English Romanticism*, p. 99.

98. See Wilson, *Shelley's Later Poetry*, pp. 174–75.

99. The scriptural quotations are from Rev. 21:22.

100. Cf. Rev. 20:1–3.

Epilogue: "The Sublime System"

1. In *Shelley and His Circle: 1773–1822*, ed. Kenneth Neill Cameron and Donald H. Reiman (Cambridge, Mass.: Harvard University Press, 1973), 4:614n., Reiman points out that Leigh Hunt's *Literary Pocketbook* for 1820 lists Blake among "eminent living artists," citing his "poetical subjects." Shelley himself does not mention Blake. Cameron concludes (in *Shelley: The Golden Years*, p. 134) that "there is no evidence that he had read Blake, and it is most unlikely that he had, for not only was Blake virtually unknown, but his method of producing his works by engraving limited his market to a handful of readers." Cameron does make brief but useful comparisons of the two writers' social and literary theories (pp. 133, 134, 188, 192, 204, 475).

To approach the question of possible influence from the other perspective, S. Foster Damon, in *A Blake Dictionary: The Ideas and Symbols of William Blake* (1965; rpt. New York: E. P. Dutton & Co., 1971), writes that Blake "must have known of the son-in-law of his friends William Godwin and Mary Wollstonecraft" (p. 314). Such an inference is plausible; Damon goes on, however, to suggest that the episode in *Jerusalem* of the Bard of Oxford "is evidently a tribute to Shelley" (p. 314), an identification that Erdman has called "attractive—but quite indefensible" (*Blake: Prophet against Empire*, p. 479). Erdman's book also contains helpful short comparisons of the two writers (see p. 375, for example, on Prometheus), as do many other critical studies. There are, for instance, numerous references to Blake in Woodman, *The Apocalyptic Vision in the Poetry of Shelley*; Rieger, *The Mutiny Within*; and

Curran, "The Mental Pinnacle," and *Shelley's Annus Mirabilis*. Also see Frye's several comments on the two writers, especially in *Fearful Symmetry*, pp. 305–306, and Bloom's in *Shelley's Mythmaking* (New Haven: Yale University Press, 1959). Bloom also has chapters on Blake and Shelley in *The Visionary Company: A Reading of English Romantic Poetry*, rev. ed. (Ithaca, N.Y.: Cornell University Press, 1971).

2. Coleridge, *Biographia Literaria . . . with His Aesthetical Essays*, ed. J. Shawcross (Oxford: Clarendon Press, 1907), 1:202.

3. Shaffer, *"Kubla Khan" and the Fall of Jerusalem*, p. 90.

4. See More, *An Explanation of the Grand Mystery of Godliness*, in *Theological Works*, pp. 43–47.

5. Shaffer, *"Kubla Khan" and the Fall of Jerusalem*, p. 7.

6. Ronald L. Grimes, "Time and Space in Blake's Major Prophecies," in *Blake's Sublime Allegory*, ed. Curran and Wittreich, p. 65.

7. See Newman Ivey White, *The Unextinguished Hearth: Shelley and His Contemporary Critics* (1938; rpt. New York: Octagon Books, 1972), p. 140.

8. Abrams, *Natural Supernaturalism*, p. 47.

9. Ibid., p. 334.

10. Baker, *Shelley's Major Poetry*, p. 283.

11. Coleridge, *Biographia Literaria*, 1:183.

12. Coleridge, "On Poesy or Art," ibid., 2:254.

13. Ibid.

14. *Collected Letters of Samuel Taylor Coleridge*, ed. E. L. Griggs (Oxford: Clarendon Press, 1956–71), 4:545.

15. Eduard König, "Prophecy (Hebrew)," *Encyclopedia of Religion and Ethics*, ed. James Hastings et al. (Edinburgh: T. and T. Clark, 1908–26), 10:391.

16. Ezek. 11:15.

17. "Dejection: An Ode," l. 47, in *Coleridge: Poetical Works*.

Bibliography

Abrams, M. H. "English Romanticism: The Spirit of the Age." In *Romanticism Reconsidered*. Edited by Northrop Frye. Pp. 26–72. New York: Columbia University Press, 1963.

———. *Natural Supernaturalism: Tradition and Revolution in Romantic Literature*. 1971. Reprint. New York: Norton, 1973.

Aeschylus. *Prometheus Bound*. In *Aeschylus*. With an English translation by Herbert Weir Smyth. 1:209–315. 1922. Reprint. Cambridge, Mass.: Harvard University Press; London: William Heinemann, 1963.

Altizer, Thomas J. J. *The New Apocalypse: The Radical Christian Vision of William Blake*. East Lansing: Michigan State University Press, 1967.

Arnold, Matthew. "The Function of Criticism at the Present Time." In *The Complete Prose Works of Matthew Arnold*. Edited by R. H. Super. 3:258–85. Ann Arbor: University of Michigan Press, 1960–77.

Auerbach, Erich. *Mimesis: The Representation of Reality in Western Literature*. Translated by Willard R. Trask. 1953. Reprint. Princeton: Princeton University Press, 1968.

Ault, Donald. *Visionary Physics: Blake's Response to Newton*. 1974. Reprint. Chicago: University of Chicago Press, 1975.

Bacon, Francis. *The Great Instauration*. In *The New Organon and Related Writings*. Edited by Fulton H. Anderson. Pp. 1–29. New York: Liberal Arts Press, 1960.

Baker, Carlos. *Shelley's Major Poetry: The Fabric of a Vision*. 1948. Reprint. New York: Russell and Russell, 1961.

Barthes, Roland. *Elements of Semiology*. Translated by Annette Lavers and Colin Smith. 1967. Reprint. New York: Hill and Wang, 1977.

Becker, Carl L. *The Heavenly City of the Eighteenth-Century Philosophers*. 1932. Reprint. New Haven: Yale University Press, 1969.

Bentley, G. E., Jr. "Blake and Swedenborg." *Notes and Queries*, 1 (1954), pp. 264–65.

———. *Blake Books*. Oxford: Clarendon Press, 1977.

———. *Blake Records*. Oxford: Oxford University Press, 1969.

Bercovitch, Sacvan. "Emerson the Prophet: Romanticism, Puritanism, and Auto-American-Biography." In *Emerson: Prophecy, Metamorphosis, and Influence*. Edited by David Levin. New York: Columbia University Press, 1975.

Berkeley, George. *A Treatise Concerning the Principles of Human Knowledge*. In

The Works of George Berkeley Bishop of Cloyne. Edited by A. A. Luce and T. E. Jessop. 2:1–113. London: Thomas Nelson and Sons, 1949.

Bicheno, J. *The Signs of the Times.* Providence, R.I.: Carter and Wilkinson, 1794.

Bindman, David. *Blake as an Artist.* Oxford: Phaidon, 1977.

Blake, William. *Blake's Job. William Blake's "Illustrations of the Book of Job."* With an introduction and commentary by S. Foster Damon. 1966. Reprint. Providence, R.I.: Brown University Press, 1967.

———. *For Children / The / Gates / of / Paradise / 1793 / Published by W Blake No 13 / Hercules Buildings Lambeth / and / J. Johnson St Pauls Church Yard.* Copies A and D. Library of Congress, The Collection of Mr. Lessing J. Rosenwald.

———. *For the Sexes / The Gates / of / Paradise.* London: W. Blake, 1793. Copy K. Library of Congress, the Collection of Mr. Lessing J. Rosenwald.

———. *The Grave: A Poem. Illustrated by Twelve Etchings Executed by Louis Schiavonetti, From the Original Inventions of William Blake, 1808.* Illustrations reprinted as *William Blake's Illustrations to the Grave.* Double Elephant–San Vito Press series, no. 3, 1969. Reprint. London: Wildwood House, 1973.

———. *The Illuminated Blake.* Annotated by David V. Erdman. Garden City, N.Y.: Doubleday, 1974.

———. *Illustrations of the Book of Job, In Twenty-one Plates, Invented and Engraved By WILLIAM BLAKE, Author of Designs to "Blair's Grave," "Young's Night Thoughts," &c.* London: William Blake and J. Linnell, 1826. Newberry Library, Chicago.

———. *Illustrations of the Book of Job, Invented & Engraved by William Blake 1825.* Reprinted with a new introduction by Michael Marqusee. New York: Paddington Masterpieces of the Illustrated Book, 1976.

———. *Jerusalem / The Emanation of / The Giant Albion / 1804 / Printed by W.Blake, Sth Molton S^{t}.* Copy A, British Museum Department of Prints and Drawings; copy I, printed ca. 1831, Library of Congress, the Collection of Mr. Lessing J. Rosenwald.

———. Pencil Sketch for *Jerusalem*, plate 41. Library of Congress, the Collection of Mr. Lessing J. Rosenwald.

———. *The Poetry and Prose of William Blake.* Edited by David V. Erdman. Rev. ed. Garden City, N.Y.: Doubleday, 1970.

———. *William Blake: Jerusalem. A Facsimile of the Illuminated Book.* London: Trianon Press for the William Blake Trust, 1951.

Bloom, Harold. "The Bard of Sensibility and the Form of Prophecy." *Eighteenth-Century Studies* 4 (1970): 6–20. Reprinted in idem, *The Ringers in the Tower: Studies in Romantic Tradition.* Pp. 65–80. Chicago: University of Chicago Press, 1971.

——. *Shelley's Mythmaking*. New Haven: Yale University Press, 1959.

——. *The Visionary Company: A Reading of English Romantic Poetry*. Rev. ed. Ithaca, N.Y.: Cornell University Press, 1971.

Bloomfield, Morton W. *"Piers Plowman" as a Fourteenth-Century Apocalypse*. New Brunswick, N.J.: Rutgers University Press, 1961.

Boswell, James. *The Life of Johnson Together with Boswell's Journal of a Tour to the Hebrides and Johnson's Diary of a Journey into North Wales*. Edited by George Birkbeck Hill and revised by L. F. Powell. 6 vols. 1934–50. Reprint. Oxford: Oxford University Press, 1971.

Bowman, J. W. "Revelation." *The Interpreter's Dictionary of the Bible: An Illustrated Encyclopedia*. Edited by George Arthur Buttrick et al. New York: Abingdon, 1962. Vol. 4.

Brailsford, H. N. *Shelley, Godwin and Their Circle*. 1913. Reprint. Hamden, Conn.: Archon Books, 1969.

Bush, Douglas. *Mythology and the Romantic Tradition in English Poetry*. 1937. Reprint. New York: Norton, 1969.

Butlin, Martin. "The Evolution of Blake's Large Color Prints of 1795." In *William Blake: Essays for S. Foster Damon*. Edited by Alvin H. Rosenfeld. Pp. 109–16. Providence, R.I.: Brown University Press, 1969.

——. "A Newly Discovered Watermark and a Visionary's Way with His Dates." *Blake: An Illustrated Quarterly* 15 (1981): 101–103.

——. *The Paintings and Drawings of William Blake*. 2 vols. New Haven: Yale University Press, 1981.

——. *William Blake*. Catalogue of an exhibition organized in association with the William Blake Trust. London: Tate Gallery, 1978.

Cameron, Kenneth Neill. "The Political Symbolism of *Prometheus Unbound*." *PMLA* 58 (1943): 728–53.

——. *Shelley: The Golden Years*. Cambridge, Mass.: Harvard University Press, 1974.

——. "The Social Philosophy of Shelley." *The Sewanee Review* 50 (1942): 457–66.

——. *The Young Shelley: Genesis of a Radical*. New York: Macmillan, 1950.

——, and Donald H. Reiman, eds. *Shelley and His Circle: 1773–1822*. 6 vols. to date. Cambridge, Mass.: Harvard University Press, 1974.

Charity, A. C. *Events and Their Afterlife: The Dialectics of Christian Typology in the Bible and Dante*. Cambridge: Cambridge University Press, 1966.

Charles, R. H. "Apocalyptic Literature." *A Dictionary of the Bible Dealing with Its Language, Literature, and Contents*. Edited by James Hastings et al. New York: Charles Scribner's Sons, 1898. Vol. 1.

——. *Studies in the Apocalypse: Being Lectures Delivered before the University of London*. 2d ed. Edinburgh: T. & T. Clark, 1915.

Chayes, Irene H. "The Marginal Design of *Jerusalem* 12." *Blake Studies* 7, no. 1 (1974): 51–76.

Cheskin, Arnold. "The Echoing Greenhorn: Blake as Hebraist." *Blake: An Illustrated Quarterly* 12 (1978–79): 178–83.

Cohn, Norman. *The Pursuit of the Millennium*. London: Secker & Warburg, 1957.

Coleridge, Samuel Taylor. *Biographia Literaria . . . with His Aesthetical Essays*. Edited by J. Shawcross. 2 vols. Oxford: Clarendon Press, 1907.

———. *Coleridge: Poetical Works*. Edited by Ernest Hartley Coleridge. 1912. Reprint. Oxford: Oxford University Press, 1969.

———. *Collected Letters of Samuel Taylor Coleridge*. 6 vols. Edited by E. L. Griggs. Oxford: Clarendon Press, 1956–71.

Curran, Stuart. "The Mental Pinnacle: *Paradise Regained* and the Romantic Four-Book Epic." In *Calm of Mind: Tercentenary Essays on "Paradise Regained" and "Samson Agonistes" in Honor of John S. Diekhoff*. Edited by Joseph Anthony Wittreich, Jr. Pp. 133–62. Cleveland: Case Western Reserve University Press, 1971.

———. *Shelley's Annus Mirabilis: The Maturing of an Epic Vision*. San Marino, Calif.: Huntington Library, 1975.

———, and Joseph Anthony Wittreich, Jr., eds. *Blake's Sublime Allegory: Essays on "The Four Zoas," "Milton," "Jerusalem."* Madison: University of Wisconsin Press, 1973.

Curtis, F. B. "Blake and the Booksellers." *Blake Studies* 6, no. 2 (1976): 167–78.

Damon, S. Foster. *A Blake Dictionary: The Ideas and Symbols of William Blake*. 1965. Reprint. New York: E. P. Dutton and Co., 1971.

Dante Alighieri. *Inferno*. In *The Divine Comedy of Dante Alighieri*. Trans. Henry F. Cary. 1805. Reprint. New York: P. F. Collier & Son, 1909.

———. *The Paradiso*. Translated by John Ciardi. Introduction by John Freccero. New York: New American Library, 1970.

Descartes, René. *Discourse on Method*. Translated by Laurence J. Lafleur. 2d ed. Indianapolis: Bobbs-Merrill, 1956.

Dobbins, Austin C. *Milton and the Book of Revelation: The Heavenly Cycle*. University: University of Alabama Press, 1975.

Eddy, Mary Baker. *Key to the Scriptures*. 1875. Reprint. Boston: Christian Science Publishing Society, n.d.

Edwards, Jonathan. *Apocalyptic Writings*, edited and with an introduction by Stephen J. Stein. Vol. 5 of *The Works of Jonathan Edwards*. Edited by John E. Smith. New Haven: Yale University Press, 1977.

Eliot, T. S. "William Blake." In *Selected Essays*. Pp. 275–80. New York: Harcourt, Brace and World, 1964.

Elton, Oliver. *A Survey of English Literature: 1780–1830*. 2 vols. New York: Macmillan, 1924.

Erdman, David V. *Blake: Prophet against Empire: A Poet's Interpretation of the History of His Own Times*. 3d ed. Princeton: Princeton University Press, 1977.

Evans, J. M. *"Paradise Lost" and the Genesis Tradition*. Oxford: Oxford University Press, 1968.

Faber, George Stanley. *A Dissertation on the Prophecies*. 5th ed. 2 vols. London: Printed for F. C. and J. Rivington, 1814.

Farrer, Austin. *A Rebirth of Images: The Making of John's Apocalypse*. 1949. Reprint. Boston: Beacon Press, 1963.

Fisch, Harold. "William Blake." *The Encyclopedia Judaica*. Jerusalem: Keter Publishing House, 1971. Vol. 4.

Fisher, Peter F. *The Valley of Vision: Blake as Prophet and Revolutionary*. Edited by Northrop Frye. Toronto: University of Toronto Press, 1961.

Fletcher, Angus. *The Prophetic Moment: An Essay on Spenser*. Chicago: University of Chicago Press, 1971.

Fox, Susan. *Poetic Form in Blake's "Milton."* Princeton: Princeton University Press, 1976.

Frei, Hans W. *The Eclipse of Biblical Narrative: A Study in Eighteenth and Nineteenth Century Hermeneutics*. New Haven: Yale University Press, 1974.

Frye, Northrop. *Fearful Symmetry: A Study of William Blake*. 1947. Reprint. Princeton: Princeton University Press, 1969.

——. "The Road of Excess." In *Romanticism and Consciousness: Essays in Criticism*. Edited by Harold Bloom. Pp. 119–32. New York: Norton, 1970.

——. *A Study of English Romanticism*. 1968. Reprint. New York: Random House, n.d.

Furth, Hans G. *Piaget and Knowledge: Theoretical Foundations*. Englewood Cliffs, N.J.: Prentice-Hall, 1969.

Garrett, Clarke. *Respectable Folly: Millenarians and the French Revolution in France and England*. Baltimore: Johns Hopkins University Press, 1975.

Gilchrist, Alexander. *The Life of William Blake*. Edited by W. Graham Robertson. 2d ed. London: John Lane, 1907.

Gisborne, Maria, and Edward E. Williams. *Maria Gisborne & Edward E. Williams: Shelley's Friends, Their Journals and Letters*. Edited by Frederick L. Jones. Norman: University of Oklahoma Press, 1951.

Godwin, William. *Enquiry Concerning Political Justice and Its Influence on Morals and Happiness*. Edited by F. E. L. Priestley. 3 vols. Toronto: University of Toronto Press, 1946.

Goodwin, Thomas. *An Exposition upon the Revelation*. In vol. 2 of *The Works*

of Thomas Goodwin. London: Printed by J. Darby and S. Roycroft, 1681–
1704.

Grabo, Carl. *A Newton among Poets: Shelley's Use of Science in "Prometheus
Unbound."* 1930. Reprint. New York: Gordian Press, 1968.

———. *"Prometheus Unbound": An Interpretation*. 1935. Reprint. New York:
Gordian Press, 1968.

Hagstrum, Jean H. *William Blake: Poet and Painter. An Introduction to the
Illuminated Verse*. 1964. Reprint. Chicago: University of Chicago Press,
1969.

Haller, William. *The Rise of Puritanism; or, The Way to the New Jerusalem Set
Forth in Pulpit and Press from Thomas Cartwright to John Lilburne and John
Milton, 1570–1643*. New York: Columbia University Press, 1938.

Halloran, William F. *"The French Revolution*: Revelation's New Form." In
Blake's Visionary Forms Dramatic. Edited by David V. Erdman and John E.
Grant. Pp. 30–56. Princeton: Princeton University Press, 1970.

Harris, Wendell V. *The Omnipresent Debate: Empiricism and Transcendentalism
in Nineteenth-Century English Prose*. DeKalb: Northern Illinois University
Press, 1981.

Harrison, J. F. C. *The Second Coming: Popular Millenarianism 1780–1850*.
New Brunswick, N.J.: Rutgers University Press, 1979.

Hastorf, Albert H., David J. Schneider, and Judith Polefka. *Person Percep-
tion*. Reading, Mass.: Addison-Wesley, 1970.

Helms, Randel. "Ezekiel and Blake's *Jerusalem.*" *Studies in Romanticism* 13
(1974): 127–40.

Hill, Christopher. *Antichrist in Seventeenth-Century England*. London: Oxford
University Press, 1971.

———. *Milton and the English Revolution*. New York: Viking Press, 1977.

———. *The World Turned Upside Down: Radical Ideas During the English
Revolution*. 1972. Reprint. Harmondsworth: Penguin, 1980.

Hoagwood, Terence Allan. *"The Four Zoas* and 'The Philosophick Cab-
bala.'" *Blake: An Illustrated Quarterly* 12 (1978): 87–90.

———. "Holbach and Blake's Philosophical Statement in 'The voice of the
Devil.'" *English Language Notes* 15 (1978): 181–86.

Holbach, Paul Henri Thiry, Baron de. *The System of Nature; or, Laws of the
Moral and Physical World*. Translated by H. D. Robinson. 1835. Reprint.
Ann Arbor, Mich.: University Microfilms, 1963.

Howard, John. *Blake's "Milton": A Study in the Selfhood*. Cranbury, N.J.:
Fairleigh Dickinson University Press, 1976.

Hume, David. *A Treatise of Human Nature*. 1739. Edited by L. A. Selby-
Bigge. Oxford: Oxford University Press, 1973.

Johnson, James William. "Lyric." *Princeton Encyclopedia of Poetry and Poetics*.

Edited by Alex Preminger. 1965. Reprint. Princeton: Princeton University Press, 1972.

Keynes, Sir Geoffrey, ed. *Drawings of William Blake: Ninety-two Pencil Studies*. New York: Dover, 1970.

King-Hele, Desmond. *Shelley: His Thought and Work*. 2d ed. Teaneck: Fairleigh Dickinson University Press, 1971.

Kiralis, Karl. "The Theme and Structure of William Blake's *Jerusalem*." In *The Divine Vision: Studies in the Poetry and Art of William Blake*. Edited by Vivian de Sola Pinto. Pp. 141–62. London: Victor Gollancz, 1957.

König, Eduard. "Prophecy (Hebrew)." *Encyclopedia of Religion and Ethics*. Edited by James Hastings et al. 10:384–93. Edinburgh: T. and T. Clark, 1908–26.

Kostelanetz, Anne T. "Blake's 1795 Color Prints: An Interpretation." In *William Blake: Essays for S. Foster Damon*. Edited by Alvin H. Rosenfeld. Pp. 117–30. Providence, R.I.: Brown University Press, 1969.

Kroeber, Karl. *Romantic Narrative Art*. 1960. Reprint. Madison: University of Wisconsin Press, 1966.

Lawrence, D. H. *Apocalypse*. 1931. Reprint. New York: Viking Press, 1971.

Locke, John. *An Essay Concerning Human Understanding*. Edited by Alexander Campbell Fraser. 2 vols. 1894. Reprint. New York: Dover Publications, 1959.

Lowth, Robert. *Lectures on the Sacred Poetry of the Hebrews*. Translated by G. Gregory. 2 vols. 1787. Reprint. New York: Garland, 1971.

Luce, A. A. *Berkeley's Immaterialism: A Commentary on His "A Treatise Concerning the Principles of Human Knowledge."* 1945. Reprint. New York: Russell and Russell, 1948.

——. *The Dialectic of Immaterialism: An Account of the Making of Berkeley's "Principles."* London: Hodder and Stoughton, 1963.

MacCulloch, J. A. "Eschatology." *Encyclopedia of Religion and Ethics*. Edited by James Hastings et al. Vol. 5. New York: Charles Scribner's Sons, 1912.

MacNiece, Gerald. *Shelley and the Revolutionary Idea*. Cambridge, Mass.: Harvard University Press, 1969.

Mannheim, Karl. *Ideology and Utopia: An Introduction to the Sociology of Knowledge*. Translated by Louis Wirth and Edward Shils. 1936. Reprint. New York: Harcourt, Brace and World, n.d.

Manuel, Frank E. *The Religion of Isaac Newton*. Oxford: Oxford University Press, 1974.

Mede, Joseph. *The Key of the Revelation*. Translated by Richard More. 2d ed. London: Printed by J. L. for Philip Stephens, 1650.

Milton, John. *Complete Prose Works of John Milton*. Edited by Don M. Wolfe et al. 8 vols. New Haven: Yale University Press, 1953– .

———. *The Works of John Milton*. Edited by Frank Allen Patterson et al. 18 vols. New York: Columbia University Press, 1931–38.

Mitchell, W. J. T. *Blake's Composite Art: A Study of the Illuminated Poetry*. Princeton: Princeton University Press, 1978.

———. "Poetic and Pictorial Imagination in *The Book of Urizen*." In *The Visionary Hand: Essays for the Study of William Blake's Art and Aesthetics*. Edited by Robert N. Essick. Pp. 337–80. Los Angeles: Hennessey and Ingalls, 1973.

More, Henry. *Apocalypsis Apocalypseos; or, The Revelation of St. John the Divine Unveiled*. London: Printed by J. M. for J. Martyn and W. Kettilby, 1680.

———. *Conjectura Cabbalistica; or, A Conjectural Essay of Interpreting the Mind of Moses, in the Three First Chapters of Genesis, According to a Threefold Cabbala: Viz., Literal, Philosophical, Mystical, or, Divinely Moral*. In *A Collection of Several Philosophical Writings of Dr. Henry More*. 4th ed. London: Printed by Joseph Downing, 1712.

———. *The Philosophical Writings of Henry More*. Edited by Flora Isabel MacKinnon. New York: Oxford University Press, 1925.

———. *The Theological Works of the Most Pious and Learned Henry More*. London: Joseph Downing, 1708.

Muirhead, J. H. *The Platonic Tradition in Anglo-Saxon Philosophy*. London: George Allen and Unwin, 1931.

Murray, E. B. "*Jerusalem* Reversed." *Blake Studies* 7, no. 1 (1974): 11–25.

Neisser, Ulric. *Cognition and Reality: Principles and Implications of Cognitive Psychology*. San Francisco: W. H. Freeman, 1976.

Newton, Sir Isaac. *The Mathematical Principles of Natural Philosophy*. Translated by Andrew Motte. 2 vols. 1729. Reprint. London: Dawsons, 1968.

———. *Observations upon the Prophecies of Daniel and the Apocalypse of St. John*. London: Printed by J. Darby and T. Browne, 1733.

———. *Opticks; or, A Treatise of the Reflections, Refractions, Inflections and Colours of Light*. Based on the 4th ed. 1730. Reprint. New York: Dover, 1952.

Newton, Thomas. *Dissertations on the Prophecies*. 3d ed. 3 vols. London: J. and R. Tonson, 1766.

Paine, Thomas. *The Age of Reason*. In *The Theological Works of Thomas Paine*. London: R. Carlile, 1819.

———. *Rights of Man*. In *The Life and Works of Thomas Paine*. Edited by William M. Van der Weyde. New Rochelle, N.Y.: Thomas Paine National Historical Association, 1925.

Paley, Morton D. *Energy and the Imagination: A Study of the Development of Blake's Thought*. Oxford: Oxford University Press, 1970.

Pastorini, Signor [Charles Walmesley]. *The General History of the Christian Church*. 2d ed. London: J. P. Coghlan, 1798.

Peacock, Thomas Love. *The Works of Thomas Love Peacock*. Edited by H. F. B. Brett-Smith and C. E. Jones. New York: AMS Press, 1967. Vol. 8

Peganius, A. B. *A Genuine Explication of the Visions of the Book of Revelation*. Translated by "H. O." London: Printed by W. G. and sold by Moses Pitt, n.d.

Piaget, Jean. *Psychology and Epistemology: Towards a Theory of Knowledge*. Translated by Arnold Rosin. 1971. Reprint. New York: Viking Press, 1972.

Priestley, Joseph. *Disquisitions Relating to Matter and Spirit. To Which Is Added the History of the Philosophical Doctrine Concerning the Origin of the Soul*. 2d ed. 2 vols. London: Printed by Pearson and Rollason, for J. Johnson, 1782.
————. *The Doctrines of Heathen Philosophy, Compared with Those of Revelation*. Northumberland: John Binns, 1804.
————. *Letters to the Right Honourable Edmund Burke, Occasioned by His Reflections on the Revolution in France, &c*. 3d ed. London: Printed by Thomas Pearson and sold by J. Johnson, 1791.

Prophetic Conjectures on the French Revolution. Philadelphia: William Young, 1794.

Pulos, C. E. *The Deep Truth: A Study of Shelley's Scepticism*. 1954. Reprint. Lincoln: University of Nebraska Press, 1954.

Reeves, Marjorie. *The Influence of Prophecy in the Later Middle Ages: A Study in Joachimism*. Oxford: Oxford University Press, 1969.

Rieger, James. *The Mutiny Within: The Heresies of Percy Bysshe Shelley*. New York: George Braziller, 1967.

Rist, Martin. Introduction to the Book of Revelation. In *The Interpreter's Bible*. New York: Abingdon, 1957. Vol. 12.

Robinson, Charles E. *Shelley and Byron: The Snake and Eagle Wreathed in Fight*. Baltimore: Johns Hopkins University Press, 1976.

Rose, Edward J. "The Structure of Blake's *Jerusalem*." *Bucknell Review* 11 (1963): 35–54.

Roston, Murray. *Prophet and Poet: The Bible and the Growth of Romanticism*. Evanston: Northwestern University Press, 1965.

Ryken, Leland. *The Apocalyptic Vision in "Paradise Lost."* Ithaca: Cornell University Press, 1970.

Sanday, W. "Bible." *Encyclopedia of Religion and Ethics*. Edited by James Hastings et al. New York: Charles Scribner's Sons, 1910. Vol. 2.

Sandler, Florence. "The Iconoclastic Enterprise: Blake's Critique of 'Milton's Religion.'" *Blake Studies* 5, no. 1 (1972): 13–57.

Schmitt, Richard. "Phenomenology." *The Encyclopedia of Philosophy*. Edited by Paul Edwards. 1967. Reprint. New York: Macmillan and The Free Press, 1972. Vol. 6.

Scholem, Gershom G. *On the Kabbalah and Its Symbolism*. Translated by Ralph Manheim. New York: Schocken Books, 1965.

Shaffer, E. S. *"Kubla Khan" and the Fall of Jerusalem: The Mythological School in Biblical Criticism and Secular Literature 1770–1880*. Cambridge: Cambridge University Press, 1975.

Shelley, Mary. *Mary Shelley's Journal*. Edited by Frederick L. Jones. Norman: University of Oklahoma Press, 1947.

Shelley, Percy Bysshe. *The Complete Works of Percy Bysshe Shelley*. Edited by Roger Ingpen and Walter E. Peck. 10 vols. London: Ernest Benn; New York: Charles Scribner's Sons, 1926–30.

——. *The Letters of Percy Bysshe Shelley*. Edited by Frederick L. Jones. 2 vols. Oxford: Clarendon Press, 1964.

——. *Shelley's "Prometheus Unbound": The Texts and the Drafts. Toward a Modern Definitive Edition*. Edited by Lawrence John Zillman. New Haven: Yale University Press, 1968.

Siegman, E. F. "Apocalypse." *New Catholic Encyclopedia*. Edited by William J. McDonald et al. New York: McGraw-Hill, 1967. Vol. 1.

Stephen, Sir Leslie. *History of English Thought in the Eighteenth Century*. 3d ed. 2 vols. 1902. Reprint. New York: Harcourt, Brace and World, 1962.

Stuhlmueller, C. "Apocalyptic." *New Catholic Encyclopedia*. Edited by William J. McDonald et al. New York: McGraw-Hill, 1967. Vol. 1.

Sullivan, Harry Stack. "Peculiarity of Thought in Schizophrenia." In idem, *Schizophrenia as a Human Process*. Introduction and commentaries by Helen Swick Perry. 1962. Reprint. New York: Norton, 1974.

Swedenborg, Emanuel. *The Apocalypse Explained*. Translated by L. H. Tafel and John Whitehead. 6 vols. New York: The American Swedenborg Printing and Publishing Society, 1911–12.

——. *The Apocalypse Revealed*. Translated by the Rev. T. B. Hayward and the Rev. John Worcester. 2 vols. Philadelphia: J. B. Lippincott and Co., 1881.

——. *True Christian Religion*. 2 vols. London: J. Phillips and J. Denis and Son, 1781.

Tannenbaum, Leslie. *Biblical Tradition in Blake's Early Prophecies: The Great Code of Art*. Princeton: Princeton University Press, 1982.

Taylor, Rupert. *The Political Prophecy in England*. New York: Columbia University Press, 1911.

Thompson, E. P. *The Making of the English Working Class*. 1963. Reprint. New York: Vintage, 1966.

Tuveson, Ernest Lee. *The Imagination as a Means of Grace: Locke and the Aesthetics of Romanticism*. Berkeley and Los Angeles: University of California Press, 1960.

——. *Millennium and Utopia: A Study in the Background of the Idea of Progress*. Berkeley and Los Angeles: University of California Press, 1949.

Warburton, William. *The Divine Legation of Moses Demonstrated*. 2d ed. New York: Garland, 1978.

Wasserman, Earl R. *Shelley: A Critical Reading*. Baltimore: Johns Hopkins University Press, 1971.

———. *The Subtler Language: Critical Readings of Neoclassic and Romantic Poems*. Baltimore: Johns Hopkins University Press, 1959.

Weaver, Bennett. "*Prometheus Bound* and *Prometheus Unbound*." *PMLA* 64 (1949): 115–33.

———. *Prometheus Unbound*. 1957. Reprint. Hamden, Conn.: Archon Books, 1969.

Wesley, John. *Explanatory Notes upon the New Testament*. 1764. New York: Lane & Tippet, 1847.

Westermann, Claus. *Basic Forms of Prophetic Speech*. Translated by Hugh Clayton White. Philadelphia: Westminster Press, 1967.

White, Newman Ivey. *The Unextinguished Hearth: Shelley and His Contemporary Critics*. 1938. Reprint. New York: Octagon Books, 1972.

Wickwar, W. H. *Baron d'Holbach: A Prelude to the French Revolution*. London: George Allen and Unwin, 1935.

Willey, Basil. *The Eighteenth-Century Background: Studies in the Idea of Nature in the Thought of the Period*. 1940. Reprint. Boston: Beacon Press, 1961.

Wilson, Milton. *Shelley's Later Poetry: A Study of the Prophetic Imagination*. New York: Columbia University Press, 1959.

Witke, Joanne. "*Jerusalem*: A Synoptic Poem." *Comparative Literature* 22 (1970): 265–78.

Wittreich, Joseph Anthony, Jr. *Angel of Apocalypse: Blake's Idea of Milton*. Madison: University of Wisconsin Press, 1975.

———. "'Sublime Allegory': Blake's Epic Manifesto and the Milton Tradition." *Blake Studies* 4, no. 2 (1972): 15–44.

———. *Visionary Poetics: Milton's Tradition and His Legacy*. San Marino, Calif.: Huntington Library, 1979.

———, ed. *Milton and the Line of Vision*. Madison: University of Wisconsin Press, 1975.

Woodman, Ross Greig. *The Apocalyptic Vision in the Poetry of Shelley*. Toronto: University of Toronto Press, 1964.

Woodring, Carl. *Politics in English Romantic Poetry*. Cambridge, Mass.: Harvard University Press, 1970.

Wright, John W. *Shelley's Myth of Metaphor*. Athens: University of Georgia Press, 1970.

Zillman, Lawrence John, ed. *Shelley's "Prometheus Unbound": A Variorum Edition*. Seattle: University of Washington Press, 1959.

Index

Abijam, 64

Abraham, 64

Abrams, M. H., 1, 189–90, 220 (n. 61)

Abstract ideas, 24–26

Accuser, 78

Adam, 74, 90

Aeneid, 151

Aeschylus, 131, 133–34

Aesthetics, 37, 39, 41–42, 47, 57, 72

Albion, 2. *See also* Blake, William: *Jerusalem*, Albion in

Allegory, 49, 53

Angel of the bottomless pit, 50

Antichrist, 56, 138, 215 (n. 1)

Anti-images, 171, 174, 182

Apocalypse, 13, 36–37, 39, 42–44, 46, 53, 56–57, 135, 137, 166, 189–90, 202 (n. 74). *See also* Bible: Revelation; Prophecy

Apocalypticism, 72, 194 (n. 3)

Apocalyptic theater, 52

Arnold, Matthew, 2

Artemidorus, 201 (n. 70)

Art of writing, 71–72

Attribution, theory of, 143, 160, 166, 168, 173, 175

Augustine, St., 29, 42

Ault, Donald, 37, 196 (n. 21)

Bacon, Francis, 65. *See also* Blake, William: *Jerusalem*, Bacon in; Shelley, Percy Bysshe: and Bacon

Barthes, Roland, 201–202 (n. 72)

Bat (symbol), 81, 87–88

Baudissin, W. W., 72

Beast, 144

Beasts, 38, 52

Becker, Carl L., 34, 36, 195 (n. 8)

Bedford, Arthur, 203–204 (n. 88)

Bercovitch, Sacvan, 204–205 (n. 93)

Berkeley, George, 5, 12, 23–33, 39, 93, 132, 139, 188–89, 215 (n. 64)

Bible, 3–4, 40, 98, 137; Ezekiel, 7, 64, 70, 75–76, 142, 180, 182, 191; Isaiah, 7, 64, 70, 75, 140–41, 183; commentaries on, 29, 45; prophecies, 29; Daniel, 40, 45, 51, 158; aesthetics of, 41; and politics, 49; Genesis, 64, 68–69, 89–91, 95, 142–43, 167, 180; Job, 64; Kings, 64; Proverbs, 64; Deuteronomy, 88; Joshua, 90–92; Esther, 142; Jeremiah, 191

— Revelation, 3, 34, 37, 40, 57, 60, 67, 76–77, 141, 169, 184; commentaries on, 5, 38, 43, 47, 49, 54–56, 63, 73; mental conformations in, 38; and radical thought, 46; symbolism of, 47–49; and history, 48; language of, 48; multiple meanings of, 49; antithetical women of, 94. *See also* Apocalypse; Blake, William: *Jerusalem*, and Revelation; Prophecy; Shelley, Percy Bysshe: *Prometheus Unbound*, and Revelation

Bicheno, James, 56–57, 204 (n. 93)

Bindman, David, 210 (n. 11)

Blake, William: and Shelley, 1–10, 28–29, 36, 43, 47, 50, 52, 56, 138, 141, 154, 168, 187–91, 224 (n. 1); and American Revolution, 2; politics in writings of, 2, 6; and revolution, 2–3; and Jesus Christ, 2–4, 44, 65, 70–71, 74–76, 190; on last judgment, 3; philosophy of mind of, 3, 28; composite art of, 4; multiplicity of meaning in works of, 4–5; symbolism of, 4–5, 60, 71–72, 80,

(Blake, continued)

85–86, 91, 99; religious reference in
poems of, 6–8; and Ezekiel, 7,
75–76, 82–83; and Isaiah, 7, 75;
and Swedenborg, 7, 63–64, 67, 73,
99; Christianity of, 7–8; and mate-
rialism, 7–8; and Holbach, 7–8;
philosophical idealism of, 7–8; epis-
temology of, 8; poetic theory of, 8;
and Newton, 21, 23, 37, 44, 65–69,
72–73, 76, 78, 80, 88, 96, 98, 210
(n. 15); and process philosophy, 28;
conflates pagan and Christian sym-
bolism, 43; on prophet, 50, 75–76,
82–83, 98; and allusiveness, 59,
65–67; and multiple perspectives,
59; and readers, 59–60, 65, 79, 81,
87, 92, 98; illustrations for Milton's
poems, 60; and dislocation, 62; and
obscurity, 59, 62, 81; and Bacon, 65;
Female Will in works of, 65, 68–69;
and Locke, 65–66, 78, 80, 98;
visions of God, 66–67, 74–75, 77;
theology of, 67, 70–71, 74–78, 80,
82–83, 87–89, 97–99; and Henry
More, 68–69, 90, 96; and enthusi-
asm, 70, 78; and *Paradise Lost*, 71;
and art of writing, 71–72; and Reve-
lation, 71–72, 76–78, 83–84, 87,
99; and allegory, 72, 80, 85–86, 91;
and cabbalism, 72; and commentaries
on Revelation, 73, 76, 79–80, 83,
92; theory of language, 73; and
Christianity, 75, 91; portrayals of
vision, 75; and imagination, 76–77,
83, 96, 99, 188, 190; and doctrines
of wrath and forgiveness, 76–78,
82–83, 87; and Bible, 77, 98; and
Moses, 77, 85, 91, 95; and Satan, 77;
humanism of, 78; ideas of time and
space, 79; and Israelism, 79, 83–85;
and rhetoric, 79; and typology, 79;
and diverse symbolism, 80; and
priesthood, 82; and doctrine of states,
85–86; and synchronism, 83–84;
and visionary aesthetics, 86; and

Zoas, 86–87; and Elohim, 89; and
henopoeia, 90; and pagan religion,
91; and Priam, 91, 95; and Berkeley,
93, 215 (n. 64); and nature, 96;
knowledge of Hebrew, 210 (n. 10);
and Hume, 214 (n. 54); and Thomas
Paine, 214 (n. 55)
—*Jerusalem*, 1–5, 10; Israelism in,
53; and the Bible, 59, 64–67, 70,
79, 84–86, 91–92, 97–98; and lib-
eration of mind, 59; and philosophy,
59–60, 65, 76, 80, 84, 91, 95, 97,
99; and prophecy, 59, 65, 70, 76, 79,
81–86, 92, 98–99; and Revelation,
60, 67, 70, 72, 79–84, 94, 99;
contains commentary on itself, 60,
79, 85; composite form of, 60, 70;
form of, 60, 70, 81; intellectual unity
in, 60, 73, 78, 80–81, 90, 94, 99;
and visionary tradition, 60, 70,
78–79, 83, 99; and narrative struc-
ture, 60–61, 80–81, 84; copies of,
61, 210 (n. 4); and Ezekiel, 64, 70,
75–76, 82–84, 86–88; and Isaiah,
64, 70, 75; Jerusalem in, 64, 68,
93–94; idealism in, 66, 75; con-
traries in, 66–67, 69, 72–73, 78, 88,
97–98; materialism in, 66–68, 74,
88–91, 95–96, 98; Noah's ark in,
67; and Genesis, 68–69; theme of
vengeance and mercy in, 69, 86–87,
89, 97–98; moral theme of, 70–71,
74, 78, 85, 91, 95; and *Paradise Lost*,
70–71; Mystery in, 71; themes of,
71–72, 74; the fall in, 72–73; Albi-
on in, 73–74, 78, 84, 87–89, 93–95,
97, 168; Divine Vision in, 74, 83, 85,
88; visions of God in, 74, 81, 83,
87–89, 94, 97; Jesus Christ in,
74–76, 78, 80, 82, 87–88, 93–94,
96; humanism in, 75; imagination in,
76, 80, 85, 93, 98–99; Los in, 82,
87–88, 92, 95; Spectre in, 82,
87–89; Luvah in, 84, 93, 95–97;
space in, 84, 86, 93; time in, 84, 93;
Golgonooza in, 85–86; mental refer-

ence of, 85– 86; war and wars in, 86, 96– 99; Zoas in, 86– 87; Enitharmon in, 89; Vala in, 89, 92– 95; creation in, 89– 91, 95– 96; and Genesis, 89– 91, 95; Female Will in, 89– 91, 95; Eve in, 90; Reuben in, 90, 95; Joshua in, 90– 92; crucifixion in, 91, 94, 96– 97; and *Paradise Regained*, 91; sacrifice in, 91; Satan in, 91; Antichrist in, 91– 92; Bacon in, 91– 93, 97; Locke in, 91– 93, 97– 98; Newton in, 91– 93, 97– 98; Covering Cherub in, 92; Rahab in, 92; Spirit of Prophecy in, 92; paradise in, 92– 93; England and Brittannia in, 93– 94; Stonehenge in, 93– 94; virgin birth in, 94; vision of serpent in, 94– 96; political reference of, 95, 97; Urizen in, 96; and French Revolution, 97; Voltaire and Rousseau in, 97; and *Prometheus Unbound*, 187– 91; pl. 2 (title-page): 66– 69; pl. 3 ("To the Public"): 63, 70– 73, 75; pl. 4: 73– 76, 78; pl. 5: 79– 80; pl. 6: 78, 81, 87– 88; pl. 7: 87– 88; pl. 14: 67, 81; pl. 32: 90– 91; pl. 33: 69, 75, 78, 81, 88; pl. 37: 75, 88– 89; pl. 43: 95– 96; pl. 45: 61– 63; pl. 48: 98; pl. 54: 93– 94; pl. 57: 67; pl. 58: 69, 88; pl. 63: 93– 95; plates 65– 66: 97– 98; pl. 72: 94– 95; pl. 74: 84; pl. 75: 94– 96; pl. 76: 65, 81, 88; pl. 86: 89– 90; pl. 88: 92; pl. 96: 93; pl. 99: 94, 98
—other works: "Adam and Eve Sleeping" (watercolor), 69; *All Religions are One*, 43, 59– 60; *America*, 62; Annotations to *The Works of Sir Joshua Reynolds*, 14, 23; *The Book of Urizen*, 63, 138; "Christ descending into the Grave," 65; "The Creation of Eve" (watercolor), 65, 69; "Death's Door" (engraving), 62– 63; *A Descriptive Catalogue*, 3; "Does thy God O Priest take such vengeance as this?", 76; "Elohim Creating Adam" (color print), 69, 94, 141; *Europe*, 68– 69; *For the Sexes: The Gates of Paradise*, 62, 69; *The Four Zoas*, 2– 3, 63, 68, 90, 96; *The French Revolution*, 2; *The Grave*, 62, 65; "The Great Red Dragon and the Woman Clothed in the Sun" (watercolor), 3, 78; "House of Death" (color print), 69, 76; *Illustrations of the Book of Job*, 75, 88, 94; "Isaiah Foretelling the Destruction of Jerusalem" (drawing), 75; "Laocoön," 94– 96; *The Marriage of Heaven and Hell*, 6– 8, 44, 73, 75; *Milton*, 2, 62, 65– 66, 76, 189; "Newton" (color print), 69; "Satan Exulting Over Eve" (color print), 69, 141; "A Song of Liberty," 2– 3; "The Soul exploring the recesses of the Grave," 65; "To Venetian Artists," 210 (n. 15); "A Vision of the Last Judgment," 43, 71, 76– 77; "Vision of the Last Judgment" (lost watercolor), 60; *Visions of the Daughters of Albion*, 5– 6
Blood, 50
Bloom, Harold, 80, 82– 83
Bloomfield, Morton W., 200– 201 (n. 66)
Boethius, 41
Book (as symbol), 48
Boswell, James, 196 (n. 23)
Bowman, J. W., 194 (n. 1), 199 (n. 56)
Brailsford, H. N., 217 (n. 24)
Butlin, Martin, 213 (n. 46)

Cabbalism, 44, 49, 54, 71– 72, 137, 211 (n. 26)
Calvin, John, 203 (n. 84)
Calvinism, 137
Cameron, Kenneth Neill, 2, 190, 216 (n. 3), 217 (n. 24), 219 (n. 41), 219– 20 (n. 52), 221 (n. 66), 224 (n. 1)
Cause, 28– 29, 32, 34, 73

Cave, 71, 151, 162, 168

Charity, A. C., 38, 203 (n. 85)

Charles, R. H., 193–94 (n. 1), 202 (n. 74)

Chayes, Irene, 63

Cheskin, Arnold, 210 (n. 10)

Chiliasm, 41–42. *See also* Eschatology; Millennium

Christianity, 12, 20. *See also* Jesus Christ

Civil War (English), 46

Cloud, 73–74, 78, 84, 99

Cognitive psychology, 28

Cohn, Norman, 46

Coleridge, John Taylor, 189

Coleridge, Samuel Taylor, 188, 190–91

Collinges, John, 209 (n. 150)

Commandments, 64, 71. *See also* Ten commandments

Composite form, 37, 58. *See also* Blake, William: composite art of; Blake, William, *Jerusalem*: composite form of

Covenants, Old and New, 44, 187

Curran, Stuart, 80, 84, 137, 142, 168, 178, 218 (n. 41), 221 (n. 66), 222 (n. 72), 223 (n. 89)

Curtis, F. B., 55

Damon, S. Foster, 224 (n. 1)

Dante, 5, 131, 134, 157, 163, 170–71, 182

Dark room, 19, 66

Darwin, Erasmus, 163

Death, 51

Descartes, René, 5, 11–14, 16, 23, 25, 30, 34–35, 40, 151, 195 (n. 4)

Dissenters, 22

Divine Vision, 62, 67

Dobbins, Austin C., 206 (n. 98)

Door, 61–63

Doubt, 30, 34

Dragon, 78, 92, 185. *See also* Great Red Dragon

Dreams, 51, 158–59

Drummond, William, 139

Dryden, John, 45–46

Dualism, 35

Earthquake, 138, 140–42, 156, 173

Easson, Roger R., 80

Edwards, Jonathan, 202–203 (n. 77)

Egypt, 53

Egyptian, 50

Elijah, 10

Eliot, T. S., 2

Elton, Oliver, 174

Empiricism, 6, 29, 33, 195 (n. 4)

Encyclopedists, 97

English Revolution, 133

Enitharmon, 68–69, 89

Enlightenment philosophers, 35

Enthusiasm, 22, 70, 78

Epic, 131

Epistemology, 8, 11–37 passim

Erdman, David V., 2, 7, 74, 86, 96, 224 (n. 1)

Eschatology, 38, 40, 46. *See also* Chiliasm; Millennium

Essence, 17, 27, 54

Ether, 151

Etymology, 54

Evans, J. M., 211 (n. 20)

Eve, 53

Faber, George Stanley, 49, 55–56, 138, 148, 215–16 (n. 1)

Farrer, Austin, 39

Fire, 64, 142. *See also* Globe of fire; Lamp

Fisch, Harold, 210 (n. 10)

Fisher, Peter F., 192 (n. 8), 197 (n. 31), 213–14 (n. 51)

Flames, 72

Fletcher, Angus, 206 (n. 98)

Flood, 67, 69, 74

Fox, Susan, 212 (n. 45)

Fraser, Alexander Campbell, 13

Freccero, John, 171, 222 (n. 81)

French Revolution, 2, 46, 55–57, 146. *See also* Blake, William: and French Revolution; Blake, William: *Jerusalem*, and French Revolution; Shelley, Percy Bysshe: and French Revolution
Frye, Northrop, 1–2, 4, 79–80, 196 (n. 14), 197 (n. 24), 213 (n. 46), 222 (n. 82), 224 (n. 95)

Garden, 47
Garrett, Clarke, 208–209 (n. 141)
Gisborne, Maria, 220 (n. 53)
Globe of fire, 61, 63. *See also* Fire; Lamp
Goats, 63
God, 33–34, 43–44, 50, 58, 64, 66–67, 70, 75–76, 88–89, 94, 98–99, 138, 141, 166
Godwin, William, 135, 137, 139, 141, 144, 146, 160, 173, 216–17 (n. 13), 217–18 (n. 27), 220 (n. 53)
Goodwin, Thomas, 38, 135
Grabo, Carl, 37, 144, 151, 178, 184, 196 (n. 21), 216 (n. 2), 218–19 (n. 41), 221 (n. 66), 221 (n. 69)
Great Red Dragon, 53, 77–78. *See also* Dragon
Grimes, Ronald L., 189
Grotius, Hugo, 50
Gunkel, H., 198 (n. 45), 200 (n. 58)

Hagstrum, Jean H., 4
Hail, 44, 141, 143, 174
Haller, William, 205 (n. 95)
Harp, 88
Harris, Wendell V., 192 (n. 2), 195 (n. 4), 202 (n. 73)
Harrison, J. F. C., 55, 82
Hastorf, Albert H., 196 (n. 18)
Helms, Randel, 83
Henopoeia, 52
Hesse, Mary, 220 (n. 56)
Hill, Christopher, 36, 45, 194 (n. 2), 205 (n. 95)
History, 34, 53, 56, 58

Holbach, Baron d', 7–9, 12, 97–98, 139, 143
Howard, John, 79
Humanism, 18, 36, 43, 53, 187. *See also* Shelley, Percy Bysshe: humanism of; Shelley, Percy Bysshe: *Prometheus Unbound*: humanism in
Hume, David, 12, 30–35, 39, 132, 137, 139, 144
Husserl, Edmund, 196 (n. 11)
Hylasmus, 52

Iconisms, 51
Idealism, philosophical, 5, 10, 12, 16–19, 26–27, 36, 41, 52. *See also* Immaterialism
Ideas, 31–32
Identity, 31
Ideology, 31, 41–42, 46, 53, 55, 57, 144
Imagery, 20, 29, 38, 43, 52, 57
Imagination, 14, 21–23, 33, 39, 41, 43, 46, 51, 55, 58, 187–88. *See also* Blake, William: and imagination; Blake, William: *Jerusalem*, imagination in; Shelley, Percy Bysshe: and imagination
Immaterialism, 29, 35–37. *See also* Idealism, philosophical
Impressions, 31
Incarnation, 29, 54, 58
Innate ideas, 13–14, 30, 40
Inspiration, 39, 70, 188
Inversional transformation, 212 (n. 40)
Irenaeus, 41
Israelism, 53–54, 79, 83–84, 211 (n. 39)

Jesus Christ, 2–4, 44, 53, 65, 70–71, 75, 136, 180. *See also* Blake, William: and Jesus Christ; Blake, William: *Jerusalem*, Jesus Christ in; Shelley, Percy Bysshe: and Jesus Christ; Shelley, Percy Bysshe: *Prometheus Unbound*, and Jesus Christ

Joachim of Fiore, 46
John, St., 5, 11, 38, 44, 48, 51,
    63–64, 70, 75, 77, 99, 135, 166, 169
Johnson, James William, 171–72
Johnson, Samuel, 196 (n. 23)
Jones, William, 29
Jupiter, 136–37. *See also* Shelley, Percy
    Bysshe: *Prometheus Unbound*,
    Jupiter in

Kant, Immanuel, 28
Kiralis, Karl, 80
Knowledge, 28, 30, 32, 39–40. *See*
    also Epistemology; Perception
Kostelanetz, Anne T., 213 (n. 46)
Kroeber, Karl, 47–48

Lamp, 63–65. *See also* Fire; Globe of
    fire
Language, 18–19, 40, 48, 51, 152. *See*
    also Shelley, Percy Bysshe: and
    language
Laocoön, 94
Lardner, Nathaniel, 204 (n. 88)
Lawrence, D. H., 53
Leviathan, 64
Liberty, 44, 55
Light, 19–23, 45, 49, 65, 67. *See also*
    Vision
Lightning, 44, 143, 174
Locke, John, 1, 12–27, 30–31,
    38–39, 66, 78, 92, 98, 143–44. *See*
    also Blake, William: and Locke
Los, 62–65. *See also* Blake, William:
    Jerusalem, Los in
Lowman, Moses, 202–203 (n. 77)
Lowth, Robert, 37, 39, 49, 81, 134,
    137, 160–61
Luce, A. A., 14, 25, 197 (n. 26)
Luther, Martin, 29
Lyrical drama, 131, 161, 171–72

MacCulloch, J. A., 202 (n. 74)
MacNiece, Gerald, 219 (n. 52)
Manna, 53

Mannheim, Karl, 12, 55–56, 58
Manuel, Frank E., 51
Marriage, 157
Materialism, philosophical, 7, 17, 21, 23,
    35–36, 44, 48, 71–72, 87–90, 98
Matterists, 27
Meaning, theory of, 28–29, 36
Mede, Joseph, 40–41, 49, 51–52, 70,
    137, 193 (n. 12), 201 (n. 70), 202
    (n. 74), 207 (n. 116)
Metaphor, 19–21, 23
Millennium, 36, 42, 139–40, 185, 203
    (n. 84). *See also* Chiliasm; Eschatol-
    ogy; Shelley, Percy Bysshe: *Pro-
    metheus Unbound*, and millenarianism
Milton, John, 46, 53, 65, 131–32, 138,
    142, 145, 155; *Paradise Regained*, 80,
    91, 214 (n. 62); *Paradise Lost*, 132–
    34, 166; *Samson Agonistes*, 145. *See*
    also Blake, William: and *Paradise
    Lost*; Blake, William: *Jerusalem*, and
    Paradise Lost; Blake, William: *Jerusa-
    lem*, and *Paradise Regained*; Shelley,
    Percy Bysshe: and Milton Shelley,
    Percy Bysshe: *Prometheus Unbound*,
    and *Paradise Lost*
Mind, 28, 32–33, 38, 42, 58
Mitchell, W. J. T., 138, 210 (n. 3), 212
    (n. 44), 214 (n. 53)
Montaigne, Michel de, 12
Moon, 65, 69, 74, 78, 94
Moral law, 71, 74, 78
Moral philosophy, 30
Moral thought, 58
More, Henry, 6, 8, 13–14, 20, 23, 29,
    36, 39–44, 47–54, 59, 68–69,
    72–73, 81, 91, 96, 137, 188–89, 200
    (n. 64), 206 (n. 95), 211 (n. 26), 211
    (n. 39)
Moses, 44, 49
Muirhead, J. H., 200 (n. 64)
Murray, E. B., 1, 59

Necessity, 169, 221 (n. 66)
Neisser, Ulric, 28

Newton, Isaac, 5, 12, 14, 20–23, 26, 28, 36, 39–40, 43–44, 50–52, 54, 57, 66–67, 72–73, 76, 78, 92, 96, 98, 151, 158, 195 (n. 4), 203 (n. 88), 210 (n. 15). *See also* Blake, William: and Newton; Blake, William: *Jerusalem*, Newton in; Shelley, Percy Bysshe: and Newton

Newton, Thomas, 45, 50, 204 (n. 93)

Noah, 67

Notion, 32–33

Obscurity, 48–49, 59, 62, 81

Ocean, 67

Onirocriticis, 40, 51, 137

Ontology, 15, 18, 22–26, 30–32, 36, 39, 42, 72

Origen, 42

Owen, Robert, 173

Paine, Thomas, 141, 145–46, 153–54, 214 (n. 55)

Paley, Morton, 195 (n. 4), 201 (n. 66), 214 (n. 57)

Particularity, 24

Paul, St., 42

Peacock, Thomas Love, 135–36

Peganius, A. B., 54, 137

Perception, 5–7, 15–16, 19–24, 26–28, 31, 33, 36, 38–39, 41–42, 58

Personal identity, 33

Personality, 33

Perspective, 36

Pharoah, 50

Philo, 211 (n. 20)

Philosophy, 11–37

Piaget, Jean, 28, 177, 202 (n. 73)

Plato, 19, 43, 151

Poetic theory, 8, 132–36, 140, 152, 158, 175. *See also* Aesthetics; Visionary aesthetics; Visionary art

Polefka, Judith, 196 (n. 18)

Politics, 1–2, 5–6, 34, 43–45, 50, 55–58, 95, 97, 132–36, 146, 148, 150, 153–54, 167, 172–73, 177, 179, 184, 186, 189

Poole, Matthew, 209 (n. 150)

Pope, Alexander, 45–46

Posture, 65

Power, 33–34

Priestley, Joseph, 35–36, 43, 55–56, 91, 136–37, 188, 204 (n. 93)

Process philosophy, 27–28, 36

Prophecy, 1–10; commentaries on, 29, 36–38, 40, 42, 44, 51–52, 54, 57–58, 137; biblical, 36–58; and concept of mind, 38, 42, 45; and vision, 39–40; composite form, 40, 58; and dreams, 40; and idealism, 40; language of, 40, 51, 56; form of, 41; and perception, 45; and history, 45–46, 50, 133; and revolution, 45–46, 56–57; ideology of, 46; multiple meanings in, 46–47, 49, 58; self-interpreting, 48, 57; figurative system, 49; and symbolism, 49–50, 52, 58, 91–92, 99; and politics, 50; and French Revolution, 55–57; art of multiple perspectives, 57, 59; and Romantic writers, 58; obscurity of, 81; and audience, 81. *See also* Apocalypse; Bible: Revelation; Romantic prophecy

Prophetic Conjectures on the French Revolution, 57

Protestant Reformation, 133

Psychology, 18, 28. *See also* Perception

Pulos, C. E., 217 (n. 25), 222 (n. 80)

Puttenham, George, 201 (n. 69)

Qualities, 16–17, 22–24

Quarterly Review, The, 160

Rain, 44

Rainbow, 66–69

Reeves, Marjorie, 204 (n. 93)

Reflection, 15–16

Reiman, Donald H., 224 (n. 1)

Religion, 1, 6–8, 34, 36, 43, 45, 60.
    See also Blake, William: theology of;
    Blake, William: and Christianity;
    Christianity; Shelley, Percy Bysshe:
    and religion; Shelley, Percy Bysshe:
    Prometheus Unbound, religious theme
    of
Revolution, 2–3, 44, 46, 55, 58, 133,
    153–54. *See also* French Revolution;
    Prophecy: and revolution
Rieger, James, 221 (n. 66)
Rigaltius, Nicolaus, 40, 201 (n. 70)
Rist, Martin, 194 (n. 3)
Robinson, Charles E., 216 (n. 4), 218
    (n. 30), 221 (n. 66)
Rock, 88–89, 97, 99, 140, 156
Romanticism, 1–10, 21–24, 35, 37, 47,
    55–58, 187–91
Romantic prophecy, 1–10, 187–91
Rose, Edward J., 80
Roston, Murray, 198 (n. 45), 205
    (n. 94)
Rousseau, Jean Jacques, 97
Ryken, Leland, 206 (n. 98)

Sanday, W., 194 (n. 1)
Sandler, Florence, 76
Satan, 77, 91, 133, 138, 140–43, 154,
    214 (n. 62)
Schechinah, 54
Schmitt, Richard, 196 (n. 11)
Schneider, David J., 196 (n. 18)
Scholem, Gershom G., 71–72
Science, 20–21, 36, 67, 183–84
Scroll, 89
Self, 33
Selves, 38
Sensation, 15–16
Serpent, 53, 94–96
Seven, 54
Seven churches in Asia, 55
Shadow, 74, 88, 153, 155, 157
Shaffer, E. S., 188
Shelley, Mary, 3, 169, 221 (n. 66)
Shelley, Percy Bysshe: and William
    Blake, 1–13, 28–29, 43, 47, 50, 52,
56, 138, 141, 143, 154, 168, 179,
187–91, 224 (n. 1); and American
Revolution, 2; and politics, 2,
132–36, 153–54, 186, 189; and revo-
lution, 2; and French Revolution,
2–3, 55, 146, 148, 150; and Jesus
Christ, 2–4, 55, 136, 145, 180, 184,
216 (n. 7); and aristocracy, 3; and
metaphysics, 3, 132, 136, 140,
151–52; and religion, 3–4, 132–33,
136–37, 186; multiplicity of meaning
in poems of, 4–5; and symbolism,
4–5, 139, 151, 154–55, 160, 168,
172–73; on language, 8–9, 152,
157–58; and idealism, 9; and idea of
history, 9–10, 133–34, 150; on
prophet, 9–10, 50, 161; and pro-
phetic art, 9–10, 133–34, 138, 153,
160; on unity of fields of thought,
9–10, 132–37, 154; and visionary
poetics, 9–10, 134–35, 139–40,
153, 160–61; and imagination, 10,
134, 138–40, 186, 188; and inspira-
tion, 10, 159–60; and Newton,
21–22, 37; and philosophy of mind,
28, 133, 140, 146; and process philos-
ophy, 28; and Hume, 31, 34, 132,
139, 144; and personal identity, 31;
on power, 34; conflates pagan and
Christian symbolism, 43; and biblical
commentators, 55; and Aeschylus,
131, 133–34, 140–42, 144–45, 147,
167, 174, 176; and epic, 131; and
lyrical drama, 131, 161, 171–72; and
Dante, 131–32, 134, 157, 163, 176,
182; intellectual philosophy of,
131–32, 134, 151–52, 155, 165, 195
(n. 4); and Milton, 131–34, 138, 142,
144–45, 154–55; and Berkeley, 132,
139; and interiorization of hell, 132,
154–55; theory of poetry of, 132–
36, 140, 152, 158, 175; and apoc-
alypse, 135, 137, 157; and Bible,
135, 138, 142, 145–46, 150, 152,
165, 180; and William Godwin, 135,
137, 139, 144, 146, 153, 173; and

philosophy, 135; and harmony of contending creeds, 135–38; and Christianity, 136; and Jupiter, 136; and myth, 136, 138, 146, 158; and Joseph Priestley, 136–37; and Bacon, 137; and Robert Lowth, 137, 160–61; and commentators on prophecy, 138; and George Stanley Faber, 138, 148, 216 (n. 1); and Enlightenment philosophy, 139; and Sir William Drummond, 139, 217 (n. 25); and Holbach, 139, 143; on relation of thoughts with things, 139, 165; and millennium, 139–40, 172–73; concept of one mind of, 140, 143, 154; humanism of, 140, 148–49, 160, 169, 176, 180; and Isaiah, 140–41; and Book of Revelation, 141; and Thomas Paine, 141, 145–46, 153–54, 219 (n. 50); and biblical prophecies, 141–42, 180; and Locke, 143–44; theology of, 143–44, 146; and theory of attribution, 143–44, 160, 166, 168, 173, 175; and ideology, 144; on immortality, 147; and the *Aeneid*, 151; and Plato, 151; and the Sibyl, 151; and science, 151–52, 163; and readers, 154; skeptical idealism of, 161, 185–86; and Erasmus Darwin, 163, 221 (n. 69); on God, 166; unification of subject and object in works of, 175, 177, 186; on Job, 176; on time and eternity, 176, 179; and the Sermon on the Mount, 180; and Genesis, 180; and Ezekiel, 180, 182–

—*Prometheus Unbound*, 1–5, 10; form of, 131; imagery of, 131; and prophecy, 131, 152–53, 158–60, 167, 169, 174–77, 179–80, 183–84; Shelley's evaluation of, 131; multiple levels of reference of, 131–32, 138, 141, 146, 148, 152, 154, 158, 173, 175, 184; and visionary poetics, 132, 160, 173; preface to, 132–34, 138–39, 157; Prometheus in, 133, 138, 141–45, 149–50, 154, 159–61,

164–65, 167–68, 175–78, 184; and Satan, 133, 138, 140–43, 154; theme of, 133, 155; and *Paradise Lost*, 133–34, 140, 154, 166; and Jesus Christ, 138, 143, 145–49, 154, 159; and Job, 138; and Samson, 138, 145; and wrathful God, 138, 140, 146, 183; and philosophy, 139; Jupiter in, 139–44, 146, 149, 154, 160–61, 164–65, 173, 180, 215 (n. 1); and Hebrew God, 140–44; and Jehovah, 141, 143; moral theme of, 141, 172–73; curse and revocation in, 141–44, 164; Earth in, 142, 150–51, 155, 177; and Esther, 142; and Ezekiel, 142, 182; Panthea in, 142, 148, 155, 158–60, 182; Phantasm of Jupiter in, 142; and Zoroastrianism, 142, 223 (n. 89); and Genesis, 142–45, 167; vengeance in, 143–46, 183; psychological framework of, 144–45, 148–49, 173; French Revolution in, 146, 148, 150; political theme of, 146, 148, 150, 167, 172–73, 177, 179, 184; Furies in, 146–49, 157, 162, 172; and Book of Revelation, 148, 150, 153–54, 157, 165, 169, 174, 179–80, 183–85, 220 (n. 61); multiple perspectives in, 148, 178–79, 182, 184; religious theme of, 148, 167; repetition in, 148, 150, 153–57, 162, 164, 171, 174; Mercury in, 149–50, 154–55, 157; metaphor of birds, 150–51; poetic unification of thought and thing in, 150–51, 157; cave in, 151, 156, 162, 168, 174–76, 179, 223 (n. 89); prophetic spirits in, 152–53, 155–56, 166; mental reference of, 153, 163, 166, 168, 180; Asia in, 154–56, 158–59, 162, 164–68, 170, 222 (n. 71); metaphor of shadow in, 155, 157, 160; Demogorgon in, 156, 162–64, 166, 167–69, 173–74, 180–81, 184–85, 221 (n. 66), 222 (n. 71); music in, 156, 162–64; and Dante's *Divine Comedy*, 157, 162–63,

(Shelley, continued)

170–71, 182; metaphorical technique of, 157–58, 165; sexual union in, 157–58, 173, 184, 220 (n. 61); parallelism of acts in, 158, 162, 165, 170, 174, 181; alleged obscurity of, 160; unity of persons in, 161; unity of time in, 161; worship in, 164; structure of, 165, 171–72, 174; paradise in, 170, 180; anti-images in, 171, 174, 182; synesthesia in, 171, 182; and millenarianism, 172–73, 177–79; symbolism in, 172–73, 177, 185; and Blake's *Jerusalem*, 173, 187–91; Earth-sphere and Moon-chariot in, 173, 182–83; new heaven and earth in, 173, 182; and Old Testament, 173; unification of subject and object in, 175, 177, 186; and secularization of scripture, 178; Spirit of the Earth in, 178–79; humanism of, 178–80; Spirit of the Hour in, 179; time in, 179; Ione in, 182; and Isaiah, 183; and science, 183–84

—other works: *A Defence of Poetry*, 1, 8–10, 43, 134, 137–38, 153, 155, 175, 188; *Essay on Christianity*, 136, 216 (n. 7); *Hellas*, 4, 170, 176–77, 180, 186; "Ode to Liberty," 3; *On Life*, 154, 174–75; *A Philosophical View of Reform*, 2–3; *Queen Mab*, 221 (n. 69); Notes to *Queen Mab*, 139, 143; *A Refutation of Deism*, 141, 145; *The Revolt of Islam*, 2–3, 164; Preface to *The Revolt of Islam*, 3, 146; *Speculations on Metaphysics*, 3

Sibyl, 151
Siegman, E. F., 199–200 (n. 58), 201 (n. 71), 202 (n. 77)
Sinai, 71–72
Skepticism, 12
Slavery, 6
Sleep, 62, 68–69, 74, 92
Smith, John, 201 (n. 66)
Sodom, 53
Solipsism, 27, 152

Space, 32
Spenser, Edmund, 46–47, 49
Spirit, 21, 27–28, 38, 42, 44, 58, 73
Spirit of Prophecy, 60
Spinoza, Baruch, 187–88
Starry sky, 68, 74
Stars, 79, 97
Stein, Stephen J., 36, 204 (n. 88)
Stephen, Leslie, 1, 30, 31
Steuernagel, C., 200 (n. 61)
Stone, 78, 85, 97
Stonehenge, 93–94
Storm, 44
Stuhlmueller, C., 206 (n. 103)
Substance, 16–17, 27, 31–32, 35, 66
Sun, 138
Swedenborg, Emanuel, 7, 38, 48–50, 54–55, 63–64, 67, 72–73, 99, 189, 210 (n. 10)
Sword, 43
Symbolism, 2, 5–6, 19, 29, 37, 39–44, 47, 51–52, 91–92
Synchronism, 6, 40, 57–58, 83–84, 165, 193 (n. 12), 202 (n. 74), 202–203 (n. 77)
Synesthesia, 171

Tables of stone, 77
Tablet, 89, 97
Talmudic tradition, 72
Tannenbaum, Leslie, 29, 53, 193 (n. 12), 197 (n. 31), 208 (n. 128)
Tasso, Torquato, 201 (n. 69)
Taylor, Rupert, 206 (n. 101)
Ten commandments, 71, 97
Theater of mind, 33, 83, 137, 174
Theater of visions, 37, 58, 131, 137
Thompson, E. P., 55
Throne, 165, 168–69, 179, 181, 184
Thunder, 44, 72, 141–42, 173–74, 177, 179
Time, 32, 41, 53–54, 189
Torah, 72
Trumpet, 88
Tuveson, Ernest Lee, 15, 20, 36, 46

Twisse, Dr., 51, 206 (n. 103)
Typology, 53–54, 79, 84, 154, 214
(n. 55)
Tyranny, 5–6, 45, 57

Urizen, 63. *See also* Blake, William:
Jerusalem, Urizen in; Blake, William:
The Book of Urizen

Veil, 135, 137, 165–66, 180–81
Vengeance, 67, 69, 75, 77, 86–87, 89,
97–98, 143–46, 183, 189
Vico, Giambattista, 51–52
Vision, 5, 11, 19–23, 28–29, 37–40,
48–50, 56, 58, 67
Visionary aesthetics, 20, 41, 56, 59, 72
Visionary art, 4–6, 19–22, 33, 37, 41,
50, 58, 60, 189
Visionary theory, 19–22, 37, 39, 57
Void, 61, 64–66, 79
Voltaire, 97

Walmesley, Charles [Sig. Pastorini], 57
War (as symbol), 43–44
Warburton, William, 200 (n. 64), 201
(n. 70), 202 (n. 72), 211 (n. 22)
Wasserman, Earl R., 1, 4, 45, 169, 173,
193 (n. 11), 216 (n. 5), 217 (n. 17),
221 (n. 66), 223 (n. 90)

Weaver, Bennett, 216 (n. 5), 222
(n. 72)
Wesley, John, 29, 53
Westermann, Claus, 199 (n. 57), 200
(n. 61)
Whirlwind, 141, 174, 177, 180
Whore of Babylon, 92, 94
Wickwar, W. H., 198 (n. 44)
Wilderness, 47, 163
Willey, Basil, 137
Williams, Kathleen, 206 (n. 98)
Willison, John, 209 (n. 150)
Wilson, Milton, 218 (n. 39), 222, (n.
71), 222 (n. 77), 223 (n. 91)
Wind, 64
Winepress, 42
Witke, Joanne, 80
Wittreich, Joseph Anthony, Jr., 7, 84,
177, 193 (n. 12), 200 (n. 66), 201 (n.
69), 205–206 (n. 95), 209 (n. 154),
212 (n. 40)
Woodman, Ross Greig, 218 (n. 39), 223
(n. 85)
Woodring, Carl, 219–20 (n. 52)
Wordsworth, William, 178
Wright, John W., 218 (n. 28)

Zoroastrianism, 142, 223 (n. 89)

About the Author

Terence Allan Hoagwood teaches English at West Virginia University. He received the bachelor of arts degree from the University of Maryland, the master of arts degree from The American University, and his doctorate from the University of Maryland. This is his first book.